PENGUIN BOOKS
IN THE SHADOW OF THE TAJ
A PORTRAIT OF AGRA

Royina Grewal has written *Sacred Virgin, Travels along the Narmada*, *In Rajasthan, a Travelogue*, as well as the *Book of Ganesha*. Her interest in history is expressed in the six son-et-lumiere productions she conceived, scripted and directed. Royina and her husband live between Delhi and an organic farm in Rajasthan.

In the Shadow of the Taj

A Portrait of Agra

ROYINA GREWAL

PENGUIN BOOKS

PENGUIN BOOKS
Published by the Penguin Group
Penguin Books India Pvt. Ltd, 11 Community Centre, Panchsheel Park, New Delhi 110 017, India
Penguin Group (USA) Inc., 375 Hudson Street, New York, New York 10014, USA
Penguin Group (Canada), 90 Eglinton Avenue East, Suite 700, Toronto, Ontario, M4P 2Y3, Canada (a division of Pearson Penguin Canada Inc.)
Penguin Books Ltd, 80 Strand, London WC2R 0RL, England
Penguin Ireland, 25 St Stephen's Green, Dublin 2, Ireland (a division of Penguin Books Ltd)
Penguin Group (Australia), 250 Camberwell Road, Camberwell, Victoria 3124, Australia (a division of Pearson Australia Group Pty Ltd)
Penguin Group (NZ), 67 Apollo Drive, Rosedale, North Shore 0632, New Zealand (a division of Pearson New Zealand Ltd)
Penguin Group (South Africa) (Pty) Ltd, 24 Sturdee Avenue, Rosebank, Johannesburg 2196, South Africa

Penguin Books Ltd, Registered Offices: 80 Strand, London WC2R 0RL, England

First published by Penguin Books India 2007

Copyright © Royina Grewal 2007

All rights reserved

10 9 8 7 6 5 4 3 2 1

ISBN-13: 978-0-14310-265-6   ISBN-10: 0-14310-265-6

Typeset in Sabon by Mantra Virtual Services, New Delhi
Printed at Deunique Printers, New Delhi

For my family, especially Neel,
and my extended family
in Agra

Contents

Acknowledgements

This book is the product of the time, words and knowledge shared so generously with me by scores of people I met in Agra. To my enormous regret, I have been able to include only a tiny fraction of these encounters: the contribution made by each, however, remains in the many nuances throughout the book. *In the Shadow of the Taj* is a very personal, selective account of the people and places, past and present, that caught my attention. It is not a history of Agra, nor is it an exhaustive document on the life of the city.

My special thanks to Reshma and Shashak Bhagat for all their help as well as hospitality at the Holiday Inn, Agra. Kamini and Rajeev Lall stood in for my family and opened many doors. Promilla Poddar provided the inspiration for the book and ongoing inputs. The consistantly helpful staff of Holiday Inn introduced me to Dr Neville Smith and Mr Puneet Dan. Dr Smith and his wife, Anugrah, provided both friendship and unfailing assistance. Among the many others, Dr K.K. Muhammad vastly enhanced my understanding of history and Puneet Dan and Mr S.P. Joshi were generous with their time and knowledge. Sarita Chopra was also a great help in many different ways. I am deeply indebted to them all.

Ravi Singh of Penguin helped me gain a sense of direction in the early stages of the manuscript, while Prita Maitra's eagle eye and sensitivity shaped this book. From Ravi and Prita I learnt that writers produce manuscripts; editors convert them into books. For their superb editorial skills, patience and support, my gratitude.

Breath of a Rose

A ram Bagh, the 'garden of leisure', high above the river
Yamuna on the outskirts of Agra, induces tranquillity,
even indolence. But there is also melancholy in its decrepitude.
In a previous time every aspect of the garden had been directed
towards eliciting pleasure. The senses were soothed by the
cool restfulness of the landscape and heightened by subtle
displays of natural beauty. Stately trees and massed flowers,
flowing streams and fountains, delicate fragrances and
harmonies of colour made up a royal retreat that was created
to recall paradise.

Aram Bagh was also known as Gulafshan, or 'flower-
scattering garden', though it is now simply called Ram Bagh.
An inappropriate name, which may have owed inspiration
to Maratha generals who controlled Agra and Delhi when
the Mughal dynasty was waning. But the imprint of the
Mughals remains everywhere, in both the natural and man-
made beauty with which the Mughals surrounded their lives.
All the emperors loved the outdoors. They were also
particularly fond of fruit and fragrant flowers, and each took
pleasure in Aram Bagh and left something of themselves

behind. To me, this garden evokes the life and times of the Mughals far more than the empty palaces of the Red Fort.

Aram Bagh particularly recalls the spirit of Zahir-ud-din Mohammad Babur, founder of the Mughal dynasty, great adventurer and military commander who initiated the conquest of the subcontinent and built this garden. Babur, who spent most of his time in the saddle on military campaigns, is said to have disliked the hot airless rooms of palaces and preferred to spend his nights under a canopy in the open. He did not build any significant royal residences, but laid out gardens, including Aram Bagh in 1528. Indeed, he governed his rapidly growing empire from this garden, meeting his nobles and generals here, and planning historic campaigns.

During his brief rule, Babur's son Humayun spent long lotus-eating days here, in a haze of opium and wine. Akbar, the dynamic far-sighted and most inspired of the Mughals, planted the first pineapples at Aram Bagh. Several thousand of the large luscious fruit were grown here every year. Jahangir and his beloved empress Nur Jahan visited this garden often and added many fragrant flowers to the plantings: pink roses, jasmine, narcissi, carnations, dahlias and lilies. They also rebuilt Babur's riverside pavilions and improved upon the *hamam*, the bathhouse that Babur felt was crucial to civilized living. Jahangir gifted the garden to his empress and renamed it, for her, Bagh-E-Nur Afsan, 'garden of spreading light'. Jahangir's son, Shah Jahan, and Mumtaz Mahal escaped here from the formality of court for rare family interludes, when the emperor shed his reserve and laughed with his wife and played with his children. In addition to these imperial personages, innumerable princes, princesses, scores of nobles and generals and, of course, generations of attendants, all enjoyed the bounty of Aram Bagh.

* * *

Today's visitors are more plebeian. On the steps of an elegant Mughal pavilion overlooking the river, an anxious young man frowns over his college books in desperate concentration. There are too many distractions at home, also, too many people. The family consists of six, including his grandmother, so this is the only place he can study alone. He needs to work hard to get a future: a B.Com. followed by an MBA and then a job with an MNC that will get him away from the crowded shanty where he now lives. For families like his (his father is a daily wage labourer), housing, even on the outskirts of Agra, is terribly expensive. But there is hope; education is inexpensive and will provide him with a glowing future.

He loves to come to this garden. He forgets all his troubles here. And when there are no examinations looming, he often comes with a group of friends; they loaf and crack jokes and throw stones into the river. Sometimes, they even bring some cheap alcohol along, but that is usually at night, when the guards are asleep. They have a few drinks, a few laughs. He doesn't know who built the garden; he doesn't really care. It is enough that it is there. There is a board outside which he read years ago, but now he has forgotten what it said. There are seldom many other people here; few tourists come to Aram Bagh; they are only interested in the Taj. He has been there once in his nineteen years, on an outing with his friends. The trip was fun. The Taj Mahal? Nice.

A little further on, pairs of young men and women snuggle together in the privacy of bushes—assignations that were unheard of a decade ago. Sadly, they are increasingly the target of righteous indignation. On the broad walkway that leads to the garden, another couple approaches, evidently newly-wed from the bright henna on the girl's hands and the red chura bangles that encircle her wrists. She teeters along on very high and very new heels and looks as though her feet are killing her. Her husband has his arm draped possessively around her shoulders. They were married just a few days ago in Delhi and are in Agra for their honeymoon. Because of the Taj, of course. So many songs in Hindi movies refer to this monument to love; whenever anyone thinks of love, they think of the Taj Mahal. They have been to the Taj once, but it was very crowded. A friend in Delhi had told them that Aram Bagh was quieter and very beautiful. This is their second visit to the garden in just four days.

* * *

This garden is where my enchantment with the Mughals and with Agra began. My husband and I were attempting to build a low-cost home and had found that a domed structure would be the cheapest option. We had come to Agra to discuss recipes for mortar with officials of the Archaeological Survey of India (better known as the ASI). The visit paid off. A lime waste mortar, used in most Mughal buildings in Agra, enabled us to construct our house at approximately one-tenth the cost of conventional building. Having got our home going, we decided that the garden should follow the Mughal style, which is what brought us to Aram Bagh. Here, we received our first and very detailed explanation of the complex and yet simple structure of a Mughal garden from a gnarled old gardener whose understanding of his charge delighted us.

'God Almighty planted the Garden of Paradise,' he told us. 'This is a temporal image of that Garden, described in the holy Koran. Here, running waters and shady walks, trees heavy with fruit and massed fragrant flowers recall the Eden of divine abundance.' I recall from my readings that the Persian word for such gardens, *Pairideza*, was the origin of the English Paradise. 'The basic design of a Mughal garden,' he continued, wiping his rheumy eyes, 'develops from a cross formed by the intersection of two walkways. This divides the site into the traditional *char bagh*, 'four gardens.'

Here at Aram Bagh there are several sets of char baghs in each of the different levels of the garden. The highest terrace overlooks the river and the fields beyond. This is an important aspect of all Mughal gardens: the view beyond. The lower terraces are enclosed. So the garden is both inward- as well as outward-looking. Our learned friend strokes his wispy, hennaed beard, deep in thought, before informing us, 'High walls and deep banks of trees enclose the garden to hold in the perfumes and keep out the sere winds.' And then there was the important element of colours, changing with every season, from the delicate yellows and whites of summer to the loud monsoon notes, from the hiatus of winter to the fragile palette of spring.

My husband and I talked to the gardener about the present and discussed ongoing efforts to restore Aram Bagh. 'But it is also the patrons that matter; they must respect the garden,' the old man said, glaring at a pair of young lovers as they strolled by, flushed, hand in hand.

* * *

Babur is recognized as a master strategist, an inspired leader of men, a general renowned for his bravery and ferocity in battle, but what is less known is that he loved nature deeply. His memoirs, the *Tuzuk-E-Baburi,* which make delightful reading, contain repeated references to flowers and especially gardens, which were, to Babur, integral to gracious living. The art of building gardens reached its apogee in Persia and Central Asia, and led to a passion for flowers so consuming that it inspired some of the finest poetry of the age.

Particularly enchanted by the rose, Babur wrote:

> My heart, like the bud of the red, red rose,
> Lies, fold within fold, aflame;
> Would the breath of even a myriad springs
> Blow my heart's bud to a rose?

He also insisted that the names of all his daughters be prefixed with *gul*, Persian for 'rose'. Thus there were Gul-chihra Begum, Gul-izar Begum, Gul-badan Begum, and Gul-rang Begum.

When Babur came to Agra, the erstwhile capital of the Lodhi Sultan whom he had defeated, he complained in his memoirs: 'Three things oppressed us in Hindustan: its heat, its strong winds and its dust.' It was to counter these inconveniences, and to develop a locale where he could live with nature, that he established this garden on the banks of the river Yamuna. The great plain by the river was landscaped to create sunken gardens where the cool air settled. Great Persian wheels drew water from the river and poured it into red sandstone channels that gurgled through the garden and irrigated its flowers and fruit trees. Water paused in shallow pools and sparkled in fountains. It fell from level to level in smooth cascades or over chutes in tumults of foam. Indeed, water was the focus of a Mughal garden, its very life and soul.

The contrast between the Islamic and the Hindu approach to water has always intrigued me. Muslims, who did not worship water, as Hindus did, nevertheless brought great ingenuity to exploring the limitless possibilities of running water and regarded it with much greater respect. Tanks in mosques and temple ponds differ tremendously in their levels of cleanliness.

Babur also built pavilions on a high terrace above the

river, positioned to catch the slightest breeze, and also to provide the perspective for wide views of the garden descending in terraces. I like to think of the emperor sitting quietly by the river, writing poetry or composing music, or recording the day's events in his journal, the *Babur Nama*, or simply falling asleep at Aram Bagh under a canopy, his body cooled by the gentle breeze off the water, his mind soothed by the soft rhythm of the river.

To combat the heat and dust of Hindustan, the new emperor also constructed a basement for his hamam. Babur recorded in his journal, 'In the heat, it is so chilly that one is almost cold.' Access to the hamam involves an acrobatic clambering over iron grilles placed, I learn later, to deter entry, onto a steep stairway. It is a magical place, with a maze of subterranean chambers that open onto the river. Baths and dressing areas lead off from a large perfectly proportioned hall with a big central water body. In an adjoining room, two chutes once channelled rushing water into a small pool with a fountain that would have sprayed scented water to cool the air.

This summer retreat, where the hot air was tempered and the body refreshed by long leisurely baths, must have gladdened Babur's heart. Hearty male laughter would have rumbled through these rooms as Babur roistered with his amirs, sluicing off the dust and grime of the day. And for cold winter days there was elaborate provision for heating water, which would fall into the pools in clouds of fragrant steam.

I step outside to look out onto the river, and try to see it as it once must have been, full-bodied and swift. It was then an important waterway, crucial to trade. Big barges would labour upriver laden with goods from distant Bengal and from important riverside towns. Smaller vessels, their sails billowing in the wind, would have tacked upstream and there, anchored in the distance, would be the imperial barge, gilded and magnificent.

An Archaeological Survey staffer explains that the hamam is frequently closed to the public since it is difficult to monitor the activities of visitors. Hence the iron grilles that presented me with so much difficulty. There are only three personnel at Aram Bagh and it is impossible for them to be everywhere. The hamam became 'a danger zone,' the official explains, 'and three dead bodies were found here over the years. It became the haunt of antisocial elements,' so it was best to close it to the public till it was possible to upgrade the staffing. As with everything else, it is a question of finance.

The Archaeological Survey of India (ASI) was established in 1860 under Major General Alexander Cunningham and has gone on to do excellent work in the excavation and protection of monuments, including, of course, the Taj Mahal. However, a letter from Cunningham to a director of the East India Company, published in the journal of the Royal Asiatic Society in 1843, proves that its founding was a politically and religiously motivated attempt directed towards showing, 'that Brahmanism, instead of being an unchanged and unchangeable religion which had subsisted for ages, was of comparatively modern origin and had been constantly receiving additions and alterations; facts which prove that the establishment of the Christian religion in India must ultimately succeed...' Cunningham was passionately interested in newly-discovered Buddhist monuments and artifacts of the second and third centuries before Christ, and felt that further excavations and the publicity that would surround them, would diminish Brahmanism. However, but for the excavations and steps for conservation conducted by the ASI, much of India's heritage would have long been lost.

Conservation is in full swing at Babur's hamam. The white

plaster, thoughtlessly applied during British occupation, is being peeled off and faint traces of the paintings on walls and ceilings are beginning to emerge. Careful restoration has also revived the form and structure of the garden. Waterways, pools and paths are all being relaid after careful research. But to truly bring the garden back to life, its channels must flow again. Once sky-blue ribbons crisscrossing broad paths of flagstones, they are today empty and forlorn. The fountains and water spouts, too, that once threw up sparkling spray, lightening the formality of the garden, are all now silent. Given the shortage of water, a closed circuit could be developed that would recycle water and minimize the necessity of replenishment. Drought-resistant fruit trees would enliven the garden with their abundance of fruit and blossom. Parterres of flowers would brighten grass plots, while sturdy local trees could be planned to create shady walks. Perennial rose bushes of a hardy local variety should edge the pathways, spilling over the stone and softening hard outlines.

But all this requires funds, for the plantings themselves, but even more for maintenance. If only Agra's hospitality sector could be associated with such a project. I envisage soirées being held here once again. Guests would recline in the Mughal manner on the soft turf, enjoying the cool evening, conversing and listening to music, gazing at the rushing water, or watching dancers perform. Later, fireworks would explode in the sky in bright showers of golden stars. Dinner would be served in the Mughal manner on a *dastakhwan*, an embroidered cloth set on the ground, dispensing with inappropriate chairs and tables. And if the cost of the evening's recreation were to include a contribution to the garden, it would be possible to restore Aram Bagh and sustain it into the future.

* * *

'So everybody told you to meet me,' says Mr Agam Prasad Mathur. It isn't a question. I have sought an appointment with this most distinguished son of Agra to find out more about his city's beginnings. He is a prominent historian, twice vice-chancellor of Agra University, and revered guru, since the age of twenty-eight, of a faction of the Radha Soami Satsangh. The sect was founded in 1861 by a banker of Agra, Siva Dayal Saheb, whose teachings were directed towards achieving union with the divine. Mr Mathur, or Dadaji Maharaj as he is called by his devotees, lives in the crowded Pipal Mandi, a very old part of the city, where his Kayastha ancestors settled with others of their community. With their pragmatic command of Persian, the Kayasthas prospered under Mughal rule and rapidly rose from being mere scribes who documented the records of the empire, to important administrative posts and often high social rank.

The lane that leads to Dadaji Maharaj's residence is quiet and well paved. Unlike the crowded, chaotic, urban muddle of the Pipal Mandi area just a few steps away, where shops selling tyres and machine parts clutter the pavement with an intrusive and greasy mess. I am shown into a spacious sitting room furnished largely in maroon with pink silk anti-macassars matched by pink silk cushions. Large portraits of previous gurus of the sect line the walls. The present incumbent is also well represented at various stages of his life. Eventually, I am ushered into the presence. Mr Agam Prasad Mathur, or Dadaji, is resting on a large bed in the centre of the room. He is wearing a pale pink kurta with a quilted jacket of a slightly darker pink and is propped up against pink pillows. A pink sequinned quilt is drawn up over him. The skirt around the bed is also of pink sequinned fabric as is the cloth covering the bedside tables. Even the walls are pink.

Dadaji is an impressive man, in his mid-seventies but much younger-looking. Replying to my query on the significance of the colour pink, he smiles, 'I like it, don't you?' Mr Mathur tells me about Agra. Many ancient cities were founded on the banks of rivers for access to water and easy transport. 'There is a beautiful S-shaped curve in the river Yamuna here,' he says, drawing on his vast knowledge, 'which made it a very attractive site from which attackers could be seen from a distance. In addition, there were a few undulations, outcrops of the Aravalli hills as well as riverside sand dunes, which made the site particularly commanding.'

Dadaji Maharaj reflects for a while. 'Of course, agro-economics was the basis for the development of the town,' he says. The region was very fertile, with deep alluvial soil enriched by the periodic flooding of the river. The crops were rich and provided the foundation for the wealth of the area. 'Moreover,' he adds, pulling up his pink quilt, 'the river provided an excellent artery of communication. It was deep and placid and easily navigable all the way to Bengal. Goods flowed out of Agra and travelled downriver.' Caravan routes converged at Agra from Central Asia, Rajasthan, Gujarat and the Indus Valley, establishing Agra's strategic importance at the crossroads of the subcontinent. Dadaji describes the growth step by step. 'As money filled the farmers' pockets, the demand for other products grew,' he explains. 'Cottage industries were set up. Trade developed. Crops and textiles were exported and other commodities imported. And as material needs were fulfilled, any surplus was given to the gods.'

According to Dadaji, the city was named after Agrasen, who governed the region on behalf of his brother Sursen, king of nearby Mathura. The word Agra is also associated with the Aggarwals of the prominent Bania community, the merchant traders who settled in the area as trade developed, and trace their origin to Maharaja Agrasen. The Aggarwals prospered over the centuries and spread out from Agra to every part of the country, and have set up businesses ranging from small village grocery stores to huge metropolitan business empires.

On the Kayasthas, Dadaji tells me, 'We are really Kshatriyas, but we took to education, preferring the pen to the sword and became scribes and clerks to many kingdoms. Over a period of time, we came to be known as Kayasthas.' He holds out his hand to his secretary, who sits on the floor near his bed. 'Educated people were rare in those days. Of course, every kingdom needed scribes, so we prospered.' He pauses a moment as his secretary puts a paan into his outstretched hand. He pops it into his mouth. 'Our forebears were originally lettered in Sanskrit but later, recognizing the vast opportunities afforded by the Mughal court, they turned their considerable skills to Persian.'

'The Kayasthas were among the first professionals,' he continues, chewing thoughtfully. 'As scribes and clerks they kept the enormous administrative machinery of the Mughal empire well oiled.' Several Kayastha families moved to Agra and they all lived in vast mansions at Pipal Mandi. After the Mughal capital moved to Delhi, many followed the court, but large numbers remained in Agra where they served the governors and later, after the Mughal empire collapsed, found work with the various dynasties that ruled in the region. With their high levels of learning, most Kayastha families did well for themselves. Many went into the administrative services and other professional cadres. 'You find them everywhere,' Dadaji says with pride. 'They are the Mathurs, Narayans, Srivastavas and Saxenas. A Kayastha of Agra, Rai Saligram Bahadur, became the first Indian Post Master-General of

Uttar Pradesh in 1881.' He was also Dadaji Maharaj's grandfather and the third guru of the Radha Soami cult.

The young Agam Prasad became guru when his father died. It was an onerous responsibility, for the cult is based on bhakti, devotion to the guru of the time as the voice of the super soul, whose discourses are regarded as divinely revealed. 'I try to preserve the basic tenets of our faith,' he says with humility. 'We have no organization, no real structure. People assemble, I preside and deliver a discourse. I am more concerned with the spirit, with helping my followers achieve a detachment from material things. To enable them to listen to the internal sound.'

Conversation returns to Agra. 'During Partition, a large number of our more distinguished and supremely talented Muslim neighbours migrated to Pakistan. That was a terrible loss to the cultural life of the city. To make matters worse, there was a huge influx of Hindu refugees fleeing Pakistan. These people brought with them the scars of Partition, including an antipathy towards Muslims, at whose hands many had suffered.' Mr Mathur polishes his glasses with the edge of his pink kurta while he remembers. 'It was a time when people of both communities went mad with fear and anger. Hindus also perpetrated atrocities on Muslims. But that is neither here nor there. What was important is that it disturbed the mingling of communities that we once had at Agra. The old brotherhood between Hindus and Muslims diminished. It is still there among us old Agra people, but no longer as pronounced as it had once been.'

Dadaji tends to speak in monologues. 'In the old days, the pre-Partition days, the city had a vibrant cultural life. *Mushairas*, where poets recited their newest compositions, were part of everyday life. Poetry and classical music, they were sublime. But today the traditional culture of our city has been terribly undermined.' He puts his hand out for another paan. 'Agra also had a rich folk tradition. There were folk songs for each occasion, lullabies, wedding songs, songs for the groom when he mounted his mare, *doli* songs for when the bride left her home, and so much else,' he says through a mouthful of betel. 'The new settlers, largely Punjabis and Sindhis, brought their own songs. And over the years our traditions became diluted.'

Life was simpler in the old days, he tells me. Economic pressures were not as severe. The family was united. Each member had a special place and responsibilities. Festivals were celebrated with joy, with none of the rush and pressure of commercialism that there is today. The entire community, the whole *mohalla*, or locality, participated. After Independence, life became more complicated. Social responsibility diminished and soon disappeared altogether. Freedom was misinterpreted as licence. Over the years, attitudes changed. The young ceased to respect the old, values disintegrated.

The new settlers from Pakistan hastened the deterioration of values. They had lost everything. 'All they were interested in,' Dadaji Maharaj declaims angrily, 'was re-establishing themselves materially. They worked very hard; every man, woman and child among them worked hard, and slowly they came up commercially, materially.' Dadaji is an experienced speaker both as lecturer and as guru, and it shows. 'These refugees,' he continues, 'had no stake in Agra. They did not feel anything for the city. It was just a shell to shelter them and to make money in. They did not care about its cleanliness, its culture; they did not care about anything. Consideration, social consciousness—all was sacrificed.'

It is possible to make improvements. But the will has to be there. And some return of social responsibility. Dadaji launches into another pet peeve. 'Everyone thinks the government should do everything for us. We look to the government for the implementation of even our own civil duties,' he says angrily. 'In the old days, extended families lived together in the same mohalla. People were considerate of their neighbours, with whom they shared bonds of kinship. Since their mohalla represented the dignity and status of their family group, it was well taken care of. But then, the mohallas became overcrowded, many people moved out and the familial character of their society broke down. So now no one cares for the next person.'

* * *

I seek out Dr Neville Smith, journalist and former head of the department of English at the Raja Balwant Singh College, who I am repeatedly told is an expert on Agra. We meet close to his home at the Coffee Shop of the Holiday Inn, where I am staying, and size each other up. Dr Smith is stocky and compact, with hair turning to silver, and quick alert eyes. There is an economy in his entire persona. He speaks quickly and quietly, is brief and to the point. His eyes convey indomitable character. I feel sure Neville Smith has never told a lie in his life. It simply would not occur to him. He is also extremely generous with information, ideas and advice. He has since given me a collection of his father's articles, *The Legacy of a Journalist*, a fascinating compilation of information on diverse aspects of the city, which enormously enhanced my understanding of Agra. Thomas Smith had been a distinguished journalist and an authority on Agra, deeply respected across communities. Because Dr Neville Smith is his son and because I know him, innumerable doors in Agra open to me.

Dr Smith suggests I should first understand the layout of

the city. We pore together over a map of Agra. 'Look,' he says in the clipped accent that singles him out, 'Agra is situated on a vast open plain on the east bank of the Yamuna. The Fort, as you can see, was on the side of the river and the city developed behind it.' The fortress was the heart and hub of old Agra. The bazaars radiated from it, as they still do. In fact, many have retained old names which once indicated their special focus. There is the Kinnari bazaar where all kinds of gold and silver borders were sold, the Kashmiri bazaar, home to the people of the region and Seb Ka Bazar, famous for its apples. All of these—and more—were as crowded then as they are today. Then there is Rawatpara, where many Marwari traders and financiers settled, and Pipal Mandi, the locality of the Kayasthas. These were all well developed areas, though they now offer a bit of everything and are a melange of different peoples.

The bazaars actually led off the great royal square to the west of the moat. The *amirs* on guard duty at the citadel pitched their tents there. The two main streets of Agra ran straight from the square and were flanked by crowded arcades of stalls offering a selection of almost everything. Warehouses behind the stalls led onto a courtyard surrounded by apartments where the families of less affluent merchants lived. Richer traders had palatial homes in other parts of the city. 'And here, close to the Fort, along the Yamuna,' Dr Smith explains, tracing the river on the map, 'were the palaces of the princes and senior nobles. See, this is the Jama Masjid, the great mosque, situated between the Fort and the city, serving both, but especially the aristocracy of the Fort.' Of course this was not the only mosque; scores of smaller ones served different localities.

As long as Agra was capital of the Mughal empire, the city grew in all directions. Beyond the imperial avenues and bazaars, a jumble of unplanned twisting streets and lanes developed haphazardly to serve the mansions and huts constructed by rich and poor alike without any thought to town planning. Foreign travellers often remarked on the contrast between the lifestyles of the rich and those of the poor, particularly commenting on the 'wretched' huts of the common people, with mud walls and thatched roofs that continue to be built in Indian villages even today. The thatch, moreover, was inflammable and caused great fires, sometimes as often as a couple of times a year.

There were gardens on the outskirts of the city, on both sides of the river. Dr Smith points out Aram Bagh, now close to the road that bypasses Agra. 'And here, on the loop of the river,' he says, 'is the Taj Mahal'. He also points out the great tomb gardens near Aram Bagh, the exquisite Chini Ka Rauza and Itmad-ud-daulah's mausoleum, located, as was usual, outside the city.

There have of course been many changes in land use over the centuries. 'Take, for example, this place, the Holiday Inn,' says Dr Smith. 'Babur's army camped here at one time.' This area was probably forested then; panthers, and tigers too, would have stalked their prey in the brush jungle. 'Later, under Akbar,' Dr Smith explains, 'it became the Armenian settlement where merchants built their palaces and Agra's first chapel. In the early nineteenth century, the British built the Central Jail here. Then, in 1976, Sanjay Gandhi launched a drive to clean up Agra and this part of the city was earmarked for a commercial area. So the jail was pulled down and is now a busy business hub complete with its Holiday Inn.' He points to the map again. 'A little further from this place is the Roman Catholic Cemetery which was once a mango grove. See, here is Akbar's church,' he says, 'and the Cathedral was also built close by.'

After the British conquered Agra in 1803, there was another spurt of development. A sprawling Cantonment and Civil Lines were carefully laid out between the old city and the Taj, incorporating much of what was the old Mughal graveyard in their new development. Churches sprang up, as well as Christian schools and colleges, all built in the neo-classical style that was sweeping Europe. These, along with the considerable demolitions that occurred in the nineteenth century, altered the cityscape completely. But even today, different time frames co-exist companionably in Agra, the old medieval city, the Raj, the modern city and the timeless though ruined river.

New settlements have sprawled haphazardly all over Agra and they continue to grow. But there have been attempts to improve matters. Encroachments that ate into the arterial Mahatma Gandhi Road, causing formidable traffic snarls, were demolished in a rare demonstration of political will that was part of a vigorous clean-up-Agra drive. Similarly, the illegal commercial establishments, often a couple of storeys high, that crammed the riverside along the Yamuna, have been replaced by swathes of trees and gardens. 'Itmad-ud-daulah's tomb across the river,' says Dr Smith, 'was previously totally hidden from view'. Not any more. Ironically, these moves were initiated by concerned outsiders, in this case by Sanjay Gandhi.

One of Dr Smith's concerns is the lack of planning in Agra. 'Huge amounts of money come into the city, largely on account of the Taj,' he avers, 'but although substantial improvements have occurred in the vicinity of the monument, much remains to be done, particularly in the old city'. A series of master plans has been prepared. In fact, there is a conference every two or three years on the development of the city. The theme is always the same: making Agra worthy of the Taj.

'The difficulty,' Dr Smith believes, 'is that many of our people, especially of the old Agra families, tend to live in the past. The city itself still lives on memories of what it once was and seems unable to move on to the present. There is a lack of vision, an absence of clarity.'

One section of the people regard Agra as a Muslim city, which spawned an enormous controversy about the date of its founding. Sultan Ibrahim Lodhi is credited with founding the city in 1504 and the year 2004 was sought to be celebrated as the 500th anniversary of Agra's birth. This plan was scuttled in consideration to those who believe that Agra was an ancient Hindu settlement.

Another impediment to the development of Agra is the lack of a work culture. 'People,' Dr Smith says, speaking slowly and thoughtfully, 'will do as little as possible and are seldom motivated to give of their best. The attitude may be a hangover from the days of the Mughals, when important positions were often obtained through connections and had little to do with ability. But the same people work very well when they work for themselves or when strict discipline is enforced.' Dr Smith's final word is on the Taj Mahal. 'As a journalist,' he says, 'I am grateful to the Taj. Almost anything to do with it makes news, even international news.'

* * *

Babur and his nobles, as well as later Mughals, planted so many gardens along the Yamuna that the local people called the area Kabul, after his homeland. The entire locality between Aram Bagh and the Chini Ka Rauza was once a continuum of Mughal gardens. Babur himself is said to have laid out at least three more in the immediate vicinity of Aram Bagh. But there has been so much construction that it is difficult to see the original lay of the land. Traces linger in the riverbank plant nurseries that have proliferated, as did gardens in another time. Agra is today a reputed source of quality plants.

At the Azad Nursery on the way to Itmad-ud-daulah's tomb, a small house on the road conceals a strip of extremely fertile land that slopes down to the river. The young son of the owner introduces himself as Dr Arvind Kumar Kushwaha. His family are *malis*, traditional horticulturists who have tended the land in this area since Mughal times. And those that were not employed in the gardens of the Mughals always found plenty of work planting avenues of trees along highways to shade travellers, an act considered pious in those times. How tragically far we have come from such traditions.

Arvind is proud of his heritage, but a little defensive about the manual labour involved in his family's vocation. His gold watch, bright against his sun-darkened skin, is a proud proclamation of success. 'Even the casual labour here are experts in plant management,' he tells me. 'They are *karigars*, expert craftsmen in planting and caring for fruit trees and flowers. All over India, you will find small roadside nurseries after the rains. They are all run by malis from Agra. Nowhere else in India will you find so many people who are so skilled at this.'

Six or seven families of descendants own the land between Aram Bagh and Itmad-ud-daulah's tomb, but now the big holdings of the past have been divided among the sons of each generation till Arvind and his brothers are now left with just a narrow strip. Arvind's father was one of the first in the community to be educated. He did his BSc. and now has a contract with the Agra Development Authority to plant trees. Arvind himself studied horticulture and obtained a Ph.D. in asters. He waxes eloquent over a cup of hot sweet tea. 'Asters are best for people who want cut flowers,' he says, taking a long, satisfied slurp. 'The flowering is very good and the season very long. They are also in great demand as floral decorations at weddings because they last well without water. Asters are as beautiful as gerberas, much more practical and, of course, far less expensive.'

Arvind's community was all but disinherited by mainstream India. Barely a generation ago, its members were dismissed as low-caste labour. And now Arvind already has a doctorate in an area directly related to his families' work of many generations. The great Indian dream is alive and well.

Earlier, till the 1970s, the family concentrated on planting fruit trees, most of the species that grew in the plains, but they specialized in citrus. 'People came from all over to buy from us,' he says with a big, white smile. 'Our quality was assured.'

Then urbanization set in. The big bungalows with vast gardens gave way to flats, and the demand for fruit trees diminished. A new requirement developed, that of ornamental indoor plants. So that is what they now grow. They have every conceivable variety of indoor plant from varicoloured crotons to exotic palms. We walk though the nursery shaded by big old trees twittering with the conversation of birds, a world far removed from the snarled traffic just a few yards away. The fragrance of wet earth and mulch is rich and sensuous. I am reminded that the Mughals named a perfume, an *ittar*, after wet earth.

On either side of the narrow strip of land owned by Arvind's family, scores of other similar plots stretch from behind the roadside retail outlets to the river. The greenery is lush and fecund. Arvind gesticulates widely, his gold watch catching the sun. 'There are over 500 plant nurseries here, all linked to the Yamuna. We exist thanks to the river. It has good sweet water, unlike the ground water which is brackish.'

Today, almost everybody has pump sets on the river. Not so long ago, in fact in Arvind's childhood, Persian wheels were used, drawn by bullocks, a method the Mughals had used to irrigate this very land when it was a series of gardens. 'See,' he says, pointing to a large sunken plot, 'this was once part of a char bagh. The water channels flowed at a higher level along raised paths. This made irrigation easier, plus, of course, it was much cooler in these lower areas. Often, when we turn the soil or dig deep, we still find bits of carved water chutes and pillars from pavilions that once adorned these gardens.'

* * *

Some say Agra existed as much as 2,500 years ago. Ochre-coloured potsherds, found at several places in and around Agra, have been dated to at least 1800 BC and seem to indicate that a thriving civilization existed at that time. Agra was certainly well known by 200 AD, when the Greek geographer Ptolemy marked it on his map of the world.

Indeed, Agra's origins reach so far back in time that its beginnings are precariously balanced between myth and reality. The region is mentioned in the epic, *Mahabharata*, as Agravan, the forest of Agra, or as some prefer, the forest ahead. Given its proximity to Mathura, birthplace of Lord Krishna, Agra is on the fringes of the mythical landscape of Vraj, the sacred land where Lord Krishna grazed his cattle, enchanted the local people, performed miracles, vanquished evil and established a doctrine of love. While anthropologists explain that Krishna was chief of a tribe of pastoralists who deified him, believers, who think of him as a god, see in him the incarnation of Vishnu, born to reestablish divine order. Krishna grew up among a community of cowherds, and the pastures and villages of Vraj where he romped with his friends were canonized by his presence. Vraj is said to have contained, differently according to various theories, twelve or thirty-two forest glades, with shady groves and lush pastures. A charmed woodland, that has become part of our collective visual imagery. Even today, legends of Krishna resonate in the groves and grasslands along the Yamuna, where, it is said, if your heart is pure and your mind is still, you may hear the faint notes of the Lord's flute quivering in the early morning air.

The Sursena dynasty into which Krishna was born, maintained an outpost at Agravan. The city, as Dr Agam Prasad Mathur had explained, is believed to have been founded during the time of Agrasen, Krishna's maternal grandfather. It probably consisted of a few huts surrounded by fields and forests and a small fortress, later converted into a prison by his uncle Raja Kans, king of Mathura and the personification of evil, whom Krishna was born to destroy. Mathura during this period was a rich and beautiful city with huge gates of gold, and Kans is said to have had hundreds of gold-plated chariots. Although such descriptions could well be mythical hyperbole, exaggerated over the centuries, Mathura was certainly a wealthy city, well situated in the fertile croplands of the Gangetic plain.

After the Sursena dynasty died out, Mathura was ruled by various local kings and went on to become an important provincial city of the major dynasties that ruled north India. It was an extremely important place of pilgrimage for Hindus, but also drew Buddhist and Jain pilgrims. The devout travellers made rich gifts to temples and religious institutions. Demand from pilgrims led to the development of crafts and a brisk trade, which contributed to the fabulous wealth of the merchants of Mathura, famous across the country as millionaire financiers. And Agra, only a small distance upstream and already an outpost of the Sursena empire, must certainly have benefited from proximity to such great prosperity.

* * *

Agra, under Babur's descendants, quickly became one of the largest metropolises of the civilized world at the time. It was as big, if not bigger, than London, Paris or Constantinople. For the subcontinent it was the centre of the universe, a city of unparalleled splendour, the fountainhead of power for the seventy years that it was capital of the Mughal empire. The centuries flew by and the Mughal capital moved to Delhi, taking with it many of the city's cultural elite and those who made their living providing for their needs. Agra was seriously depopulated. In later years the Mughal dynasty disintegrated and Agra diminished further in power and prestige. Looting by marauding chieftains followed by years of British dominance and overweening colonial values that downgraded every thing Indian, was another setback to Agra. The final blow was the exodus of some of its finest minds and most generous patrons at Partition.

There has been no major leader from Agra of sufficient national stature to promote its development. To make matters worse, large sections of the people are indifferent to their city. An attitude contributed to by the new settlers, who have no roots in Agra. No past associations. But even long-standing citizens of Agra often lack any real commitment. An attitude that is possibly rooted in the absence of any local dynasty after the Mughals. This caused a lack in Agra of any strong emotional bonding with the past, unlike in the Rajput states, for example, where the people had deep associations with the ruling family, their palaces, cenotaphs and the cities themselves, all of which reinforced a sense of belonging and commitment. Shorn of pride and identity by the compulsions of history, many people of Agra are therefore apathetic towards their city. For most, life revolves around the self and immediate family, excluding social or even community responsibility. Life is all about making a buck in difficult circumstances and difficult times. Planners, developers, even the city fathers, have focussed on Mumtaz Mahal's mausoleum and the area around it—for this is where the serious money was to be spent—largely ignoring the historic old city and other parts of the town where population has far outstripped infrastructure.

The cobble-stoned medieval streets of the old city are today flanked by open gutters and piles of garbage. The faded elegance of upper storeys is festooned with electric wires, telephone cables, television lines, snaking in and out of homes in great hazardous loops. Encroachments spill untidily onto streets while stalls and handcarts add to the confusion, each jostling for space to make a living. The narrow streets, planned for a much smaller population, and the sedate, more gracious pace of life several centuries ago, are so thronged by frenetic crowds of suppliers and buyers that they are difficult to walk through without repeated near-collisions. Everyone is in a hurry to get to a job, to clinch a deal. Consideration for others is a luxury that no one can afford. Auto-rickshaws weave past, dodging potholes, rushing for that one extra fare. Car and truck drivers lean on their horns to warn people out of their way. The chaos is overwhelming, unrestrained, tumultuous, and with a roaring anarchic vitality.

Development has passed Agra by; today there are only a few significant industries, and little real progress. This has left its people largely mired in a past with which many don't identify. Even the cottage industries derive from a previous time. And while everyone acknowledges that the perpetuation of labour-intensive craft skills and the employment of artisans are essential, industrial investment on any substantial scale is low. One of the reasons is a chronic shortage of electricity in the state, which leads to power cuts and consequent losses in production. The deficiency of electricity has spurred the manufacture of generators, making Agra one of the country's best-known suppliers of those machines. There is a sense, almost, of suspended animation, a city adrift in time. Agra is a city in transition, still searching for a new identity. Agra needs citizens who care. And a huge awareness campaign to re-instil pride in the city. But pride comes only when the stomach is full. And for many of Agra's people this requirement is still unfulfilled. Until that need is met, Agra will remain a provincial backwater, muddling through in the shadow of the Taj Mahal.

2

The Lion in Summer

Arun Dang's family moved to Agra after Partition. But he has made his mark on the city and is president of the Tourism Guild of Agra. We meet at his office in the Grand Hotel, which he owns. 'Agra has given my family everything,' he says, 'and now I am working to give something back by helping the city prosper'. He has many facts on his fingertips. 'Agra is a city of relatively young people; only six per cent are over sixty years old,' he informs me. This could be because a lot of the older migrants died during and just after Partition. Unemployment is high at forty per cent. 'Only twenty per cent of the people of Agra are associated with tourism and handicrafts. There is considerable scope to expand this sector of employment if tourism were to be boosted.' He shuffles the papers on his desk. 'Can you believe it? Agra has no air links whatsoever. There are twelve flights to Varanasi and not one to Agra, the magnet of tourists to India.' Even chartered flights have to drop off passengers and park the aircraft in Delhi till it is time for the visitors to depart.

'An airport in Agra would also benefit Delhi,' says Mr Dang, expanding on the topic. 'It would ease air traffic congestion.' The Tourism Guild has made repeated recommendations, but, Mr Dang informs me, 'The matter has been held up between the civil aviation and defence ministries.'

One of the problems regarding the development of air traffic is that the city is an important air base, with air force planes taking off and landing. 'But,' protests Mr Dang, 'Jodhpur, Goa, Pune and Siliguri have air force bases and yet they all have civilian flights. What is more, there *were* flights to Agra, but these were stopped in, I think, 2003 or 2004.' Then there is the issue of train timings. 'Most trains from Delhi arrive early in the morning and leave at night, encouraging people to make Agra just a day-trip and in too many cases depriving us of even a night's stay which, in turn, impacts hotel occupancies. The problem,' Mr Dang insists, 'is that Agra has no real ability to lobby in Delhi. Agra has never had a godfather, we've never had a political patron.'

There is a short interruption as prospective clients drop into the office to negotiate rates for events they plan to host at the Grand Hotel. One group is planning a wedding, and another, a smaller celebration for a relative who is visiting from the United States. But the refrain is always the same: 'the cheapest possible', 'just two or three things on the menu'. And when a suitably curtailed menu and its price are agreed upon, the client asks for a few more dishes at the same price! The routine never varies.

With an apology for the delay, Mr Dang gathers together the threads of the conversation. 'There is so much in Agra beyond the Taj and hardly anyone speaks of this. The Agra Fort, for instance, is also a World Heritage Site, the only fort in the world with this status, which means that it is the best fort in the world. This should receive publicity.' Then there are the gardens—the Aram Bagh, the Bagh-E-Bhist, Mehtab

Bagh, and so many others. There are also some interesting
Christian relics: the graveyard, for instance, which contains
so much of Agra's history. 'These must all be put on the
tourist map,' he says firmly.

The Tourism Guild of Agra has put forward a series of
proposals to both the state and central governments to
enhance the city's appeal. Among them is the call for an effort
to spruce up the entry points to the city of the Taj. I bring up
the need to clean up the old city, the famous streets and
bazaars, and suggest that is a priority. 'The old city has its
own charm,' Mr Dang points out, 'and it's not so different
in terms of cleanliness and order from, say, Chandni Chowk
in Delhi. There are so many difficulties involved in improving
upon the old city, so much opposition, that it is easier to
tackle new ground.' Besides, Mr Dang declares, 'Agra
generates 1,000 tonnes of garbage a day. Even in the best
case, the government cannot lift more than 800 kilos.'

'Surely there is a solution?' I ask.

His response is quick. 'Where will the money come from?'

Self-help must become a feature of life in Agra. There is a
tendency to complain, to grumble and to always pass the
buck. Few residents or tourism professionals I have met so
far are willing to do any real work for the betterment of the
city. Surely it would be possible for the industry to plough
some of their profits back into Agra, for hotels, for example,
to adopt streets in the old city and supervise their cleanliness.

Another issue that the Tourism Guild is pursuing is the
viewing of the Taj on all nights, but from the Mehtab Bagh
across the river. 'There is a proposal,' Mr Dang tells me, 'for
some kind of soft lighting that will not affect the marble,
and will not attract insects. These lights need to be on only for
an hour. It will add to our room nights, but also allow greater
numbers of people of all segments of visitors to see the Taj.'

History has given Agra an interesting mix of communities, I am informed by Mr Dang. There are the Banias, the backbone of the trading community who were also famous moneylenders. These include the Aggrawals and the Guptas. Then there are the Marwari traders who came here mostly from the Shekhavati area in Rajasthan. Many of them are Jains, such as the Oswals, Suranas, and others who call themselves simply Jains. Dozens of dialects are spoken in Agra and they often vary from street to street. Others include the Christians, the Kashmiris and, of course, the Muslims who, Mr Dang says, 'form just around sixteen per cent of the population today. Most of them went to Pakistan during Partition. Those that were left behind are mostly craftsmen and those that work with leather. Most of them are poor, though of course there are several notable exceptions.'

Each community also brought its own customs and its special cuisine. 'There is so much variety,' Mr Dang says with enthusiasm. 'Few other cities have such a range. Agra has the potential to be famous for its food. From the kachoris, jalebis and samosas to the puri aloo and the delicately flavoured vegetarian cuisine unique to UP, to the biryani, kormas and kebabs that are our heritage from the Mughals. And yet little is known about this facet of the city. It could form the basis for an entire promotion.'

* * *

From its quasi-mythical origins as a prison, the fortress at Agra grew in peace and prosperity till the latter part of the eleventh century, when it was attacked by 'Muhamad Shah, governor of Hind' on behalf of one of the descendants of Mahmud Ghazni 'who invaded India seventeen times'. Despite a valiant defence, Jaipal, the governor of the Fort, was forced to submit. This early fort of Agra is described by Niamatullah, a historian of the time, as 'built amidst the sand like a hill, and the battlements resembled hillocks.... No calamity had ever befallen its fortifications'.

Meanwhile, other Muslim conquerors who had gained their first foothold in the subcontinent in the eighth century, began to consolidate. They extended their conquests over the centuries till they controlled much of the land between the Yamuna and the Ganga, including of course, Agra. Four dynasties of sultans ruled in rapid succession till the Lodhis came to power in Delhi in 1451. It was a turbulent time in north India, and the second ruler of the dynasty, Sultan Sikander Lodhi, felt the need to establish a new capital closer to the kingdoms of recalcitrant vassals. The sultan appointed officers to survey the riverbanks downstream of Delhi and subsequently floated down the Yamuna in the royal barge to survey the site they had selected. With him were courtiers, generals and others of his court in a grand and colourful aquatic convoy. As they approached a wide bend in the river, two large mounds in the distance were pointed out to the sultan. He asked the commander of the royal barge which mound would be best on which to found his new capital. '*Age rah*,' the official replied, 'the one in front'. And so, it is said, Agra received its name, became the imperial capital and began a new phase in its development. The year was 1504.

On 6 July the same year, a terrible earthquake shook the ground and razed much of the new capital to the ground. Lofty buildings became heaps of rubble, and thousands of the populace were trapped in the ruins. An omen, murmured many, of disaster to come. But the sultan was not perturbed and quickly commenced rebuilding and further expanding Agra.

* * *

Maurice Rodgers, an amateur geologist and visitor to India whom I had met over the Net, researched the earthquake and found that its epicentre was close to Agra. Soft soils, such as the alluvium around Agra, tend to actually aggravate quakes, Maurice explained. 'It's rather like deep water waves,' he wrote, 'which can become alarmingly strong as they approach the shore'. As energy waves pass though alluvial soils, they gather momentum and can cause major damage, especially to tall and slender structures. There are well-known local faults in the vicinity of Agra that are capable of producing strong earthquakes. Whether the Taj Mahal, and especially its minarets, can withstand strong future quakes is open to question.

'Is it beyond the wit of man,' Maurice asked in an e-mail, 'to design a protective barrier? A ring of heavy energy-absorbing concrete weights, sunk into the ground with a set of dampers tuned to the appropriate resonance, could protect the monument.' Since the Taj Mahal will only be impacted when surface waves come from a certain direction, surely, these can be intercepted. An activity called micro-zoning, that has been conducted in the area around Delhi could, Maurice wrote from England, be replicated around the Taj. This would involve using sensors to assess the directions and magnitudes of incoming waves and arriving at statistics which will help interception. An intriguing possibility.

* * *

In the same year as the earthquake, Zahir-ud-din Muhammad, better known as Babur, the Lion, for his ferocity in battle, made his first raid across the high mountains. Born in Fergana, in present-day Kyrgyzstan, he was attracted to Hindustan by rumours of exceedingly rich pickings and these he found to be true.

Meanwhile, Sikander Lodhi nurtured his new capital and Agra grew rapidly into a large and prosperous town with royal palaces, grand buildings and mosques. As the centre of power, it attracted a large number of settlers, artisans and merchants. Ibrahim Lodi succeeded his father in 1517 and Agra continued to prosper under the new sultan.

But it was a difficult period, plagued with incessant conflict. Lodhi power was not strong enough to hold dissenters at bay. Intrigue and treachery were common weapons in the battle for supremacy. To make matters worse, a dangerous new factor entered the old equations. Babur descended again on the plains of Hindustan, this time not for a quick profit but for conquest. Cannons boomed and matchlocks cracked for the first time ever in north India, terrifying the Lodhis and causing their horses and elephants to panic. Even though Babur's soldiers numbered just 12,000, against the 100,000-strong Lodhi army, the invader gained a quick and decisive victory at Panipat in 1526. A date that would mark the onset of a new era.

Babur had a distinguished ancestry, reaching back to the dreaded Timur who sacked Delhi at the end of the fourteenth century. On his mother's side Babur was descended from the fierce Mongol chieftain Chingiz Khan. The term 'Mughal', in fact, derives from 'Mongol', but was also generally applied by the conquered people to all foreigners from Central Asia. Babur's conquest of India was, of course, initiated by the lure of incredible wealth. The export of huge quantities of textiles and spices for centuries before Christ had brought into India vast amounts of gold and silver bullion. This was translated into a dazzling display of wealth expressed in gilded palaces, magnificent temples endowed with rich gifts, stupendous jewellery and ornaments, frequently described by awestruck visitors in their memoirs. Babur had seen some of this opulence during his early raids, and realized there was very much more that he could access on a permanent basis.

Immediately after his victory, Babur dispatched his eldest son Humayun to Agra to seize the Lodhi treasury. His expectations of great wealth were not disappointed. Among the vast booty gained by Humayun at Agra was the great Kohinoor diamond, said to have weighed 240 carats, which was presented to the conquerors by a Lodhi vassal from Gwalior. Babur notes in his *Babur Nama* that its immense value could feed the entire world for two and a half days. Humayun dutifully gave it to his father, but Babur gave the jewel back to him. The diamond, said to have been called the Darya-E-Noor, 'river of light', was passed on to successive Mughal emperors till the early eighteenth century, when Nadir Shah of Persia invaded Delhi. He looted great treasures, including the fabled Peacock Throne, but was unable to find the enormous diamond. Finally, a lady of the harem told him the emperor always carried it in the folds of his turban. Nadir Shah then invited the Mughal to a great feast during which he proposed an exchange of turbans, a traditional gesture of friendship. The emperor was forced to comply. Nadir Shah left the festivities as soon as he could, and with feverish hands, probed for the gem. The elongated oval stone blazed with such brightness that he is said to have exclaimed, 'It is a *kohinoor*, a mountain of light!'

But the diamond brought him bad luck. Indeed, it was believed that it brought whoever owned it either world dominance or great tragedy. Nadir Shah was assassinated, as were his sons Adil Shah and Ibrahim, who also had their eyes put out before they were killed. Nadir Shah's grandson Shah Rukh was tortured till he gave the Kohinoor to Ahmad Shah of Afghanistan, whose death was followed by bloody civil wars between his twenty-three sons, till two of the survivors fled to the Punjab with the diamond.

Maharaja Ranjit Singh obtained the stone, scorning the legends of potential misfortune. But none of his eight descendants produced heirs and his entire royal line disappeared after the British defeated the Sikhs in 1849. The Kohinoor passed to the victors as part of war indemnity. It was later presented to Queen Victoria as a 'historical symbol of the conquest of India'. The Kohinoor was recut to improve its radiance in 1852, at a cost of £8,000 and its weight reduced from 186 carats to 109. Queen Victoria wore it in a tiara and then in a brooch. The legend that the Kohinoor could only be worn with good fortune by a woman seemed to have come true, for in 1877 she was proclaimed *Kaiser-I-Hind*, Empress of India. Queen Alexandra also wore the diamond and in 1911 it was set in a crown for Queen Mary. The Kohinoor was remounted in 1937 in the Maltese Cross in front of another crown which Queen Elizabeth wore at the coronation of King George VI. The queen mother's crown, kept in the Tower of London, was taken out to rest on her coffin during her funeral service.

There has been a clamour for the great diamond. The heirs of Maharaja Duleep Singh, from whom it was acquired by the British, have demanded that it be returned, since, they say, it was wrongly acquired. Other Mughal treasures that are also in British possession include a gold spoon studded with priceless rubies, a jade wine cup that belonged to Shah Jahan and the exquisitely illustrated *Padshah Nama* that documents his reign.

* * *

While Humayun was securing the Lodhi treasury and acquiring the Kohinoor, Babur took Delhi and advanced on Agra. On 10 May 1526, he entered the Lodhi capital at the head of his great army. A pragmatic commander, his first act was to distribute the spoils of war among his followers and with royal generosity. His nobles each received several hundred thousand gold *asharfi* coins, and huge amounts of loot from the Lodhi treasury were distributed among his soldiers. Every trader and servant received his munificent share. Rich gifts were also dispatched to Babur's relatives and to the holy men of his homeland, and even to those of distant Mecca and Medina. So vast was the treasure of Agra that Babur sent a silver coin to every man, woman and child in Kabul. He could afford to be generous: he had, after all, found the golden goose, or rather the 'golden bird' as the subcontinent was called at that time. But despite the riches they received, Babur's troops were not happy in Agra. They had arrived at the worst possible time of the year, during a particularly vicious summer when the sun blazed mercilessly and hot winds seared the plains. In addition to being overwhelmed by the heat, Babur's soldiers, accustomed to quick raids, were distressed by his intention of staying on in India for good. Wisely, Babur allowed all who chose to do so, to return.

Babur's Agra was surrounded by great animosity. Even the city and people of Agra itself were hostile. Local skirmishes to quell immediate adversaries took up much of his time. And Agra and its environs resounded repeatedly to the shrill blast of trumpets, the tread of armies and the rattle of battle drums. His first great confrontation was with the Rajputs, led by the legendary warrior Rana Sanga of Mewar who, incidentally, had offered to collaborate with Babur against the Lodhis whom he was anxious to oust. But Rana Sanga had not counted on Babur staying on in India and establishing an empire. He quickly realized he had introduced a new and much more dangerous element into the political rivalry of the northern plains. He called upon his fellow Rajputs to join him to repel the 'invader'. Thousands of rajas and chieftains gathered under his banner in a huge force that bested the Mughals in early encounters but were eventually soundly defeated. The success of the Mughal army rested on its use of artillery, with mounted archers and musket-bearing infantry, against the unwieldy elephants of local rajas which were easily frightened by the big guns. But there were still many battles to be fought. Babur spent most of his life galloping from one battle to another to extend and consolidate his empire and to garner further booty and access lands with rich revenues. Further conquest was now necessary to pay his growing army.

* * *

Agra's strategic importance had been established many centuries before Babur and continues to this day in the substantial military and air force presence that has a considerable impact on the dynamics of the modern city. It takes some arranging but at last I am able to see both in action. The night is cold, dark and clear. A quarter moon gently silvers acres of ploughed land on the fringes of Agra. The fragrance of freshly turned earth is pleasing, and the quiet soothing, after the cacophony of the city. The drone of a distant aircraft hums through the silence but it carries no navigation lights so it is difficult to place. Suddenly, and completely without warning, scores of faint mushroom shapes blossom in the sky. I feel as though I am watching a World War II movie. The parachutes drift to the ground in complete silence. My eyes prickle with patriotic tears.

A tall and extremely fit major tells me, 'Just before they jump, the paratroopers shout, "*Chatri Mata ki jai.* Hail to the goddess of the parachute."' A series of soft thuds around is followed by shouts as each paratrooper identifies himself and reports a successful landing. Within minutes they have folded their parachutes and boarded a truck shouting, '*Bharat Mata ki Jai.* Praise to Mother India.'

While we wait for the next pass a whipcord-lean officer in a camouflage jacket pipped with para wings, fills me in on the details. The Parachute Brigade, headquartered at Agra, moved here in the 1950s. The city was a natural base for the Para Brigade as there was already an air force base with transport aircraft for their jumps. 'Agra is known for the Taj, Ma'am,' he adds with a grin, 'and then for the Paras'.

On their connections with the air force, he tells me, 'We cooperate everywhere except in the Club.' Both arms pride themselves on being a cut above the other. Expressed in hard drinking and flamboyance which cause the odd run-in. The Agra airfield developed in World War II but an important military cantonment had been established in the city much earlier, during British rule. The same imperatives that made the city strategically important under the Mughals, and earlier, continued to be valid and indeed still stay. All over India, cantonments were established at traditional centres of power, which developed precisely because they were well linked to other parts of the country. This enabled quick deployment of troops and was crucial towards securing communications.

The Paratroopers are a tough lot, much tougher than ordinary infantry troops. Just this morning they completed a forced march of sixty-four kilometers, carrying backpacks weighing twenty-five to thirty kilos. They walked for thirteen hours. And tonight they jump. All Paratroopers are volunteers from infantry regiments, and they can leave at any time. But once a man joins this elite force, he will seldom give it up. Paras, I am informed, are held in awe in Agra for their exploits both on and off the battlefield.

An aircraft is approaching again. My focus shifts. This time I look carefully and see the bright light at the jump bay of the aircraft. What must it be like to jump from the light to the dark void, I wonder. The noise at the jump bay, the major tells me, is an incredible roaring both from the aircraft and the wind. There is a vertical bar to hold on to before the jump. Every Para has to jump at least once a year and this includes medical officers, cooks, dhobis, even pandits. They had a pandit once who was terrified. Every time it was his turn to jump, he grabbed the bar at the jump bay and swung around it to safety. He was transferred to another regiment.

The major tells me the Paras came into being during World War II. The Germans put the force to use for the first time in military history in the Netherlands, where Paratroopers were dropped, and taking advantage of the surprise factor, captured territory. The first airborne operation for the Indian Paras was during the Bangladesh operations in 1971. Then, in 1988, the brigade went to the Maldives and sorted out problems associated with the coup d'état there within twenty-four hours. In fact *Time* magazine ran a feature, based on this operation, on India's emergence as a military power. The Paras also serve as normal combat troops. They have participated in all the operations of the Indian army. 'You name it,' the major says, 'we've been there'.

My attention shifts to another group of parachutes in the sky and to their rapid rate of descent. The major is dismissive. 'That's nothing,' he says, 'these are only beginners jumping from 1,200 feet. They take about forty seconds to hit the ground. In more advanced training, we jump from 300 feet which takes ten to twelve seconds.'

* * *

Despite his martial prowess, Babur was also gentle and sentimental. The story of his death is illustrative. His son Humayun fell dangerously ill. The royal physicians were helpless and the prince seemed to be on the brink of death. His distraught father consulted a host of healers and soothsayers. A wise Tartar told him that a man could fulfil any desire if he gave up his most precious possession. Babur understood. He would offer up his life in exchange for his son's. He walked around Humayun's sick bed three times, praying that his life be taken. Suddenly, he shouted in exultation, 'I have borne it away, I have borne it away.' Humayun began to recover but within a few months Babur was dead. Just four years after his conquest of Hindustan.

I had been told earlier that Babur was laid to rest at Aram Bagh till his remains were moved to a hillside outside his beloved Kabul. Then, in a chance conversation, I heard for the first time of a monument called Char Bhurji, four bastions set in a garden where he was said to have been temporarily buried. I made many inquiries but no one seemed to have heard of it, till a caretaker at Itmad-ud-daulah's tomb, who had lived in the area since he was a child, offered to show me the way. He led me through a tiny, depressing and desperately poor settlement, a straggle of huts made from worn-out tin sheets, bits of plastic, mud and thatch. We walked past open drains clogged with plastic bags, past a litter of pigs rooting in a pile of refuse, past a mother combing her teenaged daughter's hair. The strokes of the comb, long and sure, were each a caress, an expression of deep love. I stopped to talk to a young man who was watching us but with blank, empty eyes. He was unemployed and had been so for a long, long time. He was thinking of trying to get a job selling vegetables for someone who had a handcart; he has been thinking about it for a long time. He was born and brought up in Agra, but poverty, accentuated by illiteracy, hunger, the sheer struggle to survive, had kept him a prisoner of this ghetto, with absolutely no knowledge or interest in even the city beyond. I asked him if he had ever seen the Taj Mahal. 'Taj Mahal?' he said. 'I haven't seen it, but yes, I have heard of it. It is in Delhi.'

The first resting place of the first Mughal emperor turns out to be a low building in considerable disrepair, surrounded by barbed wire and a brick wall. A few square feet of grass and packed mud on all sides of the tomb are all that are left of the marvellous Garden of Paradise Babur planned. Here is a different kind of squalor, a different kind of sorrow. A poor memorial to a man who founded a dynasty which governed India for nearly 200 years, bringing peace and a sense of unity to a beleaguered land. I am comforted by the memory that Babur was finally buried again in the Bagh-E-Kilan near Kabul, on the rising ground where he loved to sit, in eternal contemplation of the lovely view.

* * *

Humayun, lost to dreams and opium, was not a worthy successor. To make matters worse, he had inherited a fractious kingdom and was often forced to engage in battle. A rebellious Afghan chieftain, Sher Khan, a particular thorn in his side, was soon to oust Humayun to become Emperor Sher Shah, founding the short-lived Sur dynasty. He led his soldiers to victory against the Mughals at Chausa in modern-day Bihar. Humayun barely escaped with his life, almost drowning in a river nearby. A *bhisti*, a low-caste water-carrier, rescued him and ferried the emperor to safety on an inflated buffalo skin.

In a typical quixotic expression of gratitude, Humayun made him king for a day. The bhisti, it is also said, invited fellow leather-workers from all over to participate in his good fortune, establishing the foundation for Agra's considerable low-caste population and its famous leather industry. Although there were many Muslim leather-workers, others among the Hindu Jatavs also flocked to Agra to participate in the great opportunity.

* * *

Rajeev Lal, whose family has been in Agra for several generations, has a deep understanding of varied aspects of the city and its demography. He and his attractive and unfailingly sweet-natured wife Kamini, one of the nicest and gentlest people I have ever met, have been my anchor in Agra, and their home in the compound of the family-owned Lauries hotel has often been my refuge. Sitting in their airy and serene living room, we talk about shoes. Agra's leather industry, Rajeev believes, actually received its main impetus during the time of Humayun's son Akbar, who decreed that his soldiers wear shoes. Till that time the Mughal army had fought barefoot. Shoe-makers were summoned from all over the empire and work began. 'Think about the hundreds of thousands of pairs required in a single year,' Rajeev says, his face lighting up with amusement, 'and that, too, on an on-going basis'. These were, of course, the ordinary hard-wearing leather *jootis* with slightly turned-up toes, but there was also a huge demand for more delicate versions for nobles, their ladies and vast entourages.

Jootis for the nobility were covered in velvet and trimmed with gold and jewels. One particular pair made history. A wealthy noble, Jafar Khan, was hard put to keep his very beautiful begum happy. So he had a pair of slippers made for her, valued, in those days, at 100,000 rupees. No one is quite sure, but it is said that the lady in question had caught the eye of the widowed Shah Jahan, and that the slippers were her husband's way of holding her attention.

'Then there were also the Mughal shields,' Rajeev points out, 'which, at least for the common soldier, were made of leather'. It seems an anomaly that Agra, which is not a centre of tanning, is yet an important focus of the shoe industry.

The industry moved to the wholesale Hing Ki Mandi in the 1920s. 'You see,' Rajiv explains, 'asafoetida was packaged in large leather bags to retain its distinctive aroma. These were of course the perfect raw material for jootis and so, gradually, cobblers moved to Hing Ki Mandi and slowly took over the area.'

* * *

Kalim and Wassem Ahmed have been in the leather business for many years. Their warehouse is situated deep into Hing Ki Mandi. There is no trace of the asafoetida trade any more and the old bazaar is now a huge leather market. It also deals in newer materials—plastics and varying grades of PVC—and there are hundreds of shops associated with footwear. Wooden lasts are piled high in one tiny shop, another is festooned with moulded PVC soles, still others are heaped with sheets of tan leather or blue plastic for the ubiquitous 'rubber' *chappals* that have brought about a revolution in footwear.

The Ahmed family has been in the industry for at least four generations. Their company is called Jones Traders. 'Our elder brother lives in London,' Kalim explains, 'and he suggested the name'. Jones Traders deal in only men's shoes and stock around twenty-five brands. They are manufacturers as well as wholesale suppliers. They make about 500 pairs a day but sell around 3,000, the huge differential supplied by eight or ten facilities that they have contracted. 'It's all about marketing and design.' says the other brother, Wassem, his eyes shining with enthusiasm. 'One has to be on one's toes all the time to study the market, anticipate trends and create demand.' The brothers make many trips abroad, they trawl the Net, and also, of course, draw upon their own experience and creativity. Their designs are so well regarded that their shoes are stocked by many up-market outlets in Delhi and Mumbai. They now manufacture on behalf of Bata London, and also export to Sri Lanka and Dubai.

In the 1970s, the State Trading Corporation initiated the export of shoe uppers to the Soviet Union. 'All our products were entirely hand-made at that time,' Kalim says, handing me a cup of tea, 'and we couldn't produce soles strong enough for the snow. So we concentrated on uppers. We even made bootie uppers with fur lining. All the manufacturers made a lot of money. But when the Russian economy collapsed post-Gorbachev, trade with Agra, which was based on the rouble, was badly hit. Two or three big groups actually went bankrupt.' Then came PVC and machines were installed to manufacture soles, which gave a great boost to the industry. The years 2001 and 2002 were boom time for Agra. 'Then, Chinese goods started pouring in,' Kalim complains. 'That was a big setback. Now there is direct competition between India and China. Traders from India are even ordering shoes from China and selling them under their own labels.' The secret of China's success is the low cost of production because of the high degree of mechanization and the huge turnovers. After China, Agra is Asia's largest centre of footwear manufacture.

In Agra, there are still some areas of handcrafting. The lasts are made manually and some upper sewing is also done by hand. There is a substantial niche market for hand-made shoes. The Ahmed brothers wish it were possible for the shoemakers of Agra to access this business, to prevent the skills developed over centuries from being devoured by the machine age.

* * *

The number of Muslim leather-workers reduced after Partition when many fled to Pakistan. The population of Hindu craftsmen, largely of the Chamar caste, steadily increased but their social status was at the lowest end of society. Despite legislation to the contrary they were shunned by high-caste Hindus and were often not even allowed to enter temples. Many attempts towards empowerment, including the allotment of land, were vitiated by continued endorsement of high-caste superiority.

Harsh Bhaskar drives me to his family home in his up-market Sedan. He is a delightful, open-faced young man, but he carries the burden of being a Jatav, from the very lowest caste. 'In Agra,' he explains, 'Chamars, or Dalits as they are termed, are called Jatavs. It was a word coined by our leader Ambedkar and is nicer than Chamar, which has the connotations of a swear-word.' Chamars had a tradition of working with leather. In the old days, they were responsible for the skinning of dead cattle in villages, an occupation that put them beyond the pale.

Things are better for their community in Agra than in other parts of the country. 'Here we can even say that we are Jatavs,' he says rather self-consciously. 'We say it with some embarrassment, it is true, but in other places we wouldn't mention it. I think this is because we are financially better off here, because of the shoe business.' Mr S. P. Mishra, a good friend of Harsh's father, who accompanies us, concurs. 'Jatavs,' he says happily, 'can now sit freely in the presence of upper castes as opposed to earlier days when they were forced to stand with their eyes cast down.' But things are still very bad in the rest of Uttar Pradesh, and other parts of the country where they are not even allowed to use the village well. 'I remember a time,' Mishraji, who is of a higher caste, says sheepishly, 'when if a Dalit drank water in our family home, the glass was thrown away because it was regarded as polluted. Even in the mid 1950s, when I was in school, Dalit boys had to sit separately, away from other students.'

Harsh's parents made sure that all of their six children went to the best schools and colleges. 'We are all post-graduates,' he says proudly. He is an engineer from the prestigious Indian Institute of Technology at Rourkee. Even though he is well qualified and has the right political connections, Harsh has refused to take a government job. 'I felt that people would say I did not get it on merit but because I was a Dalit and jobs were reserved for us.' So he started coaching classes for the entrance examinations to the IITs and medical colleges. 'I am now at the top of the coaching line in Agra,' he says with a pleased smile, 'and this is despite the fact that everyone knows I am a Jatav. People feel it inside, I can see that, but they don't express their distaste for my caste.' He pauses for a moment, clearly distressed. 'I get very upset when people ask me what my caste is. Why do they ask? I am educated, I speak well. It hurts, it still hurts that they feel superior just because of their birth.' Despite his occasional anger, Harsh is untainted by the ugliness of discrimination though he has to face it every day in life. 'Many Jatavs adopt mainstream Hindu surnames,' he tells me sadly, 'to conceal their identity'.

Given their hereditary association with leather, the Agra Jatavs were the first to enter the manufacture of leather goods. Many became millionaires by supplying shoes and belts to the British army during World War II. That continued after Independence as well. But by the 1970s or so, non-Dalit traders entered the field. They acquired army tenders and began to fabricate leather goods, forcing many Jatav families out of business. A slow grin lights up Harsh's face. 'So now, many high-caste Hindu families, who looked down on Jatavs and their work with leather, are shoe manufacturers,' he says with satisfaction, though the labour in this industry remains around seventy per cent Jatav.'

Harsh's home is a sprawling bungalow set in an attractive garden. A gardener hosing down the granite drive moves quickly to leash a magnificent Dobermann and German Shepherd, both emblems of upward mobility. His pretty young wife greets us, slim, with hair fashionably streaked blond. She ushers us into a large drawing room with marble floors. There are two groupings of sofa sets smothered in lace antimacassars and the windows are covered by swagged velvet curtains. Harsh's mother joins us, an overweight lady who rests heavily on an orthopaedic walking-stick. She is having some difficulty with her knees. Her greying hair is hennaed. She wears a thick gold chain, small diamond earrings and bangles, all of which proclaim the wealth and standing of the family. Her weight, too, is a symbol of affluence, of having plenty without the need for manual work.

Her husband is a successful footwear manufacturer. He used to be a worker in a shoe factory, then started out on his own, working at home. He began with lots of six pairs. He couldn't afford to make more because of the cost of the leather. He worked very hard, often all night. 'I used to help him,' says Mrs Bhaskar, with a flash of spirit. 'I used to fix the insoles and foam. Now, thanks to God, we have around seventy workers.' Her elder son, Harsh's brother, took over the factory after receiving his MBA and brought in systems. Today, their shoes are in demand all over the country. 'The secret of our father's success was quality control,' Harsh adds, 'and keeping production low'. He also invented the Gola sports shoe with long laces; it was a hot-selling item in days long before Nike and the others. Mr Bhaskar also initiated direct marketing. Earlier, traders used to exploit shoe manufacturers; now, the Bhaskars have their own distributors all over the country. 'Design was a big problem in my father's time,' Harsh informs me. 'There were no training centres for design and, of course, no Internet, so he used to go to the Taj and spend hours studying the shoes of foreign tourists.'

* * *

We walk a short distance to nearby Ratanpura, a Jatav settlement. A narrow paved path snakes between a jumble of very small houses. Toddlers play on string beds placed in doorways, watched over by grandmothers. Only the very young or very old are at home. Harsh explains why. 'The men, of course, are all at work,' he says. They are mostly labourers at shoe factories. And almost all the women work as domestic help, cleaning floors, washing dishes and so on. Their earnings supplement their husbands' meagre monthly income of around Rs 2,000 for semi-skilled work, and enable the family to survive.' The hand-to-mouth existence is made even more tenuous by the short season at shoe factories where there is work largely only between August and March, catering to the huge domestic demand in winter, prompted by the festivals and weddings which peak in numbers during that period.

'Conditions are extremely difficult for these people,' Harsh says sadly. 'Large families, often three generations, live together in one room. Many contract tuberculosis, but there is not enough money for medicines. As a result, they are unable to work, and there is even less money. It is a vicious cycle.' Alcohol is their only escape and is a major problem in the community. Combined with poverty it causes men to age early. By fifty, a man is considered old, and a decade later, he is either very ill or dead.

Solutions involve the upgrading of craft skills through training centres. Those would enable the workers to command higher rates. At present, there are few really skilled workmen, which is causing serious difficulties in the footwear industry. 'We get orders,' says Harsh ruefully, 'but often we do not have the workers'.

Centuries of oppression have also created apathy among Jatavs. Harsh's father built a wedding hall in this very bustee. But he only built the shell because he believed that the community must come together to paint it. It has been a couple of years now and nothing has been done; it has also never been used. Harsh runs his fingers through his hair in frustration. 'I tried to promote a tree-planting programme here. I told the people I would pay all costs. But people say if a tree grows outside our homes, it will provide shade where people will gather; maybe even a rickshaw-stand will come up. With so many people gathering nearby, our home will be vulnerable to burglary.'

Most couples have six to eight children, so there are many mouths to feed. The people are unable to escape poverty because of illiteracy. Hardly any of the men of the current generation have studied beyond the primary level, and few of the women have been to school. Even today, many boys have to drop out of educational institutions when they are ten or twelve so they can start work and help support the family. Only about one per cent of the Jatavs are able to escape the chains of poverty which bind them. In Agra itself, there are Jatav hoteliers, shop-owners, even those who own hospitals. The tragedy however, is that once they succeed many do not want to acknowledge their 'lowly' origins. Instead of being proud of their enormous achievement, they are ashamed and conceal their caste. As a result, few do anything for the less fortunate among their community; many will not even hire fellow Jatavs.

Back at Harsh's home, conversation shifts to the upcoming festival Ram Barat, a re-enactment of the wedding of the god-king Ram, a celebration typical to Agra. The location of the festival shifts each year and this time it is in the Bhaskars' locality. One part of the neighbourhood will be decorated to simulate Ayodhya, Ram's home, the other will be Janakpuri, where his bride Sita lived. The festival is a huge extravaganza and costs over 30 million rupees collected though donations. The Bhaskars will be one of the major contributors. Harsh interjects, 'Naturally, we Jatavs are not invited to be on the organizing committee, which consists entirely of people from the upper castes. Our money is good enough but we ourselves are not acceptable,' he says with bitterness. I suggest that they link the payment to a position. Hundreds of years of enforced discretion surface in his horrified rejection of my suggestion.

* * *

Kartar Singh Bharati is a well-known lawyer and local Jatav leader. 'I am a social worker,' he announces, by way of introduction. 'If five people are selected for a committee I am always one of them.' For many years he has been the chairman of the organizing committee for celebrations commemorating the birth anniversaries of Dr Ambedkar, who dedicated his life to securing justice and equality for the so-called lower castes. As chairman of the drafting committee of the Constitution of India, he was largely responsible for the abolition by law of the concept that people were 'untouchable'. Ambedkar's birth anniversary is the biggest event among the Dalits. 'Prime ministers, ministers, governors, all attend,' Mr Bharati says, with a slightly Bugs-Bunny smile, 'so I have had a lot of exposure'.

Dr Ambedkar spent some time in Agra in 1946 and then again in March 1956, after which the city became the centre of the Dalit movement in northern India. Agra's Dalits, or Jatavs, are an extremely important factor in the politics of Agra, indeed of all UP. 'We form approximately twenty-five per cent of the total population in the Agra municipal area of 1.35 million,' says Mr Bharati. 'And ninety-five per cent of our votes go to the Bahujan Samaj Party.' Unlike other communities, every Jatav who is eligible casts a vote. 'Because,' explains the Jatav leader, 'they know that they can thus empower their leaders. The activities of the party have extended to the renaming of roads, universities and so on, after Dalit leaders.' He adjusts his lawyer's white collar. 'This is a small thing, you may say, but it is a huge step forward for our community; it has given as self-respect.' Such renaming was earlier blocked. In addition, there are now college hostels for Dalit boys, and Dr Ambedkar's writings are included in college curricula.

Following in their leader's footsteps, the community converted to Buddhism several decades ago. 'The conversion demonstrated a turning against Hindu tradition that treated us as the lowest of the low,' says Mr Bharati. 'But in Agra, adherence to Buddhist beliefs is diluted by the practice of

Hindu customs.' Several generations have worshipped Hindu gods. It is difficult to change the conditioning of centuries. Tragically, a subconscious need to identify with other higher-caste Hindus causes neo-Buddhist Jatavs to lean towards Hindu practices.

Militant Hindu organizations strongly opposed Dalit conversion to Buddhism. 'Hindus want us to agree to be included in their faith,' says Mr Bharati, 'yet they do not respect us. Even in the *Ramayana* there is a line that likens us to animals,' he swallows in agitation. 'It says that, like them, we too need to be controlled by a stick, that we should be beaten. Hindus feed and even worship cows, monkeys and snakes, but are outraged by the shadow of a Dalit, and refuse to even give him water. And now, they protest when we seek to assert our dignity by leaving the religion that has reduced our status to worse than that of an animal.'

3

Man and Angel

Agra took its first steps as the Mughal capital under Babur and Humayun, but the two spent too much time in battle to make any major impact on the city. After Akbar defeated the descendants of Sher Shah and regained Mughal territories, the city came into its own as an imperial capital. Abul Fazl, Akbar's court historian and beloved friend who was born at Agra, describes the city in his day: 'The river Jamuna flows through it for five kos and on either bank are delightful villas and pleasant stretches of meadow. It is filled with people from all countries and is the emporium of the traffic of the world.'

The most visible testimony to Akbar's rule (roughly coincident with that of Queen Elizabeth I of England) is the magnificent Agra Fort which he had constructed to replace the old one built and rebuilt over the centuries. This citadel was to be a statement of empire, and of the greatness of kings, an illustration of the young emperor's vision and a manifestation of his enormous creativity. Akbar was in his very early twenties when he conceived of his Fort. Yet, he must have had his image of empire very much in place, for such was the scale and grandeur of the enterprise that it could only be the centre of a colossal dominion. Within the forty years of his rule, he brought the whole of northern, western, eastern and central India, as well as parts of the Deccan, within his kingdom. A unification of diverse geographical and racial entities that, in fact, laid the foundation for modern India.

Conceived of by a Muslim king, built by Hindu masons, the Agra Fort is massive, perfectly proportioned and most imposing. It also proved to be impregnable. The fort consists of consecutive walls seventy feet high, with slits and loopholes for effective defence. It is further surrounded by a forty-foot-wide moat, enclosed by another high wall. It extends about half a mile along the river and has a circumference of around a mile and a half. The Agra Fort is of course on the high mound, that Ibrahim Lodhi saw when he came downriver from Delhi, and replaces much of his original fortress. Although Akbar demolished the old fort walls, he did retain sections of Ibrahim Lodhi's palaces. The lower sections of the Agra Fort are said to date back to a pre-Mughal period. Construction, which began in 1565, was completed in around eight years at the staggering cost of 3,500,000 rupees. The enormous expense was itself a statement of having arrived, for few kings could afford such a show of strength and such display of wealth. The money was well spent. According to Abul Fazal, the Fort was magnificent, the 'like of which travellers have never recorded'.

I set off, one morning, to see for myself. The main entrance to the Fort is now from the southern gateway, which was originally used by Akbar and his entourage, and was called the Akbari or Padshahi Darwaza, the emperor's entrance. It was renamed the Amar Singh Darwaza during Shah Jahan's reign. The story is told of Rao Amar Singh of Jodhpur, one of the leading nobles of the Mughal court, who was granted leave of absence of seven days for his wedding. But he returned only after fourteen days. The chief treasurer of the empire imposed a fine of 100,000 rupees for each of the seven days that he was absent without leave. Furious at the harshness of the penalty, Amar Singh refused to pay the fine. An altercation followed, during which he drew his sword and killed the offending official. Realizing this was an unpardonable crime, Amar Singh leapt on his horse and galloped towards the Akbari Darwaza, where he urged his gallant horse to jump the fort walls. The horse fell to his death. Amar Singh survived and was sentenced to die. But Shah Jahan, impressed by Amar Singh's courage, renamed the gate in his memory.

The long, steep walk up to the Fort gives me time to make the transition to a previous time. And soon I can almost hear the beat of the great *nagara* drums that preceded the emperor's processions. Foot soldiers advance, in my imagination, their tramping tread hypnotic. The cavalry follow, horses trotting, harnesses jingling. Around another bend, an elephant trumpets as the imperial cavalcade descends from the Fort. The colours come into soft focus, the rich trappings of the horses and the splendid robes of their riders, spears glinting in the sun. And then the emperor himself, in a bejewelled howdah on a magnificent elephant, the aigrette of his turban blazing his might and power.

His son, Jahangir, has left a vivid image of Akbar. He was, 'of middling stature ... rather inclining to be dark than fair', with black eyes, a sturdy body, long arms and hands. There was a fleshy wart, about the size of a small pea, on the left side of his nose, considered a sign of immense riches and increasing prosperity. Akbar had a loud, booming voice, elegant, pleasant patterns of speech and a 'visage full of godly dignity'. He did not wear a beard, favouring long, sideburns instead. The emperor was slightly bow-legged from a lifetime on horseback and was known to be able to ride hard and fast: 240 miles in a single day on one occasion, to surprise a rebellious general and defeat him decisively. Akbar was also blessed with a princely sympathy for the less fortunate and a generous forgiveness for those who offended him. Abul Fazal threw objectivity to the winds when he described Akbar: the emperor was to him 'an angel in the form of man'.

Akbar set out on military expeditions almost every year to subdue revolt, to acquire new territory or to simply make his presence felt. So it was often that the imperial cavalcade descended these steep slopes. When the emperor set off on a journey, military campaign or pleasure jaunt, he was accompanied by a couple of his hunting cheetahs, often by his favourite, Madan Kali, who had the honour of having a drum beaten before her in procession. There were also falcons and a selection of his 20,000 pigeons with bearers carrying their coops. Pigeon-flying was a very popular sport among the Mughals, an offshoot of the birds' use for carrying messages, and Akbar was a dedicated pigeon-fancier.

* * *

I had participated in some aspects of the sport with Jawahar Lal, a passionate pigeon-fancier and neighbour of my friend, philosopher and guide in Agra, Dr Neville Smith. They both live in Ghatia Azam Khan, once an enclave of gracious bungalows with large compounds, now overbuilt to house expanding families. Jawahar supports his family by the sale of milk from the ten to twelve buffaloes that he tethers at his home. In summer he supplements this by selling rush mats for desert coolers. He is tall and gangly, with grey hair, big, yellowing, paan-stained teeth and eyes crinkled from long hours of looking up at the sky.

He has always loved pigeons. As a boy he would hang out with neighbours who had birds and watch enthralled as they were released into the blue. As soon as he could, he bought a few pairs himself. That was many years ago. The pigeons laid eggs and now he has a flock of around sixty. Jawahar's birds are a mixed lot, 'some fast, some slow, some loving, some flighty,' he says, grinning widely, 'but I love them all'. He refers to them as *bachhe*, children. 'The homers are the best,' he tells me. 'In the old days they were the famous carrier pigeons and are still very popular.' He opens his eyes very wide as he makes his point. I realize that by homer, he means homing pigeons. The homer, a big bird with spots, is a very old strain and can fly further and faster than almost any other pigeon. That was important in the old days, when secret messages attached to their legs were carried long distances. Speed enabled them to outfly predators belonging to rival factions who would send up their falcons to bring down the pigeon with its message. In addition to the homer, Jawahar has other varieties, named mostly for their colours. There is the *neela*, the blue, the *lalban* which has red patches, the *chitta*, or white, and many others.

The pigeons live in a big wire mesh cage on the roof of Jawahar's home. He lets them out only once a day when he scatters seed. Then, after they have had their fill, he lets out a piercing whistle and they fly. To train them in the beginning, he used a piece of cloth, which he swung vigorously in big circular motions to teach the birds to swoop and soar. But now most of the young ones simply follow the patterns established by the others. As we walk together to his home, a cloud of pigeons flutters up from the roof, converging into a formation and wheeling through the sky. 'Isn't it a wondrous sight?' he asks, eyes shining. 'We have competitions with other pigeon-fanciers, races, you could say, to see whose flock goes furthest most quickly.' At the moment, however, it is summer and there are no competitions as the birds are sluggish at this time of the year. So Jawahar's flock is unchallenged. The birds fly in great circles around the sky, dipping, gliding and changing direction in perfect synchrony.

'I know each bird like I know my children,' Jawahar says, squinting upwards. Not all pigeons are fliers. Jawahar scratches his head, trying to find an appropriate explanation. 'The married ones,' he beams at last, delighted to find an appropriately delicate phrasing, 'they do not fly. Their hearts and minds are with their babies. Both parents participate in the rearing, feeding them regularly and with great dedication, filling their own beaks with water and transferring it to the young ones drop by drop.'

Pigeons have to be kept in peak condition for races. 'We have to take great care of them in winter. They are especially prone to colds, which lead to chronically blocked noses and coughs. Then, sometimes, they have gastric trouble and stop eating. For this, we feed them the top creamy layer of *dahi*.' Jawahar has initiated his children into the joy of pigeon-flying. 'It is a wonderful form of entertainment,' he says, widening his eyes again to make his point. 'It engages the senses, the body and the mind.'

* * *

Jawahar had told me that when his pigeons became very ill and no cure seemed possible, he took them to a shrine in Hing Ki Mandi, where he left the birds for a few days after which they were always miraculously healed. Haji Pir Khalil Baba Ka Maqbara, better known as Kabutar Wale Baba, is snuggled into a tiny corner in a very busy and very narrow street. Shocking pink walls with highlights of a virulent green, of the city *kotwali*, or police station, provide the backdrop for a grave, carpeted by hundreds of pigeons of every conceivable size, shape and colour, all pecking industriously at grain scattered by devotees. Dovecotes are built into the walls and the cooing is in counterpoint to the thunder of passing traffic.

'There are only a few birds here now. Many have flown off for the day,' Abdul Hamid, the wizened caretaker of the shrine tells me. 'In the evenings, there are nearly 2,000 here.' A large Persian beak of a nose dominates his long, deeply furrowed face, and there are only a few, rotted, teeth in his smiling mouth. Like many of Agra's Muslim citizens, he wears a checked *tehmat,* or lungi, with a long kurta. A checked cloth is wrapped around his grizzled head. He sits at a small stall outside the shrine, dispensing millet for the birds to all who seek Baba's blessing. He embarks on a long discourse, but some of it is difficult to understand because of his lack of teeth. A devotee who has just tossed grain to the birds and left a tithe for their guardian, clarifies. 'He is saying that Baba was in the fakir line (of business).' I gather that many people come here to ask Baba for a job, a child, an escape from poverty, in return for which they promise to gift two pigeons to Baba's durbar.

In the traditional medieval manner, the real grave is in an underground chamber beneath the cenotaph surrounded by the pigeons. The false grave ensures that the real resting place of the saint is not sullied by the birds or their droppings and also takes care of the requirement that no one walks over the grave. The crypt is a small room, its walls smothered in spanking new square blue and white tiles. The grave is swathed in a green and gold covering, but the headstone looks very old. 'Baba has been lying here in purdah for 970 years,' Abdul Hamid tells me with some hyperbole.

* * *

The Agra Fort contained more than 500 buildings. It was a city in itself, with well laid-out streets and many different categories of structures. There were imperial palaces, accommodations for the enormous retinue, offices for the central government and its innumerable departments, billets for soldiers, and stables. Space was also set aside for Akbar's much loved and vast menagerie of animals ranging from elephants to deer and antelope, rhinoceroses, lions, tigers and panthers, hunting cheetahs to hawks and hounds.

Of all his animals Akbar loved elephants best. He was fearless and could ride ones that others feared, stepping on their tusks and mounting them, even when they were in *musth*, rut. Of the 6,000 in the imperial stables, 101 were reserved for the emperor's personal use. Five men tended each elephant, feeding them generous portions of rice, sugar, milk and ghee every day, as well as 300 sugarcanes each during winter, when the cane ripened. A superintendent reported on the condition of each elephant to the emperor every day, and answered Akbar's detailed inquiries on any indisposition.

Only around thirty buildings remain. Many, especially on the northern segment of the Fort, were replaced by British barracks. These are now occupied by the Indian Army, and the area is currently off limits to visitors. Plans to vacate the Fort are being discussed, after which the area must be carefully landscaped. The Delhi Gate, which was earlier the main entrance to the Fort, should then also be reopened. Visitors could linger in the gardens and a method could be devised to regulate entry to the Fort, thus averting overcrowding.

Among the palaces that remain is Akbari Mahal, one of the first built by Akbar at the extreme south-west edge of the Fort. Its deserted and scarcely visited chambers were sited—

as were other palaces constructed under Akbar's instructions—
overlooking the Yamuna river. The Akbari Mahal is a simple
structure of red sandstone built around a courtyard with what
seems to be an assembly hall on one side, behind which a
deep verandah faces the river. Construction is in the Hindu
idiom, with pillars and beams held by carved brackets. The
only decorations that survive are fretted stone lattices, though
the ceilings must have been decorated and perhaps even
gilded.

I look out over towards the Yamuna now in the distance,
its landscape and environment dramatically altered from
Akbar's time. Forests have been cut down to make more and
more land available for agriculture, and these same tracts of
land are now being converted into housing. But previously,
great swathes of jungle and tall grasslands crowded the banks
of the river. The roar of traffic and the impatient horns of
today fade, as I imagine other sounds, the alarm calls of
monkeys, the barking of chital deer and in the distance, the
sawing of a leopard.

Akbar probably sat on this very verandah, looking out
over the river, dreaming dreams of empire that would make
him one of the greatest rulers of north India. Perhaps it was
here that he pondered ways to bring reconciliation to what
Tennyson called 'the warring world of Hindustan' in his poem,
'Akbar's Dream'. Akbar realized that to effectively rule the
subcontinent, he must win over the Hindus who were the
majority of his subjects. Despite enormous losses in revenue,
he abolished discriminative taxes that had long irked them.
With marvellous insight, Tennyson has Akbar saying:

> I hate the rancour of their castes and creeds,
> I let them worship as they will, I reap
> No revenue from the field of unbelief,

I cull from every faith and race the best
And bravest soul for counsellor and friend.

Akbar's secular ideas continued to influence Mughal policy in varying degrees right up to the reign of his great-grandson Aurangzeb. There was an extraordinary exercise of restraint on both sides that allowed the mingling of two totally different civilizations, and permitted, on the whole, people of both religions to live together in relative harmony. Under the Mughals, cow slaughter, for example, was banned by successive emperors despite their enjoyment of beef. There are many lessons for modern India in the tolerance and the forbearance among the Hindus and Muslims of Mughal India.

* * *

Armed with an introduction to Mahant Harihar Puri, the chief priest of the Mankameshwar temple, I set off for the structure that enshrines Shiva as the deity who fulfils all wishes. The introduction is through Dr Prabha Malhotra, of the Malhotra Nursing Home, where the mahant's wife, a doctor, is employed. The temple is in one of the oldest parts of the city, Rawat Pada, populated in the old days by Marwari traders mostly from the Shekhavati region of Rajasthan. The roads are still paved with the original slabs of red sandstone laid probably during Akbar's time with only minimal repairs across the centuries. The approach to Mankameshwar is crowded with shops that sell sacred offerings: flowers, sindoor, little lamps of ghee and sweets. But unlike other temple sites, not a single shopkeeper touts his wares or urges the devout to make a purchase. Even the beggars sit in an orderly line. At the temple, too, there are none of the usual eager hands reaching out for offerings and cash.

A temple attendant directs me to a door with an etched glass icon of Shiva. A male attendant in saffron speaks softly into a mobile phone while I settle down on a sofa upholstered in maroon brocade. A computer dominates a large, curving desk. Large photographs dominate the walls. One of them is of the preceding mahant, in white robes, wearing a benign smile and dark glasses. On either side are representations of Shiva, the deity he served, one of a three-headed image; the other seems to be an ancient linga in a pool of water.

'That is the form of Mankameshwar,' a voice behind me says. I look up into twinkling eyes behind a pair of rimless glasses. Harihar is much younger than I had expected, around thirty, casual in a kurta-pajama, a red tikka on his forehead. He is accompanied by his young wife, fair, slim and very beautiful. She is the doctor who works at the Malhotra Hospital, and her husband takes great pride in her achievements. I have misunderstood. Harihar is the elder son but it is his younger brother, Yogesh, who has been enthroned as the mahant. 'It was because of my upbringing,' Harihar explains. His mother felt that as the eldest son of the mahant, he would be thoroughly spoilt. So she was instrumental in sending him away to boarding school at a very early age. As a result he was exposed to outside influences.

Although their mother died when Harihar was just seven, their father continued his education according to her wishes. Yogesh was just four so he stayed at home and then, when he was older, went to the Sanyas Ashram in Delhi where he studied the holy books and practised the rituals. Naturally, he was better suited to be the mahant. Administration, finance and the general running of the temple and its charitable institutions are Harihar's forte. He is trying to improve things, to introduce change. He doesn't want people who come to pray to be disturbed. He tells his staff they should never hold their hands out to devotees. If they need something, they should ask the One the devotees have come to address.

Harihar recounts the legend regarding the origin of the temple. When Lord Krishna was born in Vrindavan, Lord Shiva, who lived in the Himalayas on Mount Kailash, was seized with a longing to hold the infant. So he set off on the long journey. On the way, he rested here and vowed that if his wish to hold the child was fulfilled, he would establish a linga on the very spot. When he reached Mathura the next day, Krishna's foster-mother, Yashodhara, sent him away. 'Your appearance is too terrifying,' she said, 'you will frighten my child'. Shiva insisted that he would wait, and sat down outside the hut. The divine infant started to cry and kept pointing to the visitor. Despairing of quieting the child, Yashodhara called Shiva in and he cradled the now gurgling child in his arms. On his way back to Kailash, he stopped here again and established the linga called Mankameshwar, the lord who grants all wishes made with a true and pure heart.

Harihar accompanies me to the temple. I cannot enter the sanctum, since I am inappropriately dressed in salwar kameez, stitched clothing, which is forbidden. I can only observe the image from the railing around the shrine, erected to keep other similarly impure devotees at bay. On one side of the sanctum, eleven lamps of ghee flicker gently, providing light from an era that preceded electricity. And by the other side, a deep, tiered *stambh*, the traditional pillar of light, contains hundreds of smaller lamps offered by devotees. A high dome rises above the sanctum, decorated at its apex by inlaid mirrors. 'This is the very heart of the city,' Harihar tells me. 'Mankameshwar is in the centre of Agra and he is also the Nagar Devta, the presiding deity of the city.'

We move on to a large room where discourses are held. It is lined by statues of the deities but at one end, in pride of place under a plexiglass cover, is a model of the Mankameshwar Maternity Hospital. Harihar beams with pride. 'There are lots of hospitals in Agra. Villagers from all around come to them. But here, we will go to the rural people. Can you believe it, there is not a single hospital within ten kilometres of this site and, especially, no lady doctor?' says this truly interesting young man. 'It will be a charitable venture, but not for free. Nothing that is entirely free is valued by the recipient.' And yes, this is what his wife is training for. 'The temple looks after the spirit,' he says with a grin, 'my hospital will tend to the body.'

Harihar takes me to meet Yogesh. The mahant holds an august position, with immense responsibilities, but they sit easily on his very young shoulders. He wears a white lungi and a saffron shawl, his forehead is smeared with sandalwood paste and he too wears rimless glasses. His head is shaven and he has a wide smiling mouth as well as a special aura. We speak about the creeping fundamentalism in religions. 'My father used to say all religions are the same, the differences are created by us, by us mahants, us maulvis, yes, us priests,' says Yogesh with a gentle smile. 'We are all born equal, men create the differences. Consider this: Shudras, the lowest caste, are considered to be positioned at the feet of the deity. Now tell me, what part of the deity does the Brahmin touch? The feet. And so do all the other castes. I often ask the most orthodox of Brahmins, "If you had to have a blood transfusion, would you refuse blood from a lower-caste donor?" Indeed most donors are of lower caste, because they need the money.'

Conversation shifts inevitably to the proposed and most controversial Ram temple in Ayodhya, a plan that has torn apart the state, indeed the entire nation, with the demolition of the Babri mosque. 'The site should be turned into a cancer research institute and hospital,' says Yogesh, 'and the expenses on the forces positioned there for security—which amounts to twenty-two crore a year—should be diverted to the hospital.'

* * *

Many of Akbar's palaces, especially the Jahangiri Mahal, built for his son Salim, later the emperor Jahangir, are Hindu in inspiration as well as detail. I pause to take in its ceremonial entrance. A group of men are also studying the great gateway. One among them, a dapper gentleman of medium height, is pointing out some features to his colleagues. He is Dr K.K. Muhammad, superintending archaeologist of the Agra circle of the ASI, on his daily inspection. I ask if I may listen in. Dr Muhammad points out the lotuses that are a prominent motif on either side of the entrance. 'Those bear witness to the degree to which ornamentation was influenced by Hinduism,' he explains. 'The lotus within the Hindu tradition is of course, the ultimate symbol of purity. It grows in the murk at the bottom of the lake, but rises above to emerge, pure and beautiful.'

A domed anteroom leads into the zenana, the harem of the Jahangiri Mahal. 'A house was never entered directly,' Dr Muhammad says, 'to ensure that its beauty was revealed only gradually'. Guards would have been positioned here, eunuchs, and Uzbeg women in comparison with whom, it was said, the Amazons were 'soft and timorous'. Finally, we enter a large courtyard, enclosed on all sides by a double-storeyed palace of red sandstone. It is of outrageous beauty. Dr Muhammad smiles at my stupefaction and elaborates, 'It is one of the most richly carved structures of the Fort.' The decoration is intricate and superb, creating a play of light and shade, a chiaroscuro effect that enhances the sense of varying volumes. Intricately worked pillars, lintels, eaves, fretted stone *jali* and sinuous curving brackets that recall the shapes and forms of Hindu temples, are roofed by fluted domes, some inlaid with tiles inspired by Persian architecture, others lavishly gilded and painted in the Hindu tradition. The inspired melding of Islamic form with Hindu ornamentation is a stunning visual manifestation of Akbar's deeply secular spirit.

Apartments lead into other apartments, courtyards lead on to other courtyards, each more beautiful than the last, in a bewildering but fascinating labyrinth. The planning, however, was careful, with considerable emphasis on cross-ventilation, to ensure a constant flow of fresh cool breezes off the river while the thick walls were designed to insulate interiors from both heat and cold. I wander bemused through this maze of chambers and courtyards trying to imagine what they must have looked like in Akbar's day. Carved walls, painted ceilings and rich Persian carpets of the finest wool came together in an explosion of colour and ornament, to create an ambiance of opulence and great beauty. Embroidered and jewelled hangings on the walls and over all openings, especially in winter, kept the apartments snug and accentuated their splendour. And then there were the occupants, imperial ladies of the highest rank, their attendants, slaves and musicians; crowds of jewelled women, wearing fluid, shimmering garments. In an age when it was customary to sit on the floor, the senior ladies and their companions reclined on scattered bolsters, their flowing and elaborately worked apparel rippling around them. Great silver trays piled high with sweets or fruit, others with gem-studded goblets and containers brimming with juices or simple lemonade, were placed on the carpets for their pleasure, while accomplished female musicians performed for their entertainment.

There was a continuous stream of people coming and going and a hum of voices as ladies paused to exchange greetings, poetesses recited their compositions or women scholars held forth to fascinated audiences. These empty apartments rustled with the whisper of silk, the tinkle of ornaments and resounded with laughter. There were also the high voices of children, as numerous progeny skipped and played. The daily activities of hundreds of women were also played out in these apartments. Women lived here, gave birth to their children, nurtured them, clothes were washed here, meals eaten. There were old women such as the emperor's mother, young brides, queens and commoners, Muslims and Hindus, and the different needs of each were taken into account.

During Akbar's lifetime around 300 women (some say closer to 5,000) inhabited these palaces. But the much larger number must have included the famous female Uzbeg guards as well as the hordes of women who served as attendants, slaves, musicians, dancers and entertainers, in addition to the emperor's wives and concubines. A multitude of women in one of the most splendid gilded cages in the world, imprisoned by an emphatically patriarchal world where they had no real choices. Several ladies of the harem were even stripped of their identity as Akbar insisted that they be renamed after their birthplaces. Consequently, many of them bore names such as Udaipuri and Fatehpuri.

There was a strict protocol in the zenana to minimize discord. The seniormost ladies were the emperor's wives, his mother and sisters, followed by more distant relatives, concubines, varied categories of attendants and slaves, all supervised by the eunuchs who maintained order. Each of the higher-ranking ladies had her own apartment and a monthly allowance, 'equal to her merit', from two to 1,600 rupees. She also had her own attendants and slaves ranging from twenty to a hundred depending on her personal fortune or the degree of the Emperor's favour. Jewels and clothes were either purchased by the ladies from their allowance or were gifts from their imperial husband, brother or son as the case may be. Their food came from a single kitchen, but was often served to senior ladies in their apartments.

The kitchens were also in the harem. Vast quantities of food would have been prepared every day for the legions of inhabitants, with an extensive variety to cater to a huge range of preferences. Although Akbar ate just once a day, at least a hundred dishes were kept in readiness, to be served within an hour of his demand. These were cooked under strict supervision, tasted for poison and sealed in dishes of gold and silver. As the emperor became older, his diet became more and more frugal, till he more or less gave up eating meat, exclaiming, 'Why should my stomach be the graveyard of so many animals?'

His son Jahangir notes, 'During three months of the year he ate meat, and for the remaining nine contented himself with Sufi food and was no way pleased with the slaughter of animals.' Fruit was his great indulgence, especially the melons, pomegranates and grapes of Central Asia which were imported in large quantities. Akbar was very particular about water. He preferred water from the Ganga, so elaborate arrangements were made to bring it to him when he travelled. But while in Agra he was content to compromise and drink Yamuna water instead.

The emperor usually dined in the harem. An elaborately worked dastakhwan was spread over the carpets. A large gold thali, used for communal dining, was placed on it. Sometimes, other close male members of the imperial family would join Akbar, his sons, perhaps, and more often his favourite grandson Khurram, who would grow up to become the Emperor Shah Jahan. Akbar had a special place in his heart for Khurram, a feeling that was deeply reciprocated by the young prince, who spent as much time as possible with his grandfather. Although it was not mandatory, the ladies of the harem usually ate after the emperor. But by the time the food reached the less favoured ladies, attendants and servants, it was often cold.

A double-storeyed apartment, where graceful curving brackets support the ceilings, is said to be the rooms of Akbar's Rajput wife Jodha Bai, mother of Jahangir (though her name is a matter of historical controversy). Akbar would have visited her here. Other than for brief moments of intimacy, though, their relationship was probably largely stiff and formal, bound by protocol and the demands of a political alliance. Unlike the Hindu wives of previous Muslim kings, who were often required to convert, Jodha Bai was allowed to worship in her own way at her personal shrine in her apartments. A previously unheard of liberty that demonstrated her royal husband's religious tolerance. Her brother, Man Singh, was a powerful ally who led Mughal forces to victory on many an occasion. Several other Rajput chiefs joined the ranks of the Mughal nobility, till a situation was reached when almost half the nobles of the empire were Hindus.

I move on through a suite of rooms onto a wide terrace where the Yamuna glimmers through fretted stone lattices and openings in the walls that have been carefully angled so that those inside could look out without any fear of being seen. The river is now in the distance, but in Akbar's day it flowed close to the Fort walls and bustled with activity. Pleasure boats sailed on its rippling waters, barges, each laden with three to four hundred tons of goods, cruised by in large convoys for protection against river pirates that preyed upon lone vessels. Battleships crowded with troops rode heavily on the water. Even elephants were often transported by river.

The emperor had several stepped landing stages, or ghats, built for easy access to the river. Some were for loading and unloading goods, others for bathing, with certain areas reserved for ladies of the harem. Covered passages from the Fort to the purdah ghats ensured complete privacy. And while women bathed and splashed in the crystal-clear water in one area, at another Hindu devotees offered prayers to the river and floated tiny lamps on the water.

* * *

In a hot dry climate such as that of north India, it was almost inevitable that rivers were regarded as mother goddesses, nurturing the land and nourishing the people. An entire mythology developed around each, ascribing divine origins and an entire family tree that endorsed 'her' sanctity. The Yamuna, according to legend, was the daughter of Surya, the sun, and sister to Yama, the god of death. Consequently, popular belief has it that those who take a dip in the holy waters of the river are not tormented by fear of death. Even today, the murky polluted waters are no deterrent to devotees who immerse themselves with enthusiasm in the river.

According to another school of thought, the Yamuna is particularly sacred because it flows through Vrindavan and Mathura, and was closely associated with Lord Krishna. The story goes that soon after Krishna's birth, his father Vasudeva carried the child across the river to save him from the massacre of male infants ordered by the evil king, Kans. The babe slipped momentarily from his arms and his feet trailed in the water and the river at once became sanctified. In later years, the Yamuna was further beatified when Krishna swam in it with his cowherd friends and sported in the waters with the beautiful damsels of Vraja. The Lord also cleansed himself in the pure waters of the Yamuna after he killed the demon Kesi. Given such sacred associations, it is believed that a dip in the Yamuna is a hundred times more purifying than a bath in the Ganga.

But even river goddesses are not immune to ill-treatment. Once, it is said, Krishna's older brother, Balaram, summoned the Yamuna to come to him. Thinking that he could be intoxicated, she ignored his bidding. Balaram, not accustomed to being disregarded, was furious. He took his plough, the special implement associated with him, snared Yamuna Devi's hair and started to drag her to him. To escape him, it is said, Yamuna split into multiple streams, now her tributaries, and developed the characteristic looping course.

The Yamuna rises as a spring in the high alpine meadows of the Himalayas and flows for some 1,380 kilometres, almost parallel to the Ganga, till they meet at Allahabad. Since ancient times, the Doab region, where the Ganga and the Yamuna flow, has been considered one of the most fertile areas in the subcontinent. Indeed, the river was probably the reason Agra came into being. It nourished the crops which engendered wealth and encouraged settlement.

Today, the Yamuna is separated from the Fort by a wide swathe of sand, deposited over the centuries on the outer curve of the river where its pace is slower. Politicians, including Mayavati, the previous and current chief minister of the state, and her bureaucrats, were quick to see possibilities and initiated plans for what they called a Heritage Corridor to link the Fort and the Taj Mahal. The concept was extended to provide entertainment, which they hoped would extend visits to Agra, and incorporated shopping malls, restaurants and much else. To do this, it was necessary to raise the riverbed by around twelve feet. Tractors and earth-moving machinery raised great clouds of abrasive dust deleterious to the monument. To protect the infill from being washed away by the river, construction was initiated on a long wall from the bridge near Aram Bagh to the Taj. Conservationists finally woke up to the dangers of the proposed development and the project was scuttled in a flurry of accusations. Little energy remains for the crucial remedial measures, including the dismantling of the wall and removing at least some of the sand that has raised the river level and increased the possibility of monsoon flooding.

Local opinion is, however, divided on the matter. One prominent Agra resident believes that the controversial riverside development would have actually been good for tourism, since it would have provided much needed diversion for visitors who have nothing much to do in the evenings. 'The lake,' he tells me, 'which was another component of the project, would make it possible for tourists to peddle boats while admiring the Taj.' Which he thought was a good idea. 'The hullabaloo that has erupted,' he believes, 'has caused government officials to sit back and simply push files. Now no one dares to initiate any development.'

* * *

The Yamuna is slower and far less full now than of yore. Upstream dams designed to irrigate huge areas and meet increasing water needs of growing urban populations, especially in Delhi, have depleted its flow, making it little more than a still sheet of sludge, worn down by man's lust for water. To make matters worse, there is the heedless discharge of excrescences into the holy river, and a complete breakdown of the intrinsic relationship between man and water that led to the worship of the Yamuna. And water, certainly in the urban context, is now no goddess—merely a convenience that comes out of a tap.

The Yamuna today is the most polluted river in India. The Yamuna Action Plan was set up in 1993 to tackle this enormous problem. Its offices at Agra are in hutments near the river, a cool leafy place shaded by several tall trees. I have arrived without a prior appointment and the chief engineer is most forthcoming. Mr Lakkhan Singh is an astonishingly young-looking man, gentle, considered in demeanour and very well informed. He quickly fills in some background. 'Delhi is the main culprit for upstream pollution but huge efforts have been made to improve the situation. The capacity for waste water, especially from sewage treatment plants, has been steadily increased all along the river over the years but there is still a tremendous shortfall. In addition, there are several settlements without sewerage along the banks of the river. In Delhi these amount to almost fifty per cent of the population. Industry, especially in the small-scale sector, also contributes its toxic tithe.' Upstream barrages have reduced the quantum of water in the river to a trickle, seriously compromising its ability to dilute heavy pollution, making the Yamuna itself little more than a sewer.

'The main problem in Agra,' he says with a frown, 'is urban pollution. In fact, all household effluents went directly into the river. This is still true of many parts of the old city, and of unauthorized settlements of the desperately poor. Under the first phase of the Action Plan, twenty drains have been intercepted and diverted to treatment plants and many more will be tackled in the next phase. But diverting *nallas* is not a permanent solution; it is essential to lay sewers, especially in the old city. The process is slow due to a shortage of funds and fifty per cent of the city is still unsewered.

Other problems that seriously impact water quality include the custom of immersing partially cremated bodies into the river. 'The poorer people of Agra can't afford the required quantity of wood,' another visitor who has been listening in protests. 'They would like to burn the bodies of their relatives but they can't.'

'Then there is defecation all along the river,' says Mr Lakkhan Singh. 'We have provided toilets at a nominal cost of just two rupees a visit but they don't use them.' The visitor has a ready rejoinder. 'There are roughly ten people to an average family including great-grandchildren. That means at least twenty rupees a day for the family and six hundred a month from salaries that are barely two thousand. It won't leave them enough to eat.' It is expensive to be poor.

Water shortage at Agra has led to the boring of thousands of tubewells for both agricultural as well as domestic use. These have depleted subsurface aquifers and led to a frightening drop in the water table. Recharge is therefore crucial. 'We need a barrage somewhere along the Yamuna which will receive water from monsoon surpluses and hold it basically to revive the aquifers.' Another consequence of the overuse of aquifers is their high salinity. In fact, today, seventy-five per cent of Agra's ground water is saline. This too would be alleviated by dilution from the recharge. One of the difficulties in building a barrage is the problem of finding an appropriate site. If the barrage were to be located upstream of Agra, its water level would have to be kept fairly low so as not to obstruct run-off from the city. 'Such problems do not occur in the vicinity of the Taj Mahal,' says Lakkhan Singh, in oblique reference to the Taj Corridor controversy. 'A water body near the monument would also vastly enhance the perspective, provided it is not trivialized and used for water sports.'

* * *

In Akbar's day, there were so many vessels plying the Yamuna, that the emperor was inspired to decree that all boats be decorated with lights at the time of the Hindu festival of Diwali. It must have been a magnificent sight: hundreds of oil lamps flickering in the darkness, as though the heavens were reflected on earth. Akbar particularly enjoyed Hindu festivals and customs, an inclination encouraged by Raja Birbal, a close friend and great influence on the emperor. Well known for his learning and wit, Birbal was among what came to be called the 'nine jewels of Akbar's court'. Raja Birbal, whose real name was Mahesh Das, started life as a bard and went on to become an accomplished poet. Birbal was also ruthlessly honest, a quality the emperor, who was surrounded by sycophants, deeply valued. Akbar often asked his opinion on various matters, answers to which Birbal rendered into stories that have slipped into folklore.

Favoured nobles such as Birbal held civil or military appointments. In fact, Birbal died in battle. He and all other nobles of the court received the rank of *mansabdars*, or commanders, their rank and status varying with the number of troops they were charged to supply. Handsome salaries, indeed small fortunes, were paid for the maintenance of these troops. Thus, a commander of 5,000 men received around 18,000 rupees each month, a large portion of which he could save. Some mansabdars, indeed most of the important ones, were given large jagirs, estates from which they had the right to collect revenue, which went towards the mansabdar's remuneration and the upkeep of his forces. Akbar was thus able to vastly increase his army without taking on the administrative problems associated with such large numbers. Painstaking historical analysis has postulated that the mansabdars collectively commanded nearly 200,000 horsemen.

Mansabdars were appointed only for their lifetime. The position was not hereditary and all of a mansabdar's possessions, even his horses and jewels, reverted to the emperor at the commander's death. Although, in practice, the emperor usually made provisions for heirs, both the ban on inheritance as well as the general insecurity of serving at the pleasure of the emperor, led to conspicuous consumption, an attitude of making the best of what you have while you can. This mindset was accentuated in later years during the decline of the Mughal empire, when invasions caused a general apprehension and fostered a tendency to live for the present since the future was open to question. An inclination that is at the root of north Indian ostentation even today.

4

Christians, Kashmiris and Kothewalis

The offices of the ASI, Agra Circle, are housed in a charming colonial bungalow, bow-fronted and wrapped in a deep verandah buffered by attractive gardens. The proportions inside are gracious, with high ceilings, skylights and towering whitewashed walls hung with photographs of several directors-general of the Survey. Dr K.K. Muhammad takes a break from a mountain of files. His particular passion is the conservation of Agra's lesser monuments, eroded by time and endangered by vandalism. Indeed, far from having any pride in these structures, local people view them as resources for future construction. Dr Muhammad discusses with great enthusiasm a scheme whereby corporate houses, hotels or communities can adopt a heritage site. He passes me folder after folder of such locations, each painstakingly documented, with the cost of crucial repairs meticulously detailed. 'Take this one,' he says passing me a photograph of Chini Ka Rauza, the wonderful glazed tile tomb of Allama Afzal Khan Mullah Shukrullah Shirazi, scholar, poet and

accomplished administrator who served with distinction as
Shah Jahan's chief minister. 'See the blue Persian tiles that
decorate it,' points out Dr Muhammad. 'Now it will cost
just one-and-a-half lakh to repair this magnificent
monument. Do you not think it would be worthwhile?' It is
an exquisite building, probably the finest example of tile
ornamentation in India, certainly the only one of its kind in
Agra.

The general manager of the Holiday Inn, who has dropped
in during our conversation, expresses keen interest. He is a
pleasant, athletic young man, with a commitment to the
future of Agra. He and Dr Muhammad discuss the possibilities
eagerly, throwing ideas around, their eyes alight with
enthusiasm. 'Perhaps you can hold a camp for young people
in the vicinity of a monument that is dilapidated,' says Dr
Muhammad, pausing to offer us tea the colour of honey,
served in small glass cups. It is delicious and refreshing. 'The
secret is that the water is boiled with lemon,' he explains and
addresses the general manager of the Holiday Inn again. 'You
could provide them hospitality, give them food and drink,
and hold some talks on why it is worthwhile to preserve the
monument. We will try to increase their pride in what is,
after all, their heritage, then select a core group who will
police the monument and make sure there is no further
defacement. This group will also prevent local people from
chipping away building material for use in the construction
of their homes. This is a common problem and so damaging
to the monuments.'

The hotelier concurs with enthusiasm. 'Nothing can be
done to really save these monuments without the involvement
of the local people. Until they are proud of their heritage, all
action is useless.' Dr Muhammad has already held awareness
camps where college students signed pledges to honour their

heritage and to stop defacing monuments with graffiti. This is not just a twenty-first-century phenomenon. In the mid-1800s, three men, Le Bait, Armstrong and Livingston, scratched their names on a glass pane near the entrance to the cenotaph chamber of the Taj Mahal.

A young man in kurta pajama rushes in, evidently excited. He heads straight for the desk. 'Sir,' he says, 'Sir, look at these photos. Just look at them!' Dr Muhammad examines the photographs carefully, eyes narrowing in concentration. 'Definitely Mauryan,' he murmurs with suppressed excitement. He passes one of the photographs to me, that of a wall covered in mud, but partially exposed. 'This wall is on the banks of a river and is most probably part of a temple. It is over 2,200 years old,' Dr Muhammad explains. In Mauryan times, a great highway stretched from Patna in Bihar to the North-West Frontier. The Mauryans probably had a local presence near Agra, which would explain the temple. 'And look at this,' exclaims Bhanu Partap, who is a distinguished local journalist with the newspaper *Amar Ujaala*. 'This is a photo of a nine-foot skeleton.'

'No, no,' Dr Muhammad corrects him gently, 'it is an ordinary man. You see, there was often mass burial, due to deaths caused by war or plague, and when the bones were put back together they often got mixed up.'

A very cool young man, evidently from a big city, with gelled and carefully spiked hair, scuffed jeans and boots, slopes into the room. He has an appointment and lounges lazily in his chair while he waits for K.K. Muhammad's attention. He represents a German battery manufacturer who plans to run a dealer-incentive programme. A visit to the Taj is one of the prizes. The proposed visual is of a plump blond man in swimming trunks lying on a rubber mattress in the water body in front of the Taj Mahal. Dr Muhammad pushes his glasses up from the bridge of his nose and looks directly at the young advertising executive. 'I can't stop you from printing that,' he says, 'but I can stop you from photographing the man at the Taj'. He very reluctantly agrees to permit the photographing of the water body. The man will be photographed in a hotel pool and technology will enable the superimposition of a gross image conceived by plebeian minds on to the foreground of one of the world's most sublime structures.

A fourth man has also come in. He is an organizer of dog shows. 'I have run the Agra dog show for seven years,' he informs what has now become a gathering in Dr Muhammad's office. 'And all shows we are having in five-star hotels.' He looks around with satisfaction. 'There are around eighty kennel clubs in India, but we are the best.' Akbar, he declares, also loved dogs. Even though Islam considered them unclean, he kept them in the harem as well as in special kennels at the base of the Fort. He often said that dogs had ten virtues and that if man had even one of them he would be a saint.

The dog-show man breeds pugs. They, too, we are informed, are the best in India, maybe the world. People from all over are on his waiting list. 'They are a good dog for urban living,' he explains. 'Nice size, so not too much exercise is needed. Then, also, they are short-haired, so grooming, too, is not much.' Then he returns to the business at hand. 'You must have heard of Cruft's,' he says. Dr Muhammad looks blank. 'They are the best organizers of dog shows in the world. Now, one of their most famous judges is coming to India on a personal visit. He is a VVIP for us. I request you to help us extend some courtesy to him, maybe send someone who is knowledgeable...' he trails off. Dr Muhammad nods understandingly. 'I will see what I can do,' he promises and takes down the dates.

* * *

Agra prospered under Akbar. The emperor's eclectic nature
and his fascination with beautiful things brought hordes of
craftsmen to Agra. The enormous resources of the expanding
empire provided the means for patronage from all levels of
society. Akbar's foremost Hindu ally and brother-in-law, the
Rajput Raja Man Singh of Amber, who was a great aesthete,
brought many of his best artisans to the city.

Professionals from all over the country converged upon
Agra to cater to the expanding requirements. The city became
a conglomerate of different races and religions and the
clamour of many different tongues roared in its bazaars. Ralph
Fitch, who visited Agra in September 1585, said Agra was
much larger, both in dimension and population, than
London, which, at that time had 200,000 inhabitants.

In addition to being capital of the empire, Agra was also
headquarters of the *subah*, or province, of Agra, an
exceedingly rich region with a revenue of over a million rupees
during the reign of Akbar, which almost doubled by the time
of Shah Jahan. Huge amounts of tribute from all over the
country also poured into the imperial treasury, in Agra,
creating enormous surpluses. Such was Akbar's wealth that
400 pairs of scales were kept at work day and night, for over
five months in an attempt to ascertain the quantity of gold
and jewels in the treasury.

Money was also no object to the aristocracy, and the city
rang to the sounds of construction as Mughal nobles ordered
the building of grand mansions which, Abul Fazal insisted,
'come not within the mould of description'. Most homes
were built around a series of courtyards, each with several

trees which, many visitors said, gave Agra a pleasing countrified feel despite its huge population. By 1580 Father Anthony Monserrat, the first European missionary and traveller to Agra, said it was 'a magnificent city' with fertile soil, a great river and 'beautiful gardens'. There were large numbers of artisans, ironworkers and goldsmiths. 'Gems and pearls abound in large numbers. Gold and silver are plentiful, as also horses from Persia and Tartary ...'

Although the emperor was illiterate, or, as the modern version of history suggests, dyslexic, Akbar had a phenomenal memory. He was consumed by a tremendous intellectual curiosity, which he attempted to assuage through dialogues with learned men or readings from the 24,000 hand-written manuscripts that filled his library. Imperial translators were kept hard at work, rendering Sanskrit and Greek treatises into Persian. The manuscripts were illustrated with miniature paintings inspired by the Persian style but with distinctive local additions that created the famous Mughal school. Eighteen talented painters were employed at court, of whom, Abul Fazal records, thirteen were Hindus from Rajput schools of painting who worked under the guidance of Persian masters. A synthesis evolved, producing the Mughal miniatures that are regarded among the world's finest expressions in art.

Although orthodox Islam frowned upon any representation of the forms of creation, Akbar declared that painting was a sacred discipline that exemplified man's humble attempts to imitate the works of God. He also instituted the practice, continued under Jahangir and Shah Jahan, of painting haloes around the head of the emperor, implying the divinity that Akbar came to associate with his kingship. Indeed, Akbar also initiated the custom of prostration before the emperor, even though Islam held that this kind of homage was only appropriate when paid to God.

The emperor would go on to found his own religion, or rather sect, the Din-E-Illahi, with a strong secular bias. It promulgated an ideal way of life and did not require its adherents to convert.

Akbar was also a great thinker deeply interested in the messages of all religions, but especially inclined towards the mysticism of Sufi saints. He called his eldest son Salim, Shaiku Baba, because he believed that his birth was in consequence of the benediction of a Sufi saint at Sikri, to be closer to whom, the emperor created Fathehpur Sikri.

* * *

Sufism has long interested me, and I seek to meet a Sufi at Agra without success. Then Dr Neville Smith comes to my rescue and directs me to Syed Ajmal Ali Shah who lives deep in the heart of the old city at Mewa Katra. I go there on a Sunday when the surrounding markets are closed and access is easier, although it still involves negotiating a warren of side streets, some barely wide enough for three pedestrians abreast. A large gate, flanked by shops, dominates the entrance to Mewa Katra. At the second-floor apartment, a very pleasant man in his mid-forties, wearing a white salwar kurta with a waistcoat and a small black cap, shows me into a large airy room that overlooks the street through tall shuttered windows. It is a quiet peaceful place, where a raised voice, even strong emotion, would be terribly out of place. It is also of a different time. Pistachio-green walls contain arched niches which hold objects of decoration and of use. There is a green carpet with plump cushions for seating and bolsters. A floor-level wood and rattan seat is on one side. 'It is the *gaddi*, the seat of the pir who heads our order,' my host tells me. I ask who occupies it presently. 'I have the privilege,' he

says, to our mutual and considerable embarrassment. 'I
attempt to continue the duties of my ancestors.' It had not
even occurred to me that one so young could occupy such an
exalted position.

I have injured my back and view the seating arrangements
with some dismay. Syed Ajmal Ali Shah senses my discomfort.
'I think you would prefer a chair,' he says, showing me into
another green room furnished with red velvet sofas and a
grouping of green plastic chairs on a green carpet. There are
attractive arrangements of dried flowers on low tables in the
corners of the room. Syed Ajmal Ali's forebears were well-
respected Sufis in Medina. 'Our family was closely connected
to that of the Prophet,' he says, speaking so softly that I have
to strain to hear. 'Hazrat Ali, the fourth Khalifa and son-in-
law to the Prophet, showed them the knowledge of Sufism.'
During Jahangir's time, an ancestor was well known for his
efforts to propagate the love of God. 'When the family first
came to Agra,' he recounts, 'they lived at Lodhi Khan Ka
Tila, now near the Taj Mahal. That was twelve to thirteen
generations ago. They moved here to Mewa Katra during the
time of Shah Jahan.' A *katra* implies an enclave with a single
entrance which can be easily protected, a most valuable aspect,
especially in later turbulent times.

There are four different schools of Sufism and some
branches as well. Syed Ajmal Ali is a follower of the Chisti
school. 'Among our most important beliefs,' he says in his
quiet voice, 'is that everything exists because of God and is
thus infused with a powerful energy. God said, "When I
wanted to see myself I created the world." We see God
everywhere and in everything.' He speaks slowly, thoughtfully,
synopsizing the essence of his faith for my understanding,
and with great simplicity, without succumbing to the
temptation to lead me into the intricacies of Sufi philosophy.

'God created all people, all things, and until we love them, we cannot love Him. We are taught to seize each moment of life as a gift of God, surrendering to Him at each instant with love,' Syed sahib explains. 'The Sufi will love all equally. Caste or religion never matters, humanity has always been our creed. The good relations between Hindus and Muslims are the legacy of Sufis. Followers of the early Sufis included people of both faiths,' he emphasizes. 'The poet Kabir belonged to this order. So did Nanak, the founder of the Sikh religion.'

Syed Ajmal Ali is of middling height, with an attractive gentle demeanour. Dark brown eyes with depths of kindness and compassion dominate his face, which is lit with a caring and slightly buck-toothed smile. 'Meditation is central to Sufi practice,' he says, speaking with the authority of his high office. 'When we meditate, the world vanishes and we see only God. This is somewhat similar to the teachings of Shankaracharyaji, who said the world was *maya*, illusion.' Qawaali, devotional songs in Urdu which are accompanied by the harmonium and tabla, are distinctive of the Sufi. In a considerable departure from orthodox Islam, which shuns music, Sufis see qawaali as a means to access the divine. It was popularized in the late thirteenth and early fourteenth centuries by Amir Khusrau, court poet of the Khilji sultans in Delhi. He was among the first to write poems in the language of the people, instead of in the more courtly Persian. These were rendered in qawaalis, accompanied by the clapping of hands and a rhythmic swaying, both of which sometimes induce a hypnotic religious trance.

Others have gathered during our conversation, an electrician, a shopkeeper, a dealer in tyres. Syed Ajmal Ali gets up to greet each, covering the visitor's hand with both palms in sincere welcome. Then he quickly fills them in on the current focus of our conversation so that no one feels left out, but also to spread the benefits of the conversation to everyone. He addresses us all: 'One of the most important lessons of Sufism is to be free of attachment to the world, even while partaking in its activities.' His visitors all nod in agreement. They are familiar with the theory but find it difficult to implement. 'Attachment engenders fear,' the Syed says. 'Sufi saints are free of fear because they are free of attachment.'

Sufis marry and participate in the material aspects of life. 'My father was head of the department of psychology at St John's College,' Syed Ajmal Ali tells me. 'I am a lecturer of economics at the Shobiya College. I give of my best and yet I am somewhat removed, focussed more on the life beyond'. The work of Sufis is service to all God's people, even if it means personal sacrifice. One of their duties is teaching. Significantly, their homes are called *khankha*, which means 'where the name of God is taught'.

While the Syed welcomes yet another visitor, one among those who have gathered tells me, 'When a Sufi calls on Allah, his call is the most powerful because of his direct link to the Prophet, through Hazrat Ali. After all, if one friend does not honour another friend's word, then what is left of honour?' Fundamentalists do not like Sufism, nor do priests. 'Even though the Mughal emperors were interested in Sufism,' Syed Ajmal Ali says, 'the ulema, the clergy, who were really paid servants, blocked its development.' Akbar had angered them with his secular polices, so Jahangir, and even his son Shah Jahan, had to pander to the ulema. But Akbar's great-grandchildren, the princess Jahanara and Dara, delved deep into the mysteries of Sufism.

'We don't usually go to mosques to pray,' Syed sahib clarifies. He sits very straight, every line of his body communicating inherited dignity. 'You see, the *pesh* imam, the one who leads the prayer, must be of outstanding character and must have perfect knowledge. We stand behind him, which means we are less than he, but unfortunately, not many have knowledge, character or spirituality.' He smiles with infinite love, taking the edge off his comments. 'We Sufis find that the ulema have only theoretical knowledge. Also, they earn money through their work, which to us is anathema. Since ours is an internalized knowledge, we can pray anywhere, at a temple, gurdwara or church. Sufism is of course the answer to Islamic fundamentalism, to all aspects of bigotry. If all men could regard all others as manifestations of God, the world would be far a better place.'

* * *

Akbar left his imprint on the demography of Agra. Its early settlements of Christians are directly attributed to his encouragement. Dr Smith is well acquainted with this aspect of the city. The locality where his family lives is the area where the Armenian Christians settled. 'The Armenians had traded with India since ancient times, well before the reign of Akbar,' Dr Smith explains in his clipped accent. 'But they had not established any really permanent settlement. They were only birds of passage, who came overland all the way from the land of Ararat, east of Turkey, to purchase spices and fine muslin for which India was so well known.'

During one of his visits to Kashmir, the emperor met an Armenian merchant, Jacob, to whom he took an immediate liking. Realizing, also, the great potential for furthering trade, Akbar invited him to settle in Agra and asked Jacob to persuade his friends and relatives to join him. The emperor also said he would grant them permission to build a church. Akbar's patronage and Jacob's encouragement brought many

Armenians to Agra. Several rose to high positions at court. Abdul Hai, for one, became the chief justice of the empire. The physician of the imperial harem was an Armenian lady, Juliana. Akbar was particularly fond of another Armenian, Mirza Zul Quaranain, Jacob's son, who was brought up in the imperial palace, and rose to become a grandee at the court. He acquired a considerable estate where he built a palatial home, a chapel and a graveyard. He is known as the father of Christianity in north India. 'Their Arabic-Persian names are not necessarily Islamic, but regional,' Dr Smith clarifies. 'Many Zoroastrians, for example, have Muslim-sounding names.'

Dr Smith takes me to the cemetery, which is fairly close to the Holiday Inn. It is a quiet, tranquil place, sweet with birdsong, with filtered light streaming through big old trees. We walk past graves with little domes and fluted pillars that appear Islamic, and also have Persian inscriptions. They are all Armenian graves and there are around eighty of them. Dr Smith tells me that the last Armenian to be born and to live in Agra died in 1920. Many others intermarried and their descendants continue to be among Agra's Christians even today.

We also pay our respects at the oldest European grave in northern India, of an Englishman, John Mildenhall. The lettering on it is difficult to decipher, but Dr Smith knows it well. 'Here lies John Mildenhall, Englishman,' he reads out, 'who left London in 1599 and travelling through Persia, reached Agra in 1600'. A lifetime of high adventure, of ambition and dreams, reduced to just a few words. Mildenhall is said to have met Akbar and to have presented himself, perhaps inaccurately, as an envoy of Queen Elizabeth I. I am struck by the lust for travel, adventure, the intrepid quest for great riches, that impelled men such as these to undertake the long voyage to India, and to face the considerable dangers to life that such travels entailed.

Then there is also the grave of Jerome Veronio, from Venice, who was once believed by some to be associated with designing the Taj Mahal. Dr Smith clarifies. 'During the British period, many found it difficult to believe that such a superlative structure could have been conceived of without Caucasian help. Veronio was a draughtsman and thus an obvious choice for enlightened inputs from the West. But of course, there is no truth in the story.' Dr Smith also points out the grave of the Italian lapidary, Hortenzio Bronzoni, who spent several years in the employ of Shah Jahan, before dying, in August 1677. The French jeweller, Tavernier, who visited Agra in the seventeenth century, dismissed Bronzoni's work with the remark that he cut the gemstones very badly.

A large domed structure of red sandstone, modelled generally after the style of the Taj Mahal, dominates the cemetery. It commemorates Colonel Jon Hessing, who died in 1803. He was Dutch and among the mercenaries employed by the maharaja of Gwalior in his Maratha army. The tomb was built by his wife Alice, who spent 100,000 rupees, a fortune at the time. Hessing must have been a good and devoted husband to inspire such a memorial. 'If Mrs Hessing's means and those at the disposal of Emperor Shah Jahan were to be compared,' Dr Smith smiles, 'her tribute to her husband represented a munificent gesture of deep love.'

Our last stop is at the graves of the Smith family. We pay our respects at the burial place of Dr Smith's father, Thomas Smith, who passed both his journalistic skill and his knowledge of Agra on to his son.

The story of Dr Smith's family encapsulates much of the latter history of Agra. He and his wife Anugrah still live in the old family home in Ghatia Azam Khan, near the cathedral.

It is typical of traditional small-town housing with high walls opening onto a courtyard around which the house evolves. Most of the living areas are upstairs. On the ground floor, facing the entrance, is a classic *tibari*, a long narrow room fronted by three arches where, in the old days, the men of the family entertained visitors. We settle down on comfortable wood and cane sofas, perfect for all climates, to tea and a delicious plum cake, 'made by the wife,' says Dr Smith.

The Smiths have been in Agra for seven generations, spanning over 200 years. The family settled in the city soon after the collapse of the Mughal empire. The Maratha kingdoms had become powerful, and many employed foreign soldiers of fortune, especially gunners, of whom legions came to India lured by tales of immense riches, exotic women and a lifestyle of luxury and indulgence. European artillery men were in special demand and were paid huge salaries. Captain Salvadore Smith was probably among these. Born in 1798, he came away from England as a young man, served in the army of the maharaja of Gwalior for forty years, and died in 1871, outliving his two sons. He married twice. One of his wives was called Victoria Mariam, and Dr Smith's family is descended from her. She must have been a Muslim girl, possibly called Mariam, with 'Victoria' added on after she converted to Catholicism. Far more Muslim women married Westerners than Hindus, who were fettered by fears of caste pollution and believed that even eating with non-Hindus caused them to become tainted. The Muslims, on the other hand, had no such barriers and freely mingled with the Europeans. There was, in those days, still a perceived commonality between the two religions, Christians were regarded as 'people of the book'. On occasion, young European men in love with Muslim girls from conservative families, converted to Islam and underwent the required circumcision.

Captain Salvadore Smith bought the Agra house in 1869 for Victoria Mariam. He sent two of his sons to make the purchase. They were both captains in the Scindia army of Gwalior. The son called Joseph, who also married a Muslim lady, is Dr Smith's ancestor. Dr Smith's maternal grandmother, on the other hand, came from a Hindu-Christian family. Her father was a Rajput from Alwar who fell out with his family over the distribution of family property and, in a fit of pique, left his home and became a Christian. 'Society in those days, that is, in the early nineteenth century,' says Dr Smith, settling back into the comfortable cane-backed chair, 'was in turmoil. Cultures were intermingling and identities were blurred. Our family was a product of this mixture. We have Brahmin links, Thakur links, English links. Even now, we have relatives in England, some in Australia.'

The mingling of cultures brought strong local inflexions to the lives of Indian Christians. Their mannerisms, their language, their eating habits, are all essentially Indian. 'For Christmas lunch, for example, we have biryani, korma, kebabs and shirmal,' Neville elaborates. Typical Muslim festive food. Much the same as a Muslim family would have on Id. 'Then, from the Hindus, we received the tradition of the *pakvan*. A huge cauldron of boiling oil would be set up at least two days before Christmas, in which various delicacies would be fried. Puff-ball kachoris stuffed with delicate spices, gujias with fillings of sweet coconut and gram. The Western influence was in the cake; yes, we always had homemade rich fruitcakes and doughnuts as well. We always had doughnuts.' Marriages among the Christians of Agra are arranged by parents and family elders in the same way as in other Indian communities.

Dr Smith reminisces about his childhood. 'My mother,' he says, 'was never without the large silver paan *daan*, which she had brought in her dowry.' Paan-eating was a fine art: unless you knew the etiquette, you could cause serious insult. The paan daan was part of every household and every visitor was welcomed by an offering of paan supari. It had many benefits: it was good for the gastric system, it was an elixir, and of course, it ensured the breath was always fragrant.

Since his other brothers had left Agra to work elsewhere, his mother did not want Dr Smith to leave the city. So, after completing his MA in 1962, and later his PhD., he taught English literature at Raja Balwant Singh College.

'Why English?' I ask.

'English was in our blood,' he replies. 'Remember, one of our ancestors was British.'

'But do you speak English at home?' I enquire.

'No,' he says, 'mostly Hindi'.

Dr Smith taught at Raja Balwant Singh College till he retired in the year 2000. Thereafter, he followed in his father's distinguished footsteps and became a prominent Agra journalist. An amateur historian, he is a mine of information.

Dr Smith tells me there were two kinds of Christians in Agra: the converts, commonly called Indian Christians, and the Anglo-Indian Anglicized descendants of European men who married Indian women. The British government, chary of allowing the development of a possible power base, instituted a law forbidding Anglo-Indians to own property in India. As a result, they were seriously disadvantaged. Few occupations were open to them. 'So,' Dr Smith relates, 'they went into the postal service or the railways and brought a sense of responsibility and commitment to their work.' After Independence, most of the more Westernized Anglo-Indians emigrated. The few that remain have been swamped by the Indian Christians, who are willing to be typists at low wages. Now, many are computer experts.

* * *

The Armenians stimulated Akbar's interest in Christianity.
He went on to invite Jesuits from the Portuguese colony in
Goa to his court. The priests were most graciously received
by the emperor at Fatehpur Sikri, where Akbar held long
discussions with them. Although the emperor showed no
interest in converting, he did give land to the Jesuits on the
outskirts of Agra, near the Armenian settlement, and granted
them permission to build a church. What has now come to
be called 'Akbar's church' was constructed about the year
1600 by the Jesuit fathers, paid for by the emperor himself.
The Jesuits seem to have first built a chapel, but Prince Salim
(later Emperor Jahangir), disappointed that the church in
Agra was not as large and beautiful as the one in Lahore,
donated a thousand crowns to renovate it to appropriate
magnificence.

The church is a small simple structure but with an aura of
sanctity. Canonized, perhaps, by centuries of prayer. To the
right, near the entrance, a statue of the Virgin Mary is
embedded in the wall. The image wears a veil, her hands are
joined and she stands on a lotus with shoes on her feet; an
Indian sculptor's version of what a foreign goddess would
wear! It is said to have been sculpted during the reign of
Akbar and was possibly one of the images described by
William Finch as well as Captain Hawkins, who visited Agra
during the reign of Jahangir and referred to images of Jesus
and Mary on the wall behind Jahangir's throne. It later
adorned the portico of the Agra Bank, from which the
archbishop of Agra obtained the statue.

Akbar would come to the church on Christmas morning
to see the crib. He arrived in a splendid procession, with drums
and music heralding his arrival. Church bells tolled and the

choir sang joyous hymns. The priests received the emperor
outside the church, ushering him in with censers of incense.
In the evening, the ladies of the harem and the younger princes
also visited the crib, sometimes carrying candles.

Easter festivities acquired local colour in Agra. The
Christian community observed Lent rigidly, and with great
austerity. After eating the traditional lamb on Maundy
Thursday, the church bells were muffled until Holy Saturday.
On Good Friday, Christians took out an evening procession
through the city to the church. Elements of Mughal pageantry
were incorporated, with caparisoned elephants, camels and
horses. A European walked in front carrying an effigy of Judas
Iscariot, which was later burnt, a custom unique to Agra at
the time that has ceased. The effigy was made and robed by
the wives of the merchants and the ladies of the harem, all of
whom waited with excitement for the day it would be burnt
after the Stations of the Cross.

Today, Mass is in progress. The congregation sits on the
floor and the service is in Hindi. All hymns are also sung in
the vernacular, some in literal but charming translation that
retains both spirituality and verve. The Eucharist is given by
the priest into the hand of the communicant, an adaptation
inspired perhaps by the giving of prasad in Hindu temples.
Later, the parish priest, Father Jerome da Cunha, a dark,
tubby man from Goa, tells me the parish is entirely Hindi-
speaking. Most of his parishioners are descended from converts
during the Mughal period and never learnt to speak English.
Their ancestors were Muslims and they still retain many
Islamic customs. Most still live in Padritola, on land gifted
to the Jesuits by Akbar. 'You must visit it,' says Father Jerome,
'and meet some of the older parishioners'. He calls out, 'Hey,
Cyril,' to a short, skinny young man, scarcely more than a
boy. 'His name is actually Sunil,' Father explains, 'but we

call him Cyril. Hey, Cyril, take this lady to Mrs Henry.'

Sunil's name represents a growing tendency among Christians to give their children Hindu names to help them meld with the majority. This is part of a growing movement towards a new, more Indian, identity as opposed to the earlier, more Western, bias. The Hindi Mass, the seating of the congregation on the floor and the Communion given in cupped hands, are all attempts in the same direction by a community straddling a European religion and Indian tradition.

Sunil Samuel walks with me to the Padritola settlements. He is a gentle, soft-spoken young man, on that agonizing threshold of adulthood where he sees his fading dreams in the harsh light of reality and is summoning up the nerve to move on, to find a job. Any job will do for the moment. 'All work is prestigious,' he says. 'All work is worthwhile,' he adds, almost repeating a mantra. There is a wistfulness about him that is endearing and makes me wish I could open doors to him. Sunil's dreams are a little hazy, soft-focus ideals in a fantasy world. He would like to be a footballer. Actually, he is very good at the game. He has played for his school and scored a couple of good goals. The match was in a big stadium, it was a wonderful experience, but that was a couple of years ago and he hasn't played since. Another thing he would like to do is to play in a band. He learnt to play the guitar from a visiting priest. Of course, he doesn't have his own instrument, he couldn't ever afford one, but he feels he does have talent.

Padritola actually means 'settlement of padris', or Christian priests, but for centuries it has represented a safe haven to Agra's Catholics, especially in these more troubled times, given the saffron upsurge of Hindu fundamentalism that has led to attacks on priests. There are two settlements, Upper and

Lower Padritola. Both are similar to mission compounds across the country, with neatly laid-out rows of houses on either side of a lane paved with bricks. There is cleanliness and order, welcome after the chaos of the city.

Mrs Henry is not at home, but Gabriel Benjamin is sitting on a string-bed outside his small house in Upper Padritola. He is holding forth to a group of neighbours clustered around a shiny, red motorbike, evidently new. His attractive wife sits behind him, a position she probably occupies in life. He is a big man, in his mid-thirties, dark, jowly, with a mustache and an emphatically defiant, even pugnacious attitude. He is self-employed, unlike many of the other poor fellows in his neighborhood who have to take up jobs. He is a painter and takes on big lucrative contracts. As we speak, a little girl with two front teeth missing, and wearing a red velvet dress, her hair carefully curled, flings her arms around her Papa. He is clearly the love of her life. We speak about the church. 'The church employs many people, but hardly any from here. It is the south Indians they favour,' he says angrily. 'Ever since we started getting priests and nuns from the south, all the people that work in convents or at the priest's house are from there. They have called all their relatives and friends here and deny us work.' The south Indian Christians are better educated and work for lower wages.

'There is security here in Padritola,' Gabriel says. 'We are all Christians and if there is any trouble, the fathers are close by. But we are a peace-loving people, we are not trouble-makers. In the Bible it is written that when someone slaps you, turn the other cheek.' I simply can't see Gabriel turning the other cheek. Drunkenness is a problem among Christians. Not only does it drain family financial resources, it also engenders a bellicosity that creates friction. I meet many others of the community, several of whom have Latin names. There are Verencio, Bitus, Linus, Lucas. In the old days, when Mass was conducted in Latin, they all knew enough of the language to follow the service and provide the correct responses.

In Lower Padritola, women have pulled out beds onto the little-used road, where they sit in the sun chatting, while they cut vegetables for the evening meal. Many of the younger women use lipstick and eye makeup in addition to the more common bindis. They are all relatively affluent and upwardly mobile, but as everywhere in urban India, housing here continues to be a problem. The original families who were allotted homes in Padritola have multiplied many, many times over, and the sons and their sons, and their sons across many generations, all share the same home. Many extensions built over the years are piled on the tiny homes and yet there is no sense of overcrowding. Occupants seem to take pride in their surroundings; a few have attempted to pretty up their homes with carefully tended potted plants.

Unlike the early Jesuits, who came to India for spices and souls, Father da Cunha has a refreshing perspective on an issue that has plagued the church in India. 'I am not one for conversion,' he says. 'I think it is better that a person be a good man, a good Hindu, a good Muslim, than a bad Christian. After all, apples should be apples, grapes should be grapes.'

* * *

Akbar was associated with yet another community, the Kashmiris, whose large presence in Agra is said to date to his reign. The emperor liked their fair complexion and fine features. They were generally employed as domestics in the Mughal court. Since the women did not observe purdah, it was possible for them to serve as attendants outside the harem as well as within it. Kashmiri women were also considered most attractive and often married Mughal nobles. They were also good singers and dancers and performed both at court as well as in public squares. But Kashmiri men, especially Muslims, were less popular with the Mughals, following their perceived treachery during the Mughal conquest of Kashmir. In consequence, they were debarred from the army as well as the administration. But the Kashmiris found another means to wield power. They became enormously wealthy and powerful merchants, dealing in fine wool shawls and carpets which were in great demand at the Mughal court. The less fortunate were skilful tailors and superb cooks.

Hindu Kashmiris, however, mastered Persian and many rose to high positions in successive Mughal administrations. During the Mughal period, they settled in Kashmiri Bazaar in Agra where they retained the customs and traditions of their homeland, married only within the community and established a distinct identity.

I walk through the narrow serpentine street, past the imposing gateways, graceful arches and grand havelis of Kashmiri Bazaar where traders, courtesans and dancers from Kashmir once lived. It is one of the few localities in Agra where the old buildings have not been rebuilt, possibly because, long after its fame under the Mughals, the region continued to be home to legions of dancing girls, and many of the lovely old havelis that still stand were *kothas*, in which the singers and dancers entertained their patrons till the early 1950s. But the ankle bells have long fallen silent, the balconies from which the ladies called out to their admirers are empty and the crowds that throng the bazaar are only eager shoppers who converge on stalls that have sprung up at the street level of the havelis.

It was once a vibrant neighbourhood, tinkling with music

and song as the ladies practised their art. Lovelorn swains galloped through streets thronged by pleasure-seekers and gazed longingly at windows hoping for their beloved to appear. Others sent up splendid gifts and waited anxiously for some token of love reciprocated. The ladies, of course, slept well into the day, worn out by the dancing of the night before. They would appear in the evenings after lengthy toilettes, leaning over balconies and preening. Later, the palanquins would arrive to transport them to the venues for their dance. By six o'clock in the evening the torches would be lit in the main squares of the city, the drums would beat and dancing would begin. Delighted patrons would shower their appreciation in handfuls of gold, after which the dancers were named *kanchan*, the golden ones. The dancing continued for about three hours after which the kanchan repaired to more private venues. Many of the ladies had patrons who gave them generous allowances with which they maintained their households in appropriate elegance. The money was also used to recruit and support talented dancers and singers whose abilities, hospitality and quality of jewellery added to the repute of the house. The excellence of the food served was also an important aspect.

Dr Smith's brother, Mr Ronald Smith, a debonair and more worldly version of his sibling, and a distinguished Delhi journalist, had told me that the kotha was not viewed with any opprobrium by the residents of Agra, but rather as part of the city's cultural life. 'We used to go there in the evenings,' he said rather wistfully, 'hear some chaste Urdu, enjoy witty conversation with lovely women, listen to music, watch the dancing, have a drink or two. Only on the rare occasion would the more uninhibited be permitted to spend the night.' The main room where the performances were held was always magnificent, with large chandeliers, and mattresses on the floor with brocaded bolsters to recline upon. He paused, lost in nostalgia. 'It was never tawdry or commercial, but exquisitely civilized and in the very best taste. The girls were accomplished and gracious, carefully tutored in the art of conversation and wit, they could compose poetry and were well versed in literature. Any boorish gesture was unthinkable.'

Mr Smith recalls occasionally leaving home around eight in the evening. He would first stop to have a paan, but only at a special paanwalla's, who was an *ustad*, a master, of his art. The next stop was at a perfumery, where he would take a piece of cotton soaked in the *attar* of his choice and tuck it behind his ear. Then—and only then—would he head for the kotha. Naturally, he wore kurta pajama, otherwise he would be mocked as a sahib who was slumming. But things had already begun to change. Patrons were fewer and less well heeled. Also, other entertainments had burgeoned. The cinema, for example.

Interaction between British tommies and the local ladies of pleasure was common, but inhibited by language and therefore perfunctory, reducing an elaborate social art to sweaty sheets, and gradually into ordinary prostitution. Over the years concerns were raised about disease and exploitation. Then, in the 1950s, a local doctor formed a society to enable the girls to leave their profession and do something else. There were raids on the kothas and they came to be regarded as houses to whisper about, that were bawdy—which they never were. The nicer girls left, and the tone of the kothas deteriorated till they eventually petered out.

Mr Ronald Smith remembers recognizing a courtesan riding with two children in a rickshaw. She was taking them to school, one of the best, obviously to provide the little ones with the tools for another life. 'But an unforgettable image came to me once when I was passing down the street.

It was late in the evening, about 10 p.m. during the monsoon,' he reminisces. 'A *sawan* breeze was blowing and the gauzy curtains of an upper floor billowed open. I saw a beautiful young woman with a large *nath*, a nose-ring, performing a salaam. Strains of a *thumri* floated out of the window. It was very romantic and very beautiful.'

5

Magnitude in Miniature

Salim, Akbar's eldest surviving son, born to his Rajput wife, was a long-awaited child. All the emperor's previous children had died in early childhood. The half-Rajput Mughal prince was brought up by Akbar's mother and his senior wife, both of whom doted on him. Salim and his brothers went out of the zenana for lessons in the academic disciplines of the day: science, grammar, logic, mathematics, calligraphy, poetry, Arabic and Persian. Then there were also outdoor instructions in riding, swordsmanship and the other arts of war. The deference with which the princes were treated and the cosseting within the harem led to pronounced self-indulgence and a growing dependence on alcohol and opium.

Akbar disapproved strongly of Salim's excesses, and father and son were frequently estranged, particularly after the prince came of age. The emperor distanced himself from his children as they grew older, and seemed to prefer the company of his friends and courtiers to dealing with his recalcitrant sons. Salim was terribly jealous of his father's friends, especially of Abul Fazal, to whom the emperor showed particular favour. He also chafed at his father's longevity, and the consequent delay in his own ascension to the throne. He rebelled against Akbar on a couple of occasions, once even setting himself up with all the trappings of kingship at Allahabad. One of the causes of the friction between father and son seems to have been some kind of sexual jealousy. There is the famous story of the courtesan Anarkali, whom Salim is said to have loved with desperate passion. The emperor was furious, and when he was unable to persuade his son to end the relationship, he had the unfortunate woman walled up alive. It appears that Anarkali was Akbar's concubine and that Salim had trespassed on his father's turf.

On another occasion, the prince fell in love with the beautiful daughter of Mirza Ghias Beg, an important Persian noble at his father's court. But Akbar disapproved of the liaison and had the girl quickly married off to a rising young warrior, to whom the emperor gave a jagir in distant Bengal, where he took his bride. Out of sight, thought Akbar, out of mind.

* * *

After Akbar died, his son, now thirty-six, summoned the empire's chief nobles to Agra, to witness his ascension and participate in the celebrations that would follow. His brothers Murad and Daniyal had both died so there was no real opposition to his kingship. Jahangir was probably enthroned under great pavilions of velvet and gold festooned with tassels of pearls, in the large courtyard now known as Machchhi Bhavan. The ceremony was perhaps conducted on the terrace where the black marble throne he had made during his rebellion against his father is still placed. Assembled courtiers gathered in the great square below.

The great *nagara* drums echoed off the arcaded chambers around the courtyard and heralds proclaimed his arrival.

Salim was short and stocky, with pronounced Mongol features: narrow, slanted eyes in a broad face, set off by high cheekbones, a moustache carefully combed down and luxuriant sideburns. He was resplendent in a long pleated *jama*, a robe of rich brocade which reached below his knees, and was bound around his waist with a wide sash. A diamond aigrette sparkled in his turban, great necklaces of rubies and pearls hung about his neck and cascaded down his chest. He wore jewelled armlets over his sleeves and bracelets at his wrists, and there were rings on almost all his fingers, rubies the size of walnuts, great pearls such as had never been seen: a calculated ostentation that contrasted with the simple accoutrements of Akbar.

Salim ascended the silver steps to what was once his father's throne and seated himself under the jewelled gold canopy supported by four silver lions. He placed Akbar's twelve-pointed crown, studded with gems and twelve enormous pearls (valued then at over 2,00,000 pounds) on his head and the assemblage roared its acclamation and fell prostrate before the throne as they had in Akbar's time. The new emperor declared to the assembly that since the business of kings was to control the world, he would assume the name Jahangir, conqueror of the world, and the title of Nur-ud-din, light of the faith. The *khutbah*, the sermon after Friday prayers, was read in his name. He was now emperor of India. At last.

Jahangir spoke to his amirs in Persian, for that was the language the new emperor favoured in keeping with his belief that all civilized ways emanated from Persia. He announced rewards for his supporters, making many of them mansabdars. He also gave rich gifts to loyal followers, robes of honour, elephants, daggers with jewelled hilts, drinking cups of jade inlaid with gold and precious stones, saddles decorated with silver and gold, and much else. The festivities that followed were carefully orchestrated by the department of celebrations established to handle just such an event. For forty days and nights the great drums were sounded, fragrant incense smoked gently in exquisitely wrought censers, and wax candles, injected with camphor, flickered in enormous candelabras of gold and silver. The palace resounded to laughter, music and dancers' ankle bells, while fireworks flared into the sky.

Prisoners were released and there was feasting and celebration in the gaily decorated squares of the city. Large sums of money were disbursed in charity. Grand processions wound through Agra, the new emperor occupying centre stage, flinging gold coins to the people, in a display of magnificence carefully structured to emphasize his prestige and supremacy.

* * *

Agra flourished under the new emperor. Migrants from Central Asia and Persia poured into the capital to seek their fortune. Often related to the Mughal aristocracy, they used their connections to obtain lucrative positions in the administration. Then there were also the Afghans, descendants of the Lodhis, whom the Mughals looked down upon and whom Babur had described as 'very rustic and tactless'. Over the years these and other immigrants brought further ingredients into the cauldron of Agra's multi-racial demography. These were the forefathers of India's considerable Muslim population, the second largest in the world. Like their imperial masters, the immigrants intermarried, often with local ladies, and became more and more Indianized over the centuries, so much so that few familiar can trace their origins with any degree of accuracy.

They are simply Indian.

Over 50,000 Muslims left Agra for Pakistan during Partition, altering the city's demography, its culture and ethos forever. Many were craftsmen, whose departure severely impacted the city's reputation for quality hand-crafted products. The aristocracy too, left the city, largely en masse. However, one name keeps cropping up among the ones who chose to stay: the Nawab of Sadabad. He, and a very few others like him, are the last links in a cultural chain stretching back to Ibrahim Lodhi, and the founding of modern Agra in 1505.

Nawab sahib has fortunately come to town from his estate in the country, and I am able to make an appointment. A roadside mechanic gives me directions to his house. 'Nawab sahib is the biggest man around here,' he says, rubbing grease from his fingers. 'He owns the entire area. This market, too.' A big gate leads to a driveway through a dusty forecourt, once a garden. It has evidently been rented for a recent wedding, as tables and chairs are being stacked up and decorations removed. Nawab Sadabad receives me at the spacious porch of his large bungalow with the old-fashioned courtesy and urbane speech typical of Muslim aristocracy. He has a fine head of steel-grey hair, perfectly groomed, mobile eyebrows and a fine handlebar moustache with the ends curving handsomely upwards.

Nawab sahib ushers me into a large high-ceilinged drawing room with a red carpet. One side of the room is set up with a carved sofa set, while on the other, there is a large divan, which evidently doubles as a bed. A computer with a plastic cover sits on a low table nearby. Chinese porcelain plates are escheloned on the wall, there are antlers above the pelmets and flowered polyester curtains that flutter in the wind. A glass cabinet displays porcelain figurines and bric-a-brac. A huge gilt-framed mirror, beautifully bevelled, stands on the floor near the sofa, and two other smaller ones are propped in other corners. Above the entrance is a tapestry of the holy Kaaba at Mecca.

Sadabad was a well-known urban centre in the old days. 'Our family was Rajput,' Nawab sahib tells me. 'We were converted, not by the sword, you understand, but by the influence of a great Sufi saint. Ours was a most distinguished family, our names are in the *Mathura Gazetteer*.' He has a copy at hand, which he gives me. It refers to 'the head of the Muhammadan family seated at Sadabad, ranking among the leading gentry of the district'. The family's genealogy reaches back to a Rajput chieftain of the eleventh century. Lal Singh, the eleventh scion of the house, received the title of 'Khan' from the emperor Akbar. Lal Singh's grandson, Itimad Rai, embraced Islam during the reign of Aurangzeb. A latter-day descendant purchased the Sadabad estate, comprising twenty-six villages, which then yielded an income of over 48,000 rupees a year.

With a family history of such prestige and honour, there is much to live up to. So many people depend on Nawab sahib for support, despite his comparatively reduced means. The right to collect revenue from the villages vanished after Independence. Large chunks of land have also been taken over by the state under land ceiling laws. Rentals from properties in Agra are at the old low rates, with little hope of revision, or even of evicting old tenants. Most of the trappings of aristocracy have vanished, the furniture, the silver, all sold by generations as the money ran out. All that remains is the respect the name still commands and Nawab sahib's courtly manners.

Nawab Sadabad spends most of his time at his estate. Agriculture is the fulcrum of his life. 'Eighty-five per cent of

India's people are farmers,' he says. 'Until farming is developed, Hindustan will not progress. The total economy depends on the agricultural sector: if our potato crop fails, everyone in the village suffers. Indeed, the nation suffers.'

We speak about what attracted Indian converts to Islam. 'In Islam there is no caste,' he explains. 'When we pray in a mosque, we don't think who is a raja, who is a pauper, we all stand together in one row. This was a reason that Islam became attractive to so many people.' In the old days there was no difference between the communities. 'Even today, my best friends are Hindu. In fact, I have hardly any Muslim friends,' he declares. 'In my own area, Sadabad, only two per cent are Muslims. And from 1947 to date, we have had no problems.' He runs his hand through his thick hair. 'Riots, you see, are politically motivated. The people are happy among themselves. Yes, certainly, there are problems sometimes, even among the most loving of brothers there are problems, but these are resolved within the family or within the extended family of both communities. No sparks are allowed to fly.' But this is not the case everywhere. 'Muslims across the country are feeling more and more insecure, and insecurity feeds fundamentalism, which in turn feeds insularity,' he says sadly. 'This began after Partition,' he continues. 'Today, all minorities are insecure. When passions are inflamed, ordinary, peace-loving people say, "Burn this shop because it is a Muslim shop. Molest that girl, she is a Muslim." Naturally, we are insecure as a community. I understand that no religion encourages its followers to give trouble to people of another religion, but most certainly, the leaders do.'

We speak about madarsas, the religious schools where Muslim children are taught the Koran. 'The community is conservative,' Nawab Sadabad insists. 'Many people are more comfortable sending their children, especially their girls, to madarsas, where they are protected from scorn and discrimination. Although madarsas were essentially schools of theology, where students were also taught a smattering of grammar, literature and logic, today, madarsas are beginning to cater to the needs of modern education. They are not necessarily centres of sedition.' For the Muslims of India to progress, however, education of girls, the mothers of future generations, is of critical importance. Measures, long discussed, to establish proper schools at madarsas, simply must be implemented.

Nawab Sadabad believes that things can only improve if Indian Muslims unite. If they find a strong leader who will be their voice. But it is difficult for them to come together, because they are in small pockets separated by vast distances. Also, all parties woo them. The Congress gives a ticket to a Muslim; so does the BJP and the BSP. The Muslim vote becomes fragmented. Nawab Sahib should know. After all, he was a member of the Legislative Assembly. 'It is not just religion that is being emphasized. Caste, also, is beginning to dominate. A Brahmin will vote for a Brahmin, a Jat for a Jat.' There is a brief silence as he collects his thoughts. 'It is no longer about the better candidate. It is about caste relations. The focus is on how people are different from one another, not on how they share a common humanity. And, Madam,' he says, 'believe me, this trend is being fostered by politicians'.

* * *

Jahangir started off well, implementing measures for the welfare of his subjects, measures that he had conceived during his long wait for kingship. These included mechanisms to protect peasants from the collection of illegal taxes, compensating farmers for crops damaged during war, and other enlightened actions. The new emperor had roads improved and caravanserais constructed, especially along the Grand Trunk Road, to ease arduous journeys and encourage trade. Imperial edicts were also issued, forbidding the practice of emasculating young men to create the eunuchs so sought after by the Mughal aristocracy for the protection of their large harems. Jahangir recorded in his memoirs: 'In Hindustan ... it was the custom ... to make eunuchs of some of their sons and give them to the governor in place of revenue ... and every year some children are thus ruined and cut off from procreation.'

But in a world where the size of a harem was an important indicator of status, the eunuchs' role continued to be crucial. The department of the harem, which employed thousands of eunuchs, was the largest administrative segment of the Mughal court and also of the establishments of senior nobles. Innumerable duties associated with the harem were entrusted to eunuchs. The treasury was there, as well as the royal jewels and the personal ornaments of the ladies, all of which had to be well guarded. Then there was also the management of the kitchens, the procurement of ingredients, the supervision of cooking and finally, the tasting, to ensure that no poison was added to the food. The emperor's wardrobe, also in the zenana, required regular attention, as also the robes of the imperial ladies, especially of the senior queens. The allowances of the ladies had to be disbursed, new garments and jewellery arranged for, and innumerable other personal requirements catered to. Other important chores included cleaning, decorating, refurbishing and the distribution of linen.

Senior eunuchs called *nazirs* and *khwajas* often rose to positions of power even outside the harem. Many were appointed generals and governors of provinces. The chief eunuch usually received the title of 'Aitbar Khan', the trusted one, and occupied important posts of the empire. Jahangir appointed the Aitbar Khan of his time governor of Agra.

The thousands of subordinate eunuchs were given varied responsibilities. Some were positioned at the entrance to the harem, where they kept a strict check on those entering or leaving. According to Coryat, a British traveller, they also inspected all goods entering the harem, and searched particularly for prohibited vegetables, considered to have phallic associations, such as brinjals, cucumber, white radish and so on. Other eunuchs served the ladies of the harem and were also charged with their surveillance to ensure they did not entertain lovers. But in practice many eunuchs were easily corrupted. They also developed strong loyalties to the ladies they served and participated on their behalf in the intrigues that were integral to the royal establishment. They sometimes acted as intermediaries between their mistress and her lovers and even smuggled men into the lady's apartment. A risky undertaking that could have cost them their lives, but one for which they were richly rewarded.

Eunuchs were carefully cultivated by the ladies of the harem, since their goodwill could make life easier in many ways. The eunuchs received gifts both big and small, poor compensation for their dreadful mutilation. Despite Jahangir's injunctions, thousands of boys and men continued to be emasculated to serve in harems across the Mughal empire. Many were imported, at three times the cost of a native slave, while others were prisoners of war who were castrated. Eunuchs were just too much in demand, too crucial to the medieval way of life, too profitable, for concerted action to protect them.

* * *

By the time Jahangir ascended the throne, there were already a large number of foreigners at Agra, jostling for trade. British merchants joined the legion of traders from Persia, Trans-Oxiana, Armenia and Turkey, as well as Portugal, Holland and France. Flushed with their victory over the Spanish Armada in 1588, the British also prepared to formally venture out to India. In 1600, the first charter for Eastern trade was granted to 'the Governor and Company of Merchants of London trading into East India'.

William Hawkins, captain of possibly the first British frigate to sail into the Arabian Sea, made his way to Agra in 1609 armed with a letter from his monarch, King James 1 of England, to the great Mughal. He spoke Persian as well as Turkish, caught the monarch's fancy and was delighted to accept the invitation to remain in Agra as ambassador of England. Hawkins records, in the rather exaggerated accounts in his memoirs, that the emperor greatly enjoyed his company and invited him to participate in drinking sessions where Hawkins entertained him with bawdy jokes. Jahangir's curiosity about England and the world beyond his realm was probably the basis for this friendship, though the Englishman also seems to have had an easy charm. Jahangir called him Khan Hawkins and made him a mansabdar of 400, a rather lowly rank. The emperor also gifted him an extremely beautiful Armenian concubine.

Although Hawkins did not receive formal permission for trade with England, he undoubtedly carried on a profitable personal business. He would have dealt in the gold brocades, silks and fine muslins which were sought after all over Europe. The beautiful weaves and intricate patterns that the master weavers and printers of the day were able to contrive, the range and fastness of colour created by secret dyeing techniques, had ensured a brisk trade in textiles from India as far back as two centuries before Christ. By the second half of the seventeenth century, these fabrics were to become the most valuable segment of the Company's trade into London. Dye-yielding plants were also exported, especially indigo, which fetched a high price. Hawkins would also have imported goods to sell in Agra. Hand-blown Venetian glass, blue delft plates and silks from China, ivory from Africa, wine from Persia, perhaps even the fine Arabian horses that were in great demand and which the Mughals were unable to breed.

Hawkins probably maintained a large stable of horses. When he set off for the palace, dressed in his finest Mughal robes, he would have been accompanied by an escort of personal cavalry as well as attendants and servants on foot who brandished bunches of peacock feathers and shouted to the crowds that thronged the streets to make way for Khan Hawkins. More senior nobles probably travelled with greater splendour, with four or five banners preceding them, around 500 footmen and as many as 200 horses in attendance. Such entourages, as well as those of rich merchants, added to the masses of people already on the roads on their everyday business as well as the traders, peddlers, jugglers, performing bears and monkeys, pickpockets and petty thieves, and the carts, horses and elephants that wound their way through them.

The escort was not just an indicator of prestige but a necessity in those dangerous times. Other Europeans were anxious to secure trading rights and Hawkins was a threat. Indeed, he claimed that, 'the lying Jesuits', as he called them, sought 'to worke my passage out of the world'. Then there were also the Armenians and the Dutch, who were struggling to make their presence felt. Competition was fierce for the stakes were high and intrigue the order of the day. Someone evidently succeeded, for Hawkins fell out of favour after two years. He left for England in 1612 but died at sea. His Armenian lady inherited diamonds worth 6,000 pounds.

Sir Thomas Roe, ambassador from the court of St James to the 'Great Mogul', arrived in India in 1615 and was finally able to meet Jahangir three years later in Ajmer and obtain an imperial firman, or decree, permitting the East India Company to trade. Although Roe himself did not visit Agra, a factory or trading centre was quickly established in the city. Others were set up in different parts of the country, to collect goods for onward transportation. Trade burgeoned, employment increased and both yielded taxes which enriched the exchequer and enhanced the legendary wealth of the Mughals. Both Hawkins and Roe, as well as many subsequent Occidental visitors, left records of their experiences in the imperial court. Their accounts have helped generations of historians arrive at a better understanding of the period. However, it is important to remember that the visitors themselves were not even of passing interest to the emperor. In all the formal accounts of Jahangir's reign that describe in great detail visits of Persian ambassadors, there is not a mention of the British. They were simply insignificant in the Mughal scheme of things.

Europeans slowly adapted to the rhythms of the Indian world. They spoke fluent Persian, ate Indian food with their fingers, and replaced the whisky and port to which they were accustomed, with the cooler arak, and even took to drinking tea. They lived hard, fought hard and amassed fortunes. They were not judgemental or bound by any sense of superiority and many were in awe of the wealth and sophistication of the Mughals. Since very few European women undertook the long and hazardous journey to India, several lived with Indian ladies, who helped them make the necessary adjustments to Indian life and gain a greater understanding of subtle nuances of conduct that vastly enhanced their success. Many had children. Such progeny were the earliest Anglo-Indians who, in those days, were accepted in society and considered to embody the best of both cultures.

* * *

Jahangir had imbibed from his father a basic tolerance of other religions and a somewhat casual approach to Islam. He, too, was interested in other religions but in the fashion of a dilettante. Out of respect for his Hindu subjects, he banned the slaughter of cows 'under pain of death'. Although some temples were destroyed during his reign, they were exceptions. The Sikh Guru, Arjun Singh, was also executed at Jahangir's command, but this was because the Guru was said to have aided Prince Khusrav in his rebellion against the emperor. Several of Khusrav's other supporters also met the same fate.

Jahangir was an enthusiastic supporter of Akbar's church. He permitted the Jesuit priests to preach freely and even to convert. The emperor gave them a monthly stipend of first fifty, and later 100 rupees, with an additional thirty for the upkeep of their church. For a while, Jahangir wore a locket with a picture of Jesus, and sometimes attended Mass. He insisted that a portrait of himself be kept in the church, so that the fathers would remember to pray for him. However, Jahangir was not seriously interested in the teachings of Christ. Although he encouraged the religious debates that his father had initiated, these often degenerated into occasions of raucous laughter and fun. Typically reflective of his attitude is Roe's account of Jahangir telling the Jesuits, 'If ye will cast the Crucifix and a picture of Christ into the fire....and if it burne not, I will become a Christian.' At another time, he is said to have attempted to establish the true religion by putting the names of twelve faiths on pieces of paper into a hat and having a monkey pick out one. According to the Catholic version, the name 'Catholic' came out three times in succession. And the fourth time, when this piece of paper was surreptitiously removed, the monkey refused to pick at all!

The high point for the priests came one midnight in July 1610 when the Jesuits describe being summoned to the emperor's presence. They arrived post-haste at court where, before a glittering assembly of nobles, Jahangir presented his three nephews, one aged ten, the others in their teens, all sons of his late brother Daniyal, and told the Jesuits to baptize them and bring them up as Christians. The priests were overcome. They had been waiting for years for just such an opportunity. They fell to their knees and kissed the emperor's feet. They had come to Agra to garner souls for Christ and here was a heaven-sent opportunity. Instruction commenced at once.

After three months, the good fathers declared that the princes were ready to be baptized. A glittering procession wound through the town from the Fort to the church. The three young princes, dressed as Portuguese grandees, with gold crosses around their necks, rode extravagantly caparisoned elephants. As they approached Akbar's church, the bells began to peal. The princes, holding candles, entered through clouds of frankincense, repeating after the priest the vows of baptism in Persian. They were sprinkled with baptismal water and given Portuguese names. Tahmuras was renamed Don Felipe, Baisanghar was now Don Carlos and Hoshang became Don Henrique. But four years later they 'rejected the light' and, as the fathers rather tastelessly added, returned to 'the vomit' of their usual existence and, of course, to Islam.

Another celebrated conversion was more successful. In 1781, Zeb-un-Nissa, Begum Sumroo, widow of Walter Reinhart, a soldier of fortune from Luxembourg, became a Catholic three years after she buried her beloved husband in the Catholic cemetery in Agra. It was not a decision she made lightly, as she had resisted becoming a Christian despite her marriage. The archbishop himself baptised her and named her Joanna. She went on to become a devout Catholic, the only such ruler in India, and built a famous church dedicated to the Virgin Mary at her principality Sardhana, sixty-three miles from Delhi. Begum Sumroo was just four feet six inches tall and said to be fairly thickset. Yet she was a lady of legendary charm, wit and courage, and won the hearts of at least three European soldiers of fortune. Her troops, whom she led into battle, (on one occasion helping Mughal forces defeat rebels) happily followed her diminutive sword-wielding figure to death.

In the early seventeenth century, Jahangir had the church walled up in retaliation to a Portuguese attack on a Mughal ship. But he eventually relented and worship was restored. Soon thereafter, a fire caused considerable damage to the church, its bell tower as well as the priests' residence, but they were all quickly repaired. Jean Baptiste Filose, another well-known and wealthy soldier of fortune, a general in the army of Maharaja Scindia of Gwalior, enlarged Akbar's church in 1835.

Other patrons of Akbar's church included the 'John' family who at one time owned several spinning and weaving mills along the Yamuna. The family patriarch was a Greek adventurer who came to India in 1801, enlisted in the British East India Company and changed his name from Antonius Joanides to the Anglicized Anthony John. His grandson Edwin developed the spinning and weaving business and established mills in Delhi, Meerut and Lucknow, making the family one of the biggest industrialists in the country. They owned nearly half the real estate in Agra, including the mills which stretched for a mile along the riverfront.

The John family fortunes waned after 1946 when several members migrated to England and the US. And in 1949, the mills were finally closed. The John family's philanthropy is recalled in the John's Public Library in Paliwal Park, the Queen Mary Empress Library in the cantonment, in the Agra Club which they built and in their many contributions to the Catholic churches of Agra.

* * *

Jahangir travelled through his kingdom extensively, to put down rebellions, to fight wars and to take his leisure. He found the heat of Agra 'uncongenial' and harmful to his constitution. The dust also probably aggravated the asthma from which he suffered throughout his life. He once stayed in Gujarat for two years. Although he chafed to return to Agra, an epidemic of plague that claimed about a hundred lives a day kept him away. The plague had occurred on the coast in 1616 and rapidly spread through the kingdom, with repeated outbreaks for almost eight years. The relatively primitive sanitation of medieval times, and the haphazard development of Agra made it difficult to contain the disease, both during Mughal times as well as after British occupation.

Thanks to his father's ceaseless endeavours, Jahangir inherited a stable empire that extended from Afghanistan in the west to the Bay of Bengal in the east and from the Himalayas in the north to the Godavari river in the south. Revenues from his vast kingdom poured into overflowing coffers, allowing the emperor to develop a lifestyle of unparalleled splendour. Jahangir was a great aesthete, who loved beautiful things and actively promoted the arts. He was an especially discerning connoisseur of miniature painting, able to distinguish between the styles of different artists. As he writes himself in his journal, the *Tuzuk-E-Jahangiri*, '... if there be a picture bearing many portraits, and each face be the work of a different master, I can discover which face is the work of each of them. If any other person has put in the eye and eyebrow of a face, I can perceive whose work the original face is, and who has painted the eye and eyebrow'.

Jahangir's patronage propelled the development of portraiture into a superb art form that captured not only details of appearance but also the subtle nuances of personality. The emperor gifted miniatures of himself on brooches to his courtiers, who wore them on their turbans— a practice that his son Shah Jahan would follow.

Nature was Jahangir's particular passion and he encouraged his artists to replicate the forms and creatures of the natural world with realism and great beauty. The well-stocked imperial menagerie and aviary, which provided plentiful subjects, were personally supervised by the emperor who also ensured that detailed records of their upkeep were maintained. A pair of Sarus cranes were special pets, their activities recorded with the zeal and minute detail of a born naturalist. The birds were painted by court artists, as were other favourite specimens including a zebra, seen for the first time in India, as well as the flightless dodo, at one time a popular game bird, now extinct. (These were probably executed by one of Jahangir's favourite painters, a man whom he called Ustad al-Mansur, literally 'wonder of the age', who specialized in birds and animals.)

Paintings of flowers were also produced in large numbers, each executed with botanical precision. Although flowers had been a popular motif and an element of subsidiary design, it was only with Jahangir's encouragement that they became the main subject of painting. They were usually presented against a pale background which focussed attention on the floral subject. Compositions were delicate, yet flawlessly accurate, with leaves, buds and flowers in various stages of development. An inspired addition of birds, butterflies and bees hovering over the flowers, introduced a sense of movement and reinforced the realism.

The emperor was also deeply interested in European art and is said to have importuned visitors for paintings. On one occasion, he had copies made of a painting of Roe's fiancée. These were so accurate that the Englishman could not tell the original from the imitation.

* * *

After the Mughal capital moved from Agra to Delhi, most painters also moved with the court. And when the dynasty later dwindled, diminishing patronage forced painters to find new masters and many moved to Rajasthan. Ishwar Chand Baghel, who has established the Krishna Arts and Crafts Emporium, has decided that his mission in life is to revive the art and restore the reputation of Agra as a centre of Mughal painting. He has identified local talent and is training several young men under artists from Rajasthan. Even the trainers are being re-trained. They are being exposed to Mughal miniatures and encouraged to adapt their art from the Rajasthani to the Mughal style. The word he uses is *kalam*, or pen.

His gallery, in a basement of a small market on the way to the Taj Mahal, is crammed with miniatures. On the walls, on the counters, in great stacks under glass cases, ranging in price from twenty-five rupees to several thousand. All works of his artists. Ishwar Chand produces a catalogue of the *Padshah Namah*, the famous manuscript that documents the reign of Jahangir's son Shah Jahan in a series of exquisite miniatures, and flips through the pages, pointing out aspects that he is trying to emulate. He takes a frank and rather engaging delight in art, but quite naturally with a focus on its relevance to his bread and butter. 'Look at the amazing movement in this picture,' he urges, launching into an impassioned description of a *Padshah Namah* painting. 'The limbs are treated in such a way that some figures seem about to walk right off the paper. And the faces. Each face is different, the features vary, and so do the expressions. And then there are the brilliant colours.' Baghel and his artists prepare some of their own paints, but not all. It is impossible to afford expensive ingredients like lapis lazuli and the real gold and silver used earlier. But they do their best. They also treat the paper in the old way, dipping it into a solution of alum and burnishing it with agate. 'Did you know that Rembrandt owned several Mughal miniatures?' Baghel asks suddenly. 'He said they were "stimulants", crucial to creativity.'

He pauses at the end pages of the *Padshah Namah*, where line drawings replicate the compositions. 'We use these for instruction,' he explains, 'to bring back a sense of composition'. Copying is of course the age-old method of training. Painters in ateliers or *karkhanas* of the empire repeatedly copied the original works of the great masters, perfecting various aspects of technique with each copy. Ishwar places considerable emphasis on drawing. It is the very basis of the first few months of training. 'They must learn to create flowing lines,' he says. 'But, these days, the boys are so impatient, they want to move quickly to the next stage so that they can earn money faster.' It was the patronage of the

Mughal emperors that created excellence. There was never the pressure to produce more to make a living, but an assured income that encouraged the pursuit of perfection.

After the drawing is completed, the colours are filled in, first the foreground and background, then body colours, followed by clothing, the painting in of ornaments and the reddening of hands, feet and lips. Various painters specialize in different aspects: landscape, facial features and so on, and their special abilities add to the beauty of the painting. After the miniature is complete, it is burnished on both sides for the glowing effect typical of the Mughal school.

'Mughal miniatures were, of course, water colours,' Baghel explains. 'They appear opaque due to the many layers of paint meticulously applied with extremely thin brushes made from the soft hair of a squirrel's tail.' He proudly produces a handful of brushes, some of just two hairs. 'Each aspect of a painting is made up of thousands of minute brush strokes.'

We leaf through a sheaf of new paintings that are copies of ones that had gone before. 'They are not in the same class as the originals,' Ishwar admits. 'But you must remember that these should be viewed as products of the twenty-first century, when life is more complex, when patronage is absent, when price drives the market and few are willing to pay for quality.' What Baghel does not say is that Mughal miniatures were a reflection of the society of the period. Copies made today are adrift in time.

Antique Mughal miniature paintings are terribly expensive. But fakes proliferate. For the uninitiated, these are difficult to identify as even the paper used is aged with sun and smoke, as is the painting when it is complete. Baghel says that a good test of the age of a picture is to study it with a magnifying glass. No surface is ever simply painted over in an original Mughal minature, but is made up of thousands of tiny brush strokes which gave a lifelike quality to hair, skin and clothing. Even in the best modern copies, the brush strokes are less careful, colour is often layered in and the attention to minute detail is diminished.

* * *

I had heard of the extensive renovations taking place in the imperial hamam, the bathhouse of the Fort, and now head for the office of the ASI for details. Dr Muhammad is as courteous and patient as ever. He says that the hamam was so extravagantly decorated that it captured the imagination of the British governor-general William Bentinck. He ordered the exquisitely inlaid marble that covered the walls and floors to be carefully dismantled and sent to Britain, some as a gift to the regent, later King George IV, while the rest went on auction. The sale of the panels was not a success and did not bring in the money expected.

Dr Muhammad is due to visit the site, but he has some work to finish first. He gives me a paper he has written on hamams for me to study till it is time to leave. The hamam was an important aspect in the life and culture of the Mughals, who built both private bathhouses attached to palaces and havelis, as well as hamams for public use, the latter a meritorious act of charity. They were especially useful to travellers and were frequently built near caravanserais. Unlike Turkish baths, however, Mughal hamams were only for bathing and did not provide steam.

We pick our way carefully over the uneven mud floor of the hamam from which the marble has been ripped out. The walls, too, are similarly bare. I find it difficult to visualize it as it once was. Dr Muhammad has no such difficulty. 'The Shahi Hamam is one of the finest examples of a Mughal bathhouse and was as extravagantly decorated as any part of the palace. This, of course, was the reception room,' he explains, waving his hands to indicate its spaciousness, its high-domed ceiling. It has delicately fretted marble screens, and traces of painting on the inside of the dome. Inlaid marble once decorated the walls, and fine carpets were strewn on the floors.

The actual bathing area adjoins the reception room. The debris of centuries has been removed, and the tanks for hot and cold water as well as the complex system of copper and clay pipes are exposed. The floor of the bathhouse rests on a cavernous underground chamber, supported on a series of arches. It looks very unsafe but I am told that the arches are so strong that the floor can take the weight of a couple of elephants. Unlike the Turks, the Mughals did not soak in their baths, for it was considered unhygienic to linger in water already soiled by a sweaty body. Instead, buckets were filled and poured over the emperor's person.

The precinct is enormous, consisting of a series of chambers that could house several dozen people. Dr Muhammad explains, 'The *ghusl*, or bath, was an event that approximated a courtly gathering.' Only favoured courtiers were admitted. I imagine them gathered here in the hall, awaiting their king, a glorious assembly of splendidly garbed amirs murmuring softly among themselves. It was a good time to do business with the emperor, who was relaxed and jovial during his bath. While he conducted the business of court, Jahangir sipped wine diluted with rose water and ate fruit, especially mangoes, which he relished even more than the fruits from Kabul, which all Mughals recalled with nostalgia. Of these, he wrote in his memoirs, 'Not one of them has, to my taste, the flavour of the mango.'

Only the emperor drank. The nobles were strictly prohibited from partaking of any liquor. As their ruler held forth, attendants would bring bowls of perfumed water to bathe his feet. Then, they would remove his outer clothing, his jewels, slippers, his robe. He probably would then have moved to a more private area to remove the rest of his clothes and bathe, but Mughal emperors conducted their entire lives surrounded by people who, to their imperial highnesses, were all but invisible.

After bathing in scented water, the process of dressing commenced. Finally, trays of jewels were offered for the emperor's preference, aigrettes for his turban, necklaces, bracelets, rings in staggering profusion. The discussions would continue and so would Jahangir's drinking of innumerable glasses of wine. As he got older, the effects of alcohol and drugs impaired his health. His hands shook so much that he often could not hold his own cup. On occasion, the emperor drank so much that he fell asleep. The candles were snuffed out and the assemblage filed away quietly. When he awoke after a couple of hours, food would be brought in: often the simple peasant *khichri*, boiled and mildly spiced millet and lentils that he developed a taste for in Gujarat. But he was sometimes so drunk that he had to be fed.

As Jahangir's dependence on alcohol increased, he leaned more and more on his empress, Nur Jahan. Her Afghan husband had been killed, though not, it seems, at the emperor's instructions. The lady returned to court, where she served the emperor's mother for four years, during which time she caught Jahangir's eye again. They were married in 1611, the sixth year of his reign. Jahangir made up for lost time. He changed her name to Nur Jahan, light of the world.

6

That Nightingales
May Not Weep

Nur Jahan was thirty-four, a widow with a child, at the time of her wedding to Jahangir. She was, according to some estimates, the emperor's twentieth wife. If not old, she was certainly well into middle age by medieval standards, where life expectancy was low. And yet, she captured the heart of the emperor of Hindustan, the most powerful man in her firmament, one who had the loveliest young women of the realm waiting on his pleasure. Although Nur Jahan was certainly beautiful, with large eyes and fair skin, what set her apart from all the nubile young beauties in the harem seem to have been her intelligence and sophistication. As was the custom among young women of the aristocracy, her education had been rigorous, ranging from literature and mathematics, art and music to the more martial expressions of war and the hunt. Her keen intelligence absorbed all her learning which she brought into play in everyday life.

Her training in the arts of repartee and wit equipped her to become a delightful and stimulating companion, able to conduct even an entire conversation in verse. Jahangir, who had received a similar education, found many things in common with his new empress. They were both concerned with elegance and beauty, shared a commitment to the patronage of painting, and took pleasure in gardening as well as hunting. They sparred together in verbal duels phrased entirely in verse. Nur Jahan was also a good markswoman and enjoyed hunting as much as Jahangir. On one occasion, she killed four tigers which came out of the bushes near the elephant carrying the royal couple. The emperor gestured silently to Nur Jahan, telling her to dispatch two with arrows and two with her guns. Nur Jahan quietly prepared two muzzle-loading guns and placed them within easy reach on the howdah. Then she chose two arrows, seized her bow, took careful aim and loosened two arrows in quick succession. Two tigers fell to the ground. Without pausing for a moment, the empress picked up a gun and fired, dropping the third tiger. The fourth fell with her final shot from the second gun. Jahangir was delighted. 'Such shooting has never been seen until now,' he exulted. He showered her with a thousand golden asharfis and gave her diamond bracelets worth a hundred thousand rupees.

Nur Jahan, beloved of the richest and most powerful monarch in the world, quickly made herself indispensable to the emperor. She would have spent hours at her toilette to make herself irresistibly beautiful. A routine followed by hundreds of less fortunate harem inmates who bathed and perfumed their bodies, dressed and bejewelled themselves day after day. But they were no match for the multifaceted talents of Nur Jahan. The empress also developed new fabrics and modes of apparel—an interest shared by Jahangir who was a bit of a dandy and enjoyed fine clothes and jewellery. Even the emperor's robes and turbans, which were more studied than those of his predecessors, are said to have been designed by his wife. Nur Jahan also directed her skills towards innovative patterns for brocade and lace, and is said to have fashioned new styles in garments for women. The practical and elegant *sharara*, which flowed in fluid lines along each leg but allowed freedom of movement, is said to have been her creation. For more informal occasions she wore a fitted bodice attached to a full skirt of gauzy material in the pale pastel colours that she preferred, over ornamented or striped tight pyjamas similar to today's churidar. She even created her own perfume from the distilled essence of roses which became her distinctive fragrance.

Nur Jahan shared her husband's passionate interest in plants and gardens. Although many of these were in their beloved Kashmir, which they visited five times in Jahangir's twenty-two-year reign, they also worked together to improve Babur's Aram Bagh. Two beautiful suites were built at the highest level, overlooking the river, and in front of these stood a large stone platform, in the centre of a water tank surrounded by fountains. This was a *mah-tab*, an island platform, where the royal couple and others after them would have dined surrounded by jets of water that danced along the surface of the tank, cooling the air.

Jahangir gifted the garden to his empress and renamed it in her honour, Bagh-E-Nur Afshan. The empress already owned the adjoining caravanserai, also on the Yamuna, where her officers collected duties on goods transported by river. The serai was an extensive property, with accommodation for as many as 3,000 travellers and an equal number of horses, at a fee of course.

I walk through a depressing muddle of rubble and huts to look for the remains of Nur Jahan's serai. Most of the land has been encroached upon and many of the desperately poor shanties are made of stones and bricks pilfered from the monument over the centuries. There were around eighty caravanserais for travellers in seventeenth-century Agra. Temporary homes to men of diverse nationalities who travelled immense distances largely to trade. Many of the travellers would have come by boat, others over land in enormous caravans of up to 20,000 bullocks, pack-horses, mules, camels and elephants. They rested here and spread out their wares for the empress's customs officials to evaluate and levy duties, but also possibly to sell. Bales of silk and fine brocades would have spilt out across the carpets laid out for the purpose, the finest damascened blades, fragrances, myrrh and camphor, fruit from Kabul, salt from Sambhar in Rajasthan and strange animals from Africa to catch the king's fancy.

Nur Jahan was a wealthy woman in her own right. She had received a considerable patrimony from her wealthy and powerful father Ghyas Beg who had risen to be treasurer of the realm. He had a reputation of being extremely helpful to those that filled his pockets, and had amassed a fortune. Jahangir, however, wrote of his father-in-law, '…he possessed many genial qualities and social accomplishments. His accounts were always perfect.' Nur Jahan's infatuated husband also gave her a huge dowry equivalent at that time to 7,200,000 pounds sterling, which, according to Jahangir's memoirs, was the sum she requested as 'indispensable to the purchase of jewels'. Nur Jahan managed her finances astutely. She invested her money and gradually enlarged her capital. She owned at least one ship that carried pilgrims and cargo to and from Mecca, earning her large sums of money.

* * *

The supremely talented Nur Jahan also turned her skills to creating new designs for carpets. Akbar is said to have brought the first carpet-weavers from Persia to Agra and established ateliers where local craftsmen were trained. Nur Jahan's impeccable aesthetic introduced a greater refinement to the industry with the use of silk and cashmere pashmina. A very high quality was quickly achieved, and imports all but ceased. Carpets woven under Nur Jahan's direction were softer and more lustrous than the earlier wool carpets and also allowed a greater density of knots, which created a texture like velvet. Gold and silver threads came to be used during this time; often, even the fringes of carpets were of gold thread. Design also received a new impetus with classical Persian forms being modified by local influences. The master designer of carpets, who created the actual size drawing that was the basis of the carpet, was also often a painter who illustrated manuscripts, bringing a cross-fertilization of ideas which enriched carpet design.

Hari Wattal is the doyen among carpet manufacturers in Agra. His contribution to the art of carpet design and weaving was so widely recognized that he was awarded the nation's highest award for excellence, the Padma Shri. Dr Neville Smith, whose father was a great friend of Mr Wattal, takes me to his home, Dholpur House, one of Agra's gracious mansions built during the Raj as a town residence for the rulers of the erstwhile state. It was once surrounded by stately gardens bisected by a long tree-lined drive. But large sections of the property were sold decades ago, and we now approach the lovely old house via a side lane. Stacks of rolled carpets, smothered in insect repellant, rise to the ceiling in a gracious anteroom. An enormous ballroom flanked by soaring Doric columns is completely bare, its old wooden floor illuminated by an enormous but dusty skylight, dull with disuse.

Chambers on either side are piled high with carpets. And there are still more in the small study into which we are finally ushered.

Mr Wattal is one of the most handsome men I have ever seen, even though he is in his eighties. It's difficult to identify any single outstanding feature, but he is tall, fair in keeping with his Kashmiri ancestry, with a hooked nose and animated twinkling eyes. There is a sense of youthfulness in his demeanour, reinforced by his strong handshake. 'I don't take life too seriously,' he smiles broadly, in response to my comment on his evident well-being.

The small room that is Mr Wattal's study is dominated by a large leather-covered desk with orderly piles of well-thumbed books. Wide french windows look out over fresh green trees. There are carpets everywhere, stacked, as in other rooms, with interesting samples hung behind and facing the desk. Carpets were Mr Wattal's life. He has designed and produced many great carpets and made a fortune. The ballroom, with its high skylight for natural light, was the main area for display. Beautiful carpets were hung on the walls and the pillars, and others were spread on the floor. Business was good; he entertained only the most serious buyers. But he is tired of working now and has closed the factory.

He forages in a bookcase of files, and produces folder after folder of papers impeccably preserved in plastic envelopes, and generously shares their contents. Several weavers usually worked on a carpet together, and since each knot was individually tied, it was a laborious process that took months, or even years, not just in Mughal times but in Mr Wattal's day as well, and even today for really good carpets. Mr Wattal temples his fingers. 'All artisans were, of course, a charge on the state,' he says. 'Everything they produced was the property of the emperor and they depended on him for all their needs, even the weddings of their children.'

Many carpets woven during Jahangir's reign reflect the imperial couple's passionate interest in plants and animals. There are several examples which incorporate flowers, roses, lilies, irises, violets, carnations, peonies, interwoven with vines, recalling the 'Paradise' gardens that the Mughals so loved. The entwined cypress and fruit tree, symbolizing life, death and immortality, was also a popular motif, one that Mr Wattal used often in his carpets.

There were also some lovely carpets depicting the imperial hunt. One of the best existing examples is at the Museum of Fine Arts in Boston, Mr Wattal (it is inconceivable to refer to him as Hari) tells us. 'It illustrates the level of sophistication that can be reached when the weaving skill and the aesthetics of the designer are in perfect harmony.' He shows me a framed photograph of a hunting-scene on a carpet that he created. It is executed in such detail that the species are easily identifiable: ibex, tiger, crane.

There was a huge domestic market both in the imperial court and its aristocracy, as well as among the merchants and professionals of the city whose requirement of carpets was inexhaustible. Mughal carpets were also immensely popular in Europe, so much so that Dutch and Flemish painters of the sixteenth and seventeenth centuries often depicted them in their work, in front of altars or simply draped over tables. They were also said to have been acquired by the Japanese royalty from European traders.

Mughal palaces were covered in carpets, their glowing colours and rich textures bringing the magnificent palaces of Agra's Fort to life. The converse is also true. The sense of emptiness in the vast chambers is precisely due to the absence of carpets. In addition to covering the floors and providing seating, they were also hung, for privacy and to keep cold winds out, from the arches that front so many apartments. Then there were also the prayer rugs, woven with a *mihrab* motif simulating the niche in a mosque which indicated the direction of Mecca. Carpets were also placed in the Diwan-I-Am, below the throne, where emissaries and petitioners stood before the emperor. But my favourite carpet story is the one about Jahangir's visit to the home of his brother-in-law, on the Persian new year's day. In honour of the imperial visit, Asaf Khan had carpets laid all the way from his house to the palace!

Mr Wattal searches his mind for more facts to share. 'Carpets need special care when they are in use,' he says. 'Dust kills carpets. It acts like hundreds of tiny saws on the delicate fibres. If you collect dust off a carpet by simply running your finger over it, and then brush your finger on a mirror, you will find the glass scratched.'

Mr Wattal is irritated with questions about Kashmiris. 'I am not just a Kashmiri,' he says waspishly, 'I am Indian'. After some reassurance that I am not looking for differences but rather exploring the great patchwork that is Agra, he gives me some background. Although many Kashmiri Pandits came to Agra during the time of Akbar, the real migration started in the early eighteenth century, during the reign of the Pathan governors of the region. Hindus were discriminated against and there was also a lack of employment in proportion to their abilities. 'Kashmiri Pandits have always been learned,' he grins self-consciously. 'They were more literate, law-abiding and intelligent than most other communities and easily found employment on their way down from the Valley.' His grandfather stopped at Bharatpur, where he became extremely powerful and was even able to influence succession. 'The Kashmiri Pandits couldn't keep from meddling in state affairs,' Mr Wattal says with a big smile, 'for the good of the state and, of course, their own gain.' Under the British, they rose quickly to the bar where they were able to interpret Persian documents. Motilal Nehru, father of India's first prime minister, was born in Agra and started his legal practice there.

We talk about Agra past and present. 'I used to walk to the Baptist school every morning when I was a child,' he says. 'The road was washed every single day.' Part of the problem today is congestion. 'When I was a schoolboy, the population of Agra was 200,000.' In 2001 it had grown six times, and must have risen considerably today. His forehead creases in a frown. 'People in Agra just do not pull their own weight.' He thinks for a moment. 'There is a certain mental fatigue; we go on repeating old adages that are now meaningless. This tendency is typical of what is commonly called the Hindi belt in large parts of Uttar Pradesh.' In addition, Mr Wattal believes, 'Agra has seen only unidimensional development. There is no real focus on art or music, on scholarship or literature,' he says angrily. 'The only thing that is important is making money. And many in Agra have made a lot of it. There is so much they could do. Libraries, for example. There are hardly any decent public libraries in Agra. Nor many well-read people either. I have been trying for months to find a copy of the *Vayu Purana* and not a single person I know has one.' Agra also has no museum of either miniature paintings or carpets. The human mind must be stimulated to be truly productive. The Mughals, for example, were the product of centuries of civilization. 'Babur did not drop like a stone into a pond,' he says. 'You have to study his ancestry, the libraries of the time, the scientific instruments, the mathematics, yes, even the gardens, to appreciate the multi-faceted development he brought with him.'

Mr Wattal had organized the Archaeological Society of Agra, of which Dr Neville Smith's father, Thomas Smith, was a prominent member. They met on the second Saturday of each month. There would be a lecture followed by a discussion. And there was no fee. He ferrets among his files again and produces a series of large registers, with detailed hand-written minutes of each meeting. The subjects were varied and their concerns many. Where are their modern-day representatives? 'Up to date, nothing much has been done,' says Mr Wattal. 'But,' he adds, 'this time span is minuscule in the history of the city.'

* * *

Nur Jahan grew in power and prestige. Both derived from the deep love of her imperial husband and his belief in her love for him. A sentiment she gave him no reason to regret. Even when his body was weakened by alcohol, indulgence and asthma, she nursed him carefully, reducing his intake of wine and restructuring his diet to exclude foods that did not suit him. Jahangir also trusted Nur Jahan implicitly and bestowed upon her power greater than any woman had ever wielded. All royal orders, the firmans, that Jahangir executed also bore the imprint of the empress. The emperor even entrusted her with the royal seal, making her the virtual ruler of the empire with unbounded influence. Jahangir even invited her to sit with him at the audience window to hear petitions. He gave instructions that coins be minted in her name. A thousand-*muhar* coin, freshly minted, was inscribed with a couplet, which translates to:

'By the order of Jahangir, gold attains a hundred times its beauty/

When the name of Nur Jahan, the First Lady of the Court,

is impressed upon it.'

Nur Jahan was capable and certainly most ambitious. She consolidated her own position. With her father, Mirza Ghyas Beg, already prime minister of the realm, honoured with the title of Itmad-ud-Daulah, pillar of the empire, she also ensured high positions at court for her brother Asaf Khan and later her nephew Shaista Khan. Her niece Arjumand Banu married Khurram, the heir to the throne. And as the emperor turned increasingly to wine and opium, she came to rule in her husband's name. But even so powerful an individual was constrained by gender. She ruled through her father and brother and in her husband's name.

Mirza Ghyas Beg tutored his daughter in the intricacies of diplomacy and statecraft. He showed her, by example, how to wield power and how to moderate it with compassion. Nur Jahan frequently interceded on behalf of those who came to her for help and was regarded as the 'asylum for all sufferers'. Her father passed away in 1622, a year after his wife. The devastated empress turned her grief into planning a suitable memorial. At first, she planned a tomb of pure silver, but her brother Asaf Khan pointed out that so opulent a structure would invite plunder. Nur Jahan focussed her creativity towards designing the most inspired building the Mughal world had seen, a unique tribute from an empress to beloved parents.

As was customary, Itmad-ud-daulah's tomb is set in a serene Char Bagh on the bank of the Yamuna. This was the first mausoleum on the river bank which till then had been a sequence of beautiful pleasure gardens. It is the most delicate building imaginable, surrounded by water channels and tanks and fountains which once veiled it in a fine haze of spray. The broad waterways were flanked by deep-green cypress which gentled the glare off the marble, while massed flowers of varying heights and colours were a perfect foil to the stark whiteness of the mausoleum.

Itmad-ud-daulah's tomb marked a huge step forward in the art of mosaic and inlay. It was also the first structure in Agra to be built entirely of white marble. Rare, precious and semi-precious gems are set into the marble in patterns that would later inspire the work at the Taj Mahal. Delicate marble lattices regulate the ingress of light, inducing a sense of soothing solemnity, while opulently decorated ceilings bring dimensions of imperial grandeur. These were so heavily encrusted with gold, that during the turmoil that followed the disintegration of the Mughal empire, marauders set fire to parts of the ceiling to melt the gold and scrape it off. Some segments of the painted ceilings were restored in 1905 by Lord Curzon, Viceroy of India, to prepare for the visit of the Prince of Wales. Jawaharlal Nehru was among the legions of travellers who greatly admired Nur Jahan's memorial to her parents and regularly advised visitors to Agra to be sure to see this most 'eclectic' structure.

Restoration work is in full swing in various parts of the tomb precinct. There is work being done in stone and mortar, as well as the more tedious replacement of inlay, all with materials and tools used in medieval times. Craftsmen wield the traditional emery saw, rather like a large bow, carefully shaping slivers of stone to the exact size of those that require replacement. The modern work is almost indistinguishable from the old.

Nur Jahan would have come here often to pay her respects to her parents. There would have been private visits as well as more formal occasions, when she participated in religious commemorative rites. Her brother Asaf Khan, his daughter Arjumand and her husband, Khurram, crown prince of the empire would have accompanied her. On occasion, even the emperor would have joined the mourning family. They would have come here by boat, and as I look from the riverfront pavilion, I imagine the imperial barge drifting downstream. There would have been bridges of boats, or pontoons, in the distance for the army to cross. And here and there bobbing heads would have appeared on the surface of the water as poorer people crossed the river on inflated buffalo skins, or floated across lying over the mouth of a big earthen pot.

I settle down to watch the river meandering around sandbanks. There is a sense of convergence of time in the river's flow. The idea that we contain the past, indeed are products of the past, is inescapable. How would the Mughals have viewed us, who are the culmination of their times? With dismay, with amusement, with horror?

* * *

The French traveller Bernier speaks of Nur Jahan's 'transcendent abilities' and her supreme competence in governance. She dealt with the affairs of the kingdom and the various crises with wisdom and charm. Pelsaert, a Dutch merchant who was at the imperial court, recorded that any petitions to the king were referred to Asaf Khan who took no decision without consulting his sister.

Nur Jahan was unable to give her husband the one thing that would perpetuate her power, a child. So she sought to safeguard her position by marrying her daughter Ladli Begum from her previous marriage, to Jahangir's youngest and least accomplished son, Prince Sharyar, and began to plot to secure the crown for him. Khurram, who was married to her niece Arjumand, was sidelined in a move that forced the prince into rebellion and the empire into civil war. But Nur Jahan's brother Asaf Khan, father of Arjumand and father-in-law of

Khurram, saw to it that she failed. When Jahangir died on his way back from Kashmir, Asaf Khan ensured the coronation of his son-in-law.

Nur Jahan retreated from the public eye and lived in seclusion. She received a yearly stipend of a quarter-of-a-million sterling. The former empress, famous for her fashionable attire, wore only white and devoted what remained of her life to building the tomb of her husband and nurturing its garden. She had a very small grave built for herself near her husband's at Lahore, inscribed with these haunting lines: 'On the grave of this traveller, be so good as to light no lamps nor strew any roses. This will ensure that the wings of moths are not singed and that nightingales will not sigh and weep and lament.'

I wonder if things would have turned out differently if she had given Jahangir a son.

* * *

Jahangir was forty-two when he married Nur Jahan and had already sired three sons in earlier marriages. However, according to infertility specialist Dr Jaideep Malhotra, years of indulgence in alcohol and drugs could well have left him infertile by the time Nur Jahan became his wife. She, too, had already had a child but it is possible that her reproductive system had been damaged, either during the birth of her child or due to some sexually transmitted disease that she had got from either her previous husband or Jahangir.

Both Dr Malhotra and her husband, as well as his parents, are gynaecologists, and together run the popular Malhotra Nursing Home. Hospitals have always been big business in Agra, serving patients from smaller towns and villages for miles around. Although there were several government hospitals, people increasingly preferred to consult doctors in the private sector. Medical facilities proliferated, catering to every kind of ailment—including insanity, for which Agra's mental asylum is well known. In recent years the problem of childlessness has been increasingly addressed. The fertility clinic at the Malhotra Nursing Home is among these, and is largely Jaideep's baby. It is a spotless, completely sterile facility and I have had to remove my shoes before entering. The waiting room, with shining granite floors and lots of blond wood, is crowded by women as well as men.

Male infertility is quite common and is one of the problems that Jaideep frequently encounters in her considerable practice. When a couple is unable to conceive, she runs tests on the male partner first. Initially, there was some resistance from her patients, many of whom were from conservative backgrounds and were conditioned to blame the woman for failing to conceive. Also, male infertility used to be seen as a diminishment of manhood, but Jaideep conducts extensive counselling to encourage people to view it as simply a medical problem which can be treated. This is an important part of her work, the counselling, a crucial factor towards helping patients understand and deal with the problem without negativity.

Male infertility is easier and much cheaper to diagnose and treat. In almost fifty per cent of Jaideep's cases, the inability to conceive arises from some clinical problem of the male partner. As a matter of fact, in every hundred men, fifteen have no sperm. And many more have low sperm counts. While previous World Health Organization guidelines considered a normal sperm count to be around 60 to 120 million, today it mentions just 20 million.

There are many causes of male infertility. Excessive intake of alcohol, smoking, the use of pesticides, and sexually transmitted diseases are all significant contributing factors. Then, of course, there are genetic issues, which account for one or two per cent. But most important of all, modern living, with all the pollutants and toxic substances that are steadily ingested, have dramatically impacted sperm counts. Soya and soya products, which have become such a major part of vegetarian diets, also have a negative effect on males. Stress, too, is a major factor.

Jaideep is petite and most attractive, with tumbling curls around a lovely face. She is also very articulate, and judging from her huge practice, evidently supremely competent. Test tube babies are her specialty. When the sperm count is too low to be viable, she injects the husband's sperm into an egg from his wife in a test tube. And when there is no sperm at all, she uses donor sperm, carefully matched to the racial and physical characteristics of the father. 'One of the most difficult things is persuading a man with a zero sperm count to allow his wife's ova to be fertilized using donor sperm, says Jaideep. 'I try to explain to them, saying "If you were dying, would you think about whose blood you were receiving?" Here there is a choice of racial characteristics, even eye colour. You can seldom tell that a donor sperm baby is not actually its father's child.'

Patients come from all over, many from smaller urban centres around Agra, others from as far away as Bangladesh, Jaideep informs me. They come after trying everything else. The tragedy is that it is sometimes too late. When a woman is over thirty-five, the fertility of her eggs diminishes, so even a test tube baby becomes a difficult proposition and success rates diminish.

Jaideep bundles her hair back as we talk. 'I had a patient once who walked into the clinic with two wives, one on either side of him. He was married to one for twenty-five years. His second wife was a widow who had a child from a previous marriage. The man turned out to be azospermic; he had a zero sperm count. Often when there are no children, men marry again and again—in the hope that the new woman will conceive—either on their own volition or due to family pressure.'

The psychological impact of infertility is considerable, though men, by and large, handle it fairly well. They are able to immerse themselves in other activities. But for women it is worse. They are often unable to leave their homes and have plenty of time to brood. Also, women are subject to taunts and harassment by other women in the family who traditionally consider there is nothing worse for a woman than to be barren. Such women become introverted; they become very reluctant to leave the house for fear of having to confront other women who ask them what is wrong with them, why they have not had children.

There are, of course, many different kinds of treatment for infertility, depending on the problem. But the catch is that the processes and medicines are still extremely expensive. For IVF, for example the all-inclusive cost is around 65,000 rupees—of which around 40,000 rupees go on medicines which are largely imported. Jaideep is only too aware of the high cost and often performs the procedures free for young couples who are unable to afford the expenses. She boots her laptop and shows me a video on cell division for a test-tube baby. 'It is so beautiful,' she says, as the images unfold, 'the cell grows so fast and becomes a baby. I think I have the best job in the world. Helping couples create children.'

7

The Golden Mile

Nur Jahan's niece, Arjumand Banu Begum, later renamed Mumtaz Mahal, grew up in enormous luxury. Her grandfather was chief minister of the empire and her father a very important noble. Both were extraordinarily wealthy, even by Mughal standards. The palatial family home on the right bank of the river Yamuna, where other prominent aristocrats lived fairly close to the Fort, was in an area said to contain the highest accumulation of affluence in the world, a golden mile.

The magnificent mansions, often three to four storeys high, were more like city blocks than homes, with innumerable courtyards and living accommodation, not just for the extended family but also for personal staff, hordes of attendants and slaves. The exteriors of the havelis, however, were simple, with nothing much to see except high walls. The huge contrast between the stark outer walls and the dazzling gem-encrusted interiors, is explained in a saying that the *sharam*, the modesty, of a home should always be concealed, its beauty revealed only gradually as the rooms emerge one after another. Arjumand's family's haveli would have had outer courtyards to stable their elephants, horses and palanquins, and to house the scores of men who cared for them. Another courtyard would have been home to slaves, dancing girls, musicians, servants and numerous other members of the household staff. The handsome and ornamented Diwan Khana, the public area where the head of the family met his visitors, would be flanked by apartments for the male members of the family. An elaborate hamam was probably close by, with a silver fountain shaped like a nine-headed serpent, which sprinkled perfumed water into a silver trough. The women's section, the zenana, in the well-protected centre of the mansion, consisted of several interconnected courtyards greened by formal gardens with shady walks and massed flowers.

The courtyard has always been an important architectural feature in the subcontinent, incorporated for climate control. Cool air settled into its green depths, where it was freshened by contact with lush vegetation as well as the fountains, pools and channels of running water. The cooled air flowed into surrounding chambers, creating convection currents, reducing temperatures and making the hot weather more bearable. For especially hot periods, there were also basement *tehkhanas* with water bodies and cascades, where big cloth fans suspended from the high ceilings swung lazily.

Arjumand's home was probably three-storeyed and topped with a flat roof, where the family would spend summer evenings enjoying the breeze off the river. She would have often slept out on the roof on dew-cooled sheets in garments that consisted of two or three shifts of muslin, so fine that each weighed not even an ounce and cost forty to fifty rupees, in addition to the gold lace trim. These were often given away to servants in the morning and a fresh set used each night.

The interiors would have been extravagantly ornamented.

Walls were finished in the *araish* plaster of marble dust and eggshells, polished to a high sheen. Arabesques of painted flowers and geometrical motifs decorated the walls and the lintels of doors would have been beautifully carved. Gemstones would gleam from chests and low writing tables. Priceless tapestries embroidered in gold and silver and embedded with precious stones would underscore the opulence of the rooms in which Arjumand wandered as a child and, later, as a young woman.

* * *

I walk along the riverfront trying to see it as it once was, this series of beautiful havelis with gardens and trees, reaching down to the Yamuna. Today, Agra's riverfront is the modern city's greatest betrayal of its heritage. It was till recently a cargo hub, where trucks roared in at all hours of the day and night, unloading freight which was then stacked in unlovely heaps awaiting redistribution. The noise, the chaos, the grease and the pollution were in horrifying contrast to what once was. The truck depot has mercifully moved to a new Transport Nagar, outside the city.

Many of the old havelis were demolished by the British in 1837 to make way for the riverside Strand Road, constructed as part of famine relief. By 1845, a German captain, Leopold von Orlich, describes riding along the Yamuna and passing 'the ruins in which the nobles resided …. Here are walls so colossal and solid that they are preserved in spite of all the violence which they have suffered. We saw pieces ten feet thick united by a cement which nothing but gunpowder can break up.' However, a few havelis were saved with just their frontage destroyed and their riverfront perspective altered. Tragically, the vandalism was perpetuated by Agra's citizens and many more havelis were torn down or converted into godowns. Only a few ornamented facades remain and even these, streaked with soot and grease, are being devoured by encroachments.

Kamini and Rajeev Lall arrange for me to visit one of the few havelis that retain some semblance of former glory. We enter the Khandelwal mansion via a barren forecourt, a dust bowl really, that was once encased in trees, gardens and running water. Today, lumber is stacked on one side and a small squalid wooden cabin clings to a soaring façade on the other. An elegant three-storeyed tower teeters gently towards imminent oblivion. Its roof has fallen in and patches of sky are visible through ruined windows.

A flight of steps, sweeping up to the main haveli, retains faint traces of former grandeur but it has been repaired many times and is now a leprous patchwork of cement. It takes a while to see past the dilapidated buildings, to imagine the grand structures and river-facing chambers at one time reserved for the most important members of the family. Some of these are still occupied, entered through a rear verandah where string beds are laid out. A white Pomeranian, tied to the leg of one bed, barks indignation at our intrusion. The lady of the house appears, a sari drawn demurely over her head. She has large lovely eyes and must have once been very beautiful. Since we are friends of friends, Mrs Khandelwal is gracious and welcoming. She accompanies us to a garden where a broken fountain once plashed into a carved bowl. Some woebegone flowering plants still struggle on: hibiscus, rose bushes, sweet-scented jasmines, frangipani. A sumptuously carved temple stands to one side. Although it, too, has seen better days, it is still in good repair. 'We still worship there every evening,' Mrs Khandelwal says, 'my mother-in-law and

I.' And the flowers they offer the gods are gathered from their garden.

The more formal *mardana*, the men's section where guests were entertained, is ornamented with rhapsodic indulgence. It has gilded and painted ceilings, etched glass and inlaid mirrors. The paintings are not very good, but there is a sense of the uninhibited enjoyment of painter and patron, an unabashed revelling in glitter and ostentation. Carved Victorian furniture, with fading upholstery, is arranged in formal symmetry, and huge chandeliers shrouded with dust covers crouch close to the painted ceiling. The room smells slightly musty. It is usually closed up and we have come at short notice. Some windows are boarded up, the glass in their panes long broken. 'The last time it was really used was for my sister-in-law's wedding,' the lady of the house tells us, serving tea in dainty cups. 'Then, it looked wonderful, the whole house looked wonderful, all decorated and lit up. Now it is sometimes used as a film set. That is our only real revenue from the property.' These huge rambling places are so difficult to maintain. Her husband works for a nationalized bank and there is only his salary.

Many years ago, a rumour of buried treasure sustained hope for better times. The family tried to find it but eventually realized they would spend a fortune in the search and perhaps find nothing. There is a story about Itmad-ud-Daulah's haveli, where Mumtaz Mahal grew up. Everyone who owned it in later years looked for treasure said to be concealed on the premises and lost everything in the quest. The haveli was also destroyed in the process. This haveli once spread over a huge area. Mrs Khandelwal points out rows of houses beyond the boundaries of the compound, behind the garden. 'It stretched for almost an entire city block,' she says wistfully.

Year by year, the family sold off bits and pieces of land.

Some parts were rented, and they are now encumbered by tenancy rights. 'The wood and coal storage area out in front—you must have seen it as you entered—that, too, has been rented,' she explains sadly. 'And we can never get it back.' She indicates the lovely crumbling tower near the forecourt. 'It was the oldest part of the house,' she says, pulling the pallav of her sari over her head, 'probably from Mughal times. This is where my husband's great-grandfather and his friends used to gather. They say the carousing went on far into the night, he seldom woke up till the next afternoon, and then it all began all over again.'

The property was originally purchased by an ancestor who had made a fortune in trade. The Khandelwals are Banias. Their forefathers were shrewd businessmen and among the earliest settlers of Agra, lured here by the fertility of the land. The Banias purchased agricultural produce at harvest time from farmers who did not have holding power, and sold it later, building up such enormous profits that they often financed the wars of kings. To spread their network and to hedge their bets, sons were sent to establish businesses in neighbouring kingdoms. These Nagar Seths as they were called, often funded battles between monarchs, and it was not uncommon for two brothers to finance opposing armies. That way, the family was always ahead. The Banias thrived under the Mughals who recognized their legendary financial skills. A large number of the top revenue officials of the Mughals were either Hindu Banias or Brahmins.

But despite the astronomical profits they made, the rot, in personal values, had already set in during British rule. Prominent Bania patriarchs vied with one another for the privilege of being allowed to sit in a chair in the presence of an Englishman. Priorities had begun to change, the simplicity of their lifestyles modulated by Westernization. I recall a collection of portraits I had seen at the home of a prominent Agra Bania. The first was of an ancestor in a dhoti with a black waistcoat and white turban, a shawl across his shoulders. He had a serene expression, a confidence in his power and status. A descendant was pictured in a dhoti with an achkan and a colourful pugree, but seated in a chair. His son wore a brocade achkan with pyjamas and a hat replaced the turban. In the fourth portrait, headgear had been abandoned altogether and the achkan was a severe black. The most recent portrait depicts the father of the current generation wearing a white suit and tie.

At one time, this family owned huge chunks of real estate in Agra. When they started associating with the British, they began to drink, womanize, and gamble on the stock exchange, and the outflow of money began. Two generations did hardly any work at all. Stories are legion of the exquisite courtesans who frequented the haveli and of the hangers-on who sponged off the Khandelwal grandfather. He was said to have been the protector of several beautiful women from the Kashmiri Bazaar, including a particularly lovely lady who went on to become a well-known film star, on whom he showered expensive gifts. The money gradually drained away, till there was nothing left. What else was the family to do but rent out their premises? Similar circumstances caused losses all along the riverfront, and forced families to compromise, to rent, to sell, just to survive.

* * *

Arjumand grew up in the zenana with her mother, grandmother and aunts. There was a comforting familiarity in the harem, a cossetted luxury. There were many diversions too. Female performers regularly entertained the ladies:

acrobats, musicians, dancers and storytellers who wove entrancing tales. The ladies played cards, chess and *chaupar*, a kind of ludo, among themselves, or with their attendants. There were excursions, perhaps to Aram Bagh or other garden palaces that lined the Yamuna. They had pets—talking mynahs and fan-tailed pigeons that cooed in the garden. Visits to the palace to meet Arjumand's aunt, Empress Nur Jahan, in heavily veiled palanquins, were exciting events. At the palace, she enjoyed many forms of entertainment, including the royal Meena Bazaar, a market in the Fort run by women, exclusively for women.

At the Fort, I walk between two rows of arched facades, crumbling and, like many other places in Agra, under repair. The stalls of the Meena Bazaar were converted during British dominance to barracks and are now being restored. This used to be a happy, busy place that resounded to laughter and the low intense negotiations of bargaining as women from the fort and the harems of various nobles crowded stalls in a rare shopping spree far from male eyes. Female vendors displayed their wares under bright awnings in front of the shops. There were rich silks, velvets, brocades, muslins, jewelled embroidery, gemstones, gold jewellery, exotic cosmetics and much, much else. Shopkeepers competed fiercely to be allowed to send their wives with their merchandise to this most exclusive of markets, for prices offered were the top of the line.

Men were only allowed into the Meena Bazaar on certain specified days, such as the Persian New Year, Navroze. These were lighthearted occasions when ladies of the highest aristocracy posed as shopkeepers, offering their wares to the nobles. Bargaining was often drawn out into a sophisticated ritual, where courtiers queried prices in verse and the ladies responded with saucy flirtation. Music played, torches flared and oil lamps flickered, generating an ambience of romantic illusion. The young blades of court swaggered by, showing off to the women. Among them was Prince Khurram, the handsome sixteen-year-old son of Jahangir. Although he was not very tall, he was broad-shouldered, fair, with clean chiselled features. He had a wide forehead, large eyes, an aquiline nose and wore a moustache and beard, possibly to hide scars from a bout of smallpox. Khurram had few Mongol racial characteristics except for his fairness, and was more like his Rajput mother.

Prince Khurram strolled through the crowds in Meena Bazaar and his eye fell upon Arjumand, just turned fifteen, busy at her stall. She was a classic Persian beauty with perfectly proportioned features and almond-shaped eyes. Khurram went up to her and happily paid the fortune she asked for, for a piece of glass, his normally serious demeanour transformed.

Khurram approached his father, and his stepmother, Nur Jahan, Arjumand's aunt. To his great joy the betrothal was agreed upon. Arjumand's parents would have been delighted, for not only was Khurram a prince, but already the most likely to succeed to the throne. Khusrav, his eldest brother, had been blinded in punishment for daring to rebel, while his other brothers, Parvez and Shahriyar, were considered not to be as accomplished. Arjumand's own joy must have been beyond measure. She had fallen in love with the handsome prince. Khurram and Arjumand were betrothed in 1607, but their wedding was delayed. Political considerations governed imperial marriages, and Khurram wed a Persian princess in 1610. Arjumand was heart-broken but is said to have channelled her sorrow into learning the Koran by heart. Within a short while she was consoled by rumours that the couple was estranged. And soon after the birth of a daughter, the Persian princess left Agra for her homeland, laden with gifts.

Arjumand and Khurram were finally wed on 10 May
1612. The emperor and his bridegroom son rode in grand
procession with their relatives and nobles to the riverside
mansion of Itmad-ud-daulah, grandfather of the bride and
father-in-law of Jahangir himself. Musicians and dancers
accompanied the procession and the great drums pounded
tidings of their approach. Celebratory fireworks thundered
along the way and shot into the sky in brilliant showers of
gold and silver. The entourage showered fistfuls of gold coins
upon the bystanders, who acclaimed the emperor and blessed
the bridal couple. As the father of the bride, Asaf Khan
received the distinguished visitors, and the marriage contract
would have been formally signed in the presence of religious
elders. Arjumand's father represented her interests and
indicated her concurrence. A sumptuous banquet followed,
with dancing girls and singers. And while the feasting and
merrymaking lasted far into the night, the bride was
undergoing rituals to cleanse and ornament her body in
preparation for the ceremonies at the palace next morning.

Arjumand's elaborate make-up of several layers of wax
and powder took several hours. A delicate tracery of henna
was applied to her hands and feet. Her eyes were outlined in
kohl, and gold leaf was carefully applied to her hairline which
was further ornamented by a band of diamonds. Gemstones
were woven in her hair, and tassels of pearls set with diamonds
and emeralds draped across one side of her forehead. After
she was dressed and bejewelled, Arjumand was escorted to
an enormous decorated palanquin. Musicians began to play
and the bridal procession of palanquins that carried her
attendants, escorted by horses and elephants, moved off to
the Fort. Arjumand's name was changed, as was the custom.
She would now be called Mumtaz Mahal, crown of the palace.

Finally, the prince looked upon his princess for the first

time in five years. She was nineteen years old and even more beautiful than he remembered. The royal poets, who of course had never set eyes upon Arjumand, wrote paeans of praise to her beauty. Her loveliness was such, they wrote, that the moon hid its face and the stars extinguished their light, fearful of comparisons with her radiant beauty.

* * *

Weddings are big business in Agra, and Lauries hotel, with its huge stretch of land and central location, is a popular venue. I stop, on one occasion, to take a closer look at an enormous bamboo and cloth extravaganza, elaborately turretted and domed, which is being erected. The brother of the bride is overseeing the arrangements. 'Many of the more conservative families prefer this venue over five-star hotels, which have restrictions on decorations and catering,' he says, 'plus they are also much more expensive'. He shows me around. The rough mud will be carpeted, the ceilings hung with gold lamé and lit by elaborate chandeliers. Then there are the flowers, not the cheaper and more usual marigolds, but orchids from Thailand. Why orchids? 'Nothing is too good for my sisters,' he says grandly. It turns out that two of his sisters will be married on the same day, a good business decision. Guests? Well, there will be at least 2,000 and they will all be lavishly entertained at three functions. Musicians and singers, from among the best in the country, are being flown in to entertain the guests. 'A particular advantage of Lauries over the other hotels, which insist on providing the food themselves,' the young man explains, 'is the freedom to use caterers of the clients' choice. That way we can serve our traditional delicacies, all vegetarian, of course, like samosas made of butter and stuffed with dry fruit, special paans and so on.'

The wedding lehengas are being made by a prominent Delhi designer, 'a real page-three person', who has also designed the outfit my friend will wear. 'No one in Agra has ever seen such clothes,' he says, 'they cost literally lakhs'.

The girls have not yet met their fiancés though photographs have been exchanged. 'It's the family that matters,' their brother says, rather sanctimoniously, 'their status, the fact that they will be able to provide. And I can tell you, neither of my sisters will lack for anything.' Their parents went to a lot of trouble to find the right 'boy' from the right family. In many ways, both the grooms' families are very similar to those of the brides. That way, the differences that the girls will have to cope with are minimized. The customs, the food and, of course, the community, are the same.

He proudly escorts me to view the dowries which are laid out in a large hall. Two glossy sedan cars tied with big gold bows parked just outside have gathered a group of admiring viewers. Inside, too, there are two of everything, fridges, washing machines, steel cupboards, sets of bedroom furniture, fifty-one saris each, all embellished with gold, and of course, the jewellery: eleven sets, each comprising earrings, necklaces, bracelets and rings. Diamonds are predominant, with pairs of enormous solitaire earrings for everyday wear and large looping necklaces for more formal occasions. Another section is devoted to a display of gifts for the grooms' families. Saris, shawls, jewellery, watches, suit lengths and so on and on in an opulent display of wealth that endorsed family prestige and standing.

* * *

There is some controversy about what Arjumand actually looked like. Since male painters were not allowed into the harem, portraits of her are often discounted. But there were women painters and the images that have come down to posterity were the product of their work. I grew up with one such painting of Mumtaz Mahal, which my mother inherited from her father, a famous collector in the 1920s. I had been drawn by the gentle thoughtfulness of her expression, and the hint of a smile that hovered around her small rosebud mouth. All attempts to look for the woman behind the painting were frustrating; she remained elusive. Hence, my passionate interest in the Mughals, and in Agra.

Khurram took a third wife five years after his wedding to Mumtaz and was married a fourth time to a Rajput princess. Mumtaz was deeply anguished by these liaisons even though she understood that they were marriages of political expediency. As befitted a man of his station, Khurram also had numerous concubines, whom he visited to avoid rumours of waning potency. But in a gesture of his love for his wife, he had several ladies abort their pregnancies. A cruel and terrible consequence, but a concession to Mumtaz who is said to have pleaded that he never raise children by any other women, 'lest her children and mine should come to blows over succession'.

Mumtaz's first child was a daughter, Chammani, a lovely little girl loved by all. But she died within a few years, possibly of smallpox. Her parents were wracked with sorrow. Not even their wealth or privilege could protect them from further tragedy. Thirteen more children were born in quick succession, but only seven survived: four princes and three princesses. Jahanara, Dara Shukoh, Shah Shuja, Raushanara, Aurangzeb, Murad Bakhsh and Gohanara, Mumtaz's last child.

Mumtaz and Khurram were inseparable. She insisted on accompanying him even to the battlefield. A departure from the days of Babur who had said, 'He that has wives and mistresses on the battlefield has given hostages to fortune.' A huge domestic contingent travelled with the army, the royal children, their wet nurses, tutors, pets, toys, and scores of attendants, musicians, dancers and entertainers. Then there were also merchants, who sold fabric, jewellery, perfumes, and other, smaller, luxuries, seamstresses who sewed royal garments, and several others.

Khurram rose rapidly in his father's favour. After his victory over the Rajput Rana of Mewar, whom even his grandfather Akbar had been unable to subdue, Jahangir raised his son to the rank of commander of 20,000. Khurram's prestige soared. He also campaigned successfully in the Deccan and laid great riches at his father's feet, for which he received the title of Shah Jahan. Everything changed suddenly when Nur Jahan betrothed her daughter from her previous marriage to Jahangir's youngest son, Shahriyar. Shah Jahan felt threatened, and when Jahangir ordered him to go back to the Deccan, he demurred, and then rebelled. Shah Jahan became a fugitive pursued by his father's forces. With him were his wife and children, who were hounded from one place to another for three whole years. They had to press on even during Mumtaz's pregnancies. Eventually, Shah Jahan wrote to his father begging his forgiveness. Jahangir granted him full pardon, but insisted Shah Jahan send his sons Dara and Aurangzeb to court as hostages.

Jahangir died in 1627 of a spasm of coughing brought on by his chronic asthma. As Shah Jahan was in the Deccan at the time, Mumtaz's father, Asaf Khan, then the most senior minister of the realm, dispatched a secret messenger with the news. To gain time and to sidetrack Nur Jahan's ambitions for her son-in-law, her wily brother had Khusrav's son temporarily installed as emperor. Shahriyar was easily defeated, blinded and imprisoned. Shah Jahan set out for

Agra as soon as he heard the news, but first sent a message to Asaf Khan to eliminate all possible contenders for the throne. Accordingly, five princes of the royal line were murdered in cold blood, a casual cruelty typical of the times. There was a saying that just as two swords could not fit in a scabbard, there could never be two claimants to the throne.

* * *

Shah Jahan entered Agra in triumphal procession. The great state drums pounded in proclamation of his approach and the gaily decorated streets were thronged with his subjects who loudly acclaimed their new king. There were the usual celebratory darbars, with much receiving and giving of gifts. Mumtaz, who was always sympathetic and ready to help for a good cause, was besieged with petitions. Her intercession often caused the emperor to set aside judgments, and on occasion to even waive the death penalty. She devoted much of her time to good works, gave gifts in charity, supported several indigent families and also set about establishing a system to help widows and orphans. The new empress often sat behind the purdah during durbars and familiarized herself with her husband's work. Brought up by astute politicians in her grandfather and father, Mumtaz's observations were often insightful. Shah Jahan came to rely on her judgement and consulted her on all important issues. Eventually, he entrusted her with the royal seal, the precious Muhr Uzak, the ultimate symbol of power, of such high significance that once a document was stamped with it, even an emperor's command could not reverse its authority.

Those were halcyon days. The empire was at peace, allowing its new inheritors to enjoy its fruits. Shah Jahan began to design white marble palaces with exquisite inlay to replace some of the red sandstone ones that his grandfather Akbar had built. Architecture had always been of special interest, and even at the age of fifteen, he greatly impressed Jahangir with the elegant renovation of his chambers in Kabul. Now, he was older, widely travelled and sophisticated. Itmad-ud-Daulah's tomb had already ignited his imagination and he would perfect the monument's innovations in his new palaces. He refurbished a suite of rooms, richly inlaid with precious stones, for his beloved Mumtaz in an octagonal bastion, the Mutthamman Burj, the Jasmine Tower, overlooking a bend in the Yamuna. This pavilion would be Shah Jahan's last refuge, as he lay dying. Also on the royal drawing board was a palace of mirrors, the Sheesh Mahal, where the emperor planned to imbed tiny convex mirrors into ceilings and walls to contrive multiple reflections of extraordinary beauty. In the emperor's fertile mind, there were also plans for the new Diwan-I-Khas and a Diwan-I-Am so large and so magnificent that they would fill the civilized world with wonderment. Shah Jahan would have drawn up the basic concept of these new buildings himself and then left the details to the numerous architects and draftsmen in his employ. But the boldness of vision, the grandeur of concept, were, undoubtably, Shah Jahan's. It has been rightly said that while Akbar laid the real foundation of the Mughal empire, it was Shah Jahan who built it.

Like his father and grandfather, Shah Jahan was a great connoisseur of gems, and added to the incredible collection of great stones that filled the Mughal treasuries. Expert craftsmen from across the globe were employed in imperial workshops where they produced treasures such as the world had never seen. The Venetian Geronimo Veroneo and the Frenchman Austin de Bordeaux were among them. Both prospered beyond their wildest dreams.

* * *

Mr Ghanshyam Mathur is Agra's foremost authority on Mughal jewellery, or on any jewellery for that matter. I meet him at the Kohinoor Jewellers, which he owns. An unimpressive door leads to an uninspiring ante-room, but the establishment beyond is luxurious and elegant. Each aspect, from the wall-to-wall beige carpeting to the subdued but comfortable furnishings and the simple display cases of wood and glass, is designed to be unobtrusive, to set off rather than detract from the jewellery. When I remark on it later to Mr Mathur, his eyes light up with a quiet smile. 'A setting for a great stone should be tasteful but simple, so, too, the surroundings of great jewellery.'

But for the moment he is busy with a large group of upmarket tourists. He produces for them a dazzling array of precious stones, emeralds as green as a parrot's plumage, pigeon blood rubies, diamonds of the first water, sapphires as blue as the skies of Kashmir, strung or set to be perfect accessories to Western clothes. Mr Mathur describes the high points of each piece, but without any hint of being pushy. If anything, restraint, and a subdued sophistication seem to characterize the man and everything about him and his surroundings. He wears a dove-grey suit, and a white shirt, its carefully shot cuffs gleaming with discreet gold links.

Much later, when business is over, we talk. His ancestors lived in Delhi and catered to the Mughal court with considerable success. After the uprising of 1857, when the exiled Mughal emperor came to Agra on his way to Rangoon, the Mathur family accompanied him and stayed on in Agra. They lived in Pipal Mandi at the time, with other Kayasthas in the Mathur Mohalla and moved here to M.G. road in 1860, to establish the shop in 1862. Mr Mathur is a passionate collector of beauty in its manifold manifestations in art, of paintings, antique silver and gold objects, and old jewellery—especially the gem-studded pieces so popular with the Mughals. Ghanshyam speaks of his collection, which is not on display. 'Jewellery should be handled, not just looked at,' he says. He learnt about jewels very young, from his father who was a well-known connoisseur. Even though he became blind at the age of fifty-four, he continued to guide his son. 'I became his eyes,' Ghanshyam says solemnly. 'It was a great privilege. My father could tell everything about a gem by merely touching it. What kind? That was easy. Then what colour, what density of colour, what quality, what price. He developed a seventh sense, you could say. Sometimes, someone would jokingly put a stone into his hand and say, 'How's this moonstone?' And he would say angrily, 'Don't fool me, it is a star sapphire.' Slowly, and over many years, Ghanshyam learnt from him and gradually acquired his father's ability. Even today, while choosing an important stone, he rolls it between his first two fingers and thumb.

Ghanshyam's father taught him to understand gems in an unusual way by helping him select vegetables and fruit for the family. He showed his son how to recognize the very best colour for a brinjal, an apple, a tomato; he taught him to appreciate quality and perfection. Ghanshyam was sent to Jaipur to be trained at the famous jewellery market, the Johri Bazaar. He started from scratch, sorting stones according to colour, quality and, of course, size. This is the most important part of the training: the secret is in the sorting. The sapphire, for example, can be of twenty-two different shades. 'Yes,' Ghanshyam admits, speaking with quiet intensity, 'I like coloured stones best. Diamonds are cold. You look at them and they look back at you. The appreciation of coloured stones is like scuba diving. You go into the bed of the ocean and discover the beauty within. You delve deep to discover the impeccable balance of colour and clarity.'

His favourite stone? The emerald. The first of the seven heavens of Islam is believed to be made of emerald. The Mughals loved these green gems, which they wore as talismans and often had them inscribed with sacred texts. Legend has it that Jesus Christ used an emerald bowl at the Last Supper. 'Western craftsmen have created the myth that emeralds are fragile and prone to shattering,' Ghanshyam says angrily. 'This is because these craftsmen are always in a hurry. They do not work with their hands or take the time to properly study the stone. Emeralds have inclusions and if you cut against these, naturally they break. It is all a matter of technique. But the emerald is harder than quartz, you can scratch glass with it. In ancient Egypt, marble was worked with emerald-tipped tools.'

We talk about Mughal jewellery and its distinguishing characteristic. 'It's the craftsmanship,' he says. 'Each piece is unique, even if the designs are similar. When you hand over a packet of stones of mixed shapes, sizes and weights to an Indian jeweller, he can still produce a piece so perfectly balanced that it is difficult to tell how he accommodated an octagonal diamond on the right side with a round diamond on the left.' Twenty-two-carat gold settings were used, in which the gold was turned around the stone. Most of kundan jewellery was based on flat-cut diamonds of varied sizes and shapes and the challenge was to place them in such a manner that each stone appeared perfectly positioned in the overall design.' Then there is the delicate enamel work, meenakari, on the back of each piece of jewellery, applied for perfection of finish.

We speak of the French jeweller Tavernier, who travelled to India in the seventeenth century, and observed that Mughal lapidaries only smoothened the rough edges of gemstones, or cut them *en cabouchon* without facets, to avoid reducing the weight of the gem. 'They did not facet because they did not know how to,' Ghanshyam explains. 'Stones were chosen for colour and clarity and rareness. They were simply cleaved. This was especially true of the long, heavy necklaces of multiple strings of spectacular rubies, emeralds, sapphires, even diamonds, that the Mughals favoured.'

The conversation shifts to the concept of excellence. 'More and more today,' he says, 'one is forced to cater to mediocrity. It is sweeping the world.' Among the beautiful things that he loves, Ghanshyam Mathur also has an interesting collection of embroidery. He accompanies me to an upper room, which appears to be surrounded by blank walls. One by one, shutters slide up with great drama, and the embroideries, if one can call them that, are revealed. My attention is riveted to what Ghanshyam describes as needle painting, incredibly detailed 'pictures' that are made up of millions of tiny stitches, so carefully shaded that from a distance they look like paintings.

Needle painting, Ghanshyam explains with the quiet intensity that he brings to all conversation, is an adaptation of zardozi, a form of three-dimensional embroidery popular among the Mughals, created with several layers of gold and silver threads. Precious stones were then sewn in, their colours in contrast to the ornate embroidery. Over the years, the cost of production increased. Demand diminished and an enterprising master craftsman began to use silk, instead of gold or silver thread. To further reduce costs and yet retain the effect, he developed a delicate padding over which the stitches were then applied. Then there it was a short step to evolving portraits, landscapes and depictions of entire events.

Ghanshyam Mathur is a patron of the art and arranges for me to meet Raes Khan, son of the late master embroiderer,

Shams-ud-din. 'He's well travelled,' Ghanshyam warns me. 'He's been to the United States several times and met with three US Presidents, not to mention innumerable Indian dignitaries.'

* * *

I drive deep into the city, armed with directions to the home of Raes Khan. Little cameos leave me smiling. A goat with a cloth tied around its horns to prevent it from harming any one. A woman sitting with her cow near a crossing, a bundle of grass beside her. Passers-by seeking religious merit purchase her grass to feed her cow. My favourite scam. A group of disgruntled and tired men, unshaven and crumpled, lounge on sofas and chairs dumped haphazardly on one side of the street. There has been a wedding, I discover, and the furniture is part of the bride's dowry. It is awaiting transportation. Meanwhile, these members of the groom's family, exhausted by the festivities, take their leisure.

The city unfolds street by street, a collage of greys and beiges, with the occasional splash of blinding white where a house has been recently whitewashed. But for the most part there is seedy neglect. Homes that once housed single families have now been divided up among many sons and sons of sons. Multiple ownership has made collective action towards maintenance difficult and of course, there is always a shortage of money. Deeper into the old city, the streets become narrower and flagstoned, lined with open drains as they must have been many hundreds of years ago. Small shops bustle with commerce, ordinary and humdrum, but with magical insights into what people crave. Children's clothes, in all shapes and sizes in shop after shop, testify to a retailer's understanding of parental aspirations as a primary lever of purchase. Footwear comes next, in many stalls that sell PVC chappals and bring on nostalgia for the *mochi*, the cobbler, especially in a city famous for its leather products. But the PVC revolution has provided cheap shoes for an entire generation that was previously barefoot. Electronics comes a slow third, with small shops selling watches, calculators, mobile phones, goods coveted by expanding needs, carefully created and nurtured by advertising. Next to many of these, are facilities that repair these very items. Then there are of course the little neighbourhood grocery and vegetable stalls, since above the shops are two floors and more of homes screened by pillared facades, carved balconies and elegant arcades. Decaying remnants of a more gracious time. Many have intricate latticework to conceal ladies in purdah, yet allow them to look out without being seen. In certain parts of the old town, women move from rooftop to rooftop, visiting friends, attending weddings, births and funerals, participating in the rituals of life.

Steam billows out of a cavernous room where Agra's famous confectionery, *petha*, is being made from ash gourd. Huge piles of the pumpkin-like vegetable are attacked by knife-wielding men who reduce the pile to bite-sized pieces in an incredibly short time. They are transferred to concrete bins and soaked in a solution of quick lime, to make the petha 'tight', I am told, firm. Then the petha is beaten vigorously with a multi-tined instrument to promote the absorption of sugar, and finally boiled in a sugar solution.

Further on, the lanes become so narrow that we have to abandon the car and walk. Raes Khan's house is around the corner. The home, similar to many others in the area, is set around a courtyard crammed with potted plants, the traditional jasmines, roses and hibiscus, with more modern palms and crotons. Raes Khan is a distinguished-looking man,

tall and fair with beetling eyebrows. He takes me to the upper
floor where embroiderers work in several rooms, carefully
sewing tiny stitches One worker is putting the final touches
to a large needle painting of a Crowned African Crane,
standing in a clump of reeds. Raes Khan bends to inspect the
final stitches. 'My father was a great naturalist, who delighted
in capturing nature's charms in embroidery,' he says. 'He saw
this bird on one of his African safaris.' The composition
measures sixty-eight inches by twenty-nine inches, and is
made of countless stitches, the colours carefully graded to
create fine nuances of shading from claws to beak. It is very
beautiful—and completely authentic. A needle painting of a
tiger has also just been completed, with at least forty shades
of brown, from dark mahogany to the palest gold. The
padding to construct varying volumes and depths is
ingeniously contrived, conveying a sense of rippling muscles.
Subtle shades of colour flow delicately, one into another.
'Father was a combination of two things,' says Raes seriously,
'artist and craftsman. There was only one other person in the
world like him, an Italian called Michelangelo.'

In another area, a young man is walking up and down
drawing out threads. 'He is blending two shades of greens,'
Raes explains. The difference between the two colours is
almost imperceptible. Today, Raes employs forty embroiderers,
each trained by his father. Together they turn out around 200
pieces a year, big and small. Average monthly earnings for
individual craftsmen are around 5,000 rupees, but since this
is based on an hourly rate, it varies according to the work
put in. Raes dreams of being able to employ 100 craftsmen.
But that would mean an expense of around 50,000 rupees a
month on salaries alone, plus of course all the materials, the
thread, the velvets, the embroidery frames and the rest.

The family has been in Agra for fourteen generations and

developed to become specialists in zardozi. There was plenty of work, hangings for palaces, robes for royalty as well as the lesser nobles and their ladies. In 1911, coronation robes for Queen Alexandria were made on these very premises. We adjourn to the family's private apartments. A long narrow room with two beds at one end, a TV at their foot and a dressing table next to the beds. A wooden sofa set with cushions is grouped around a Formica-topped table at the other end of the room. Raes shows me photographs of his father and himself with various dignitaries, Presidents of India, Rajender Prasad and Radhakrishnan, prime ministers Nehru and Indira Gandhi, as well as three American Presidents. Of particular pride is a photograph of a embroidered portrait of Abraham Lincoln being presented to President Ford at the White House in 1976. Raes produces a file and draws out a letter from Ronald Reagan addressed to his father, where he said he was 'honoured that you have created such a magnificent piece of art for me'. 'Ronald Reagan was known to be an arrogant man,' Raes interjects with great satisfaction. 'He was the man who dismembered the Soviet Union. But even he had to bow before art.' He gives me the prized letter. 'Read on,' he urges, 'see, he adds, "The jewellery box you sent for Nancy will be treasured for years to come." See the tone,' he says proudly. 'It's like members of a family communicating with one another—such informality.'

Raes shows me a photograph of the famous needle painting of Moses and the Burning Bush. It is alive with movement and effectively communicates the drama of the divine visitation. Viewed from a distance, it could well be an exquisite painting. Several years ago, three million dollars were offered—today it is beyond price.

* * *

Over the course of time, many wondrous gems had come into the possession of the Mughal emperors. Shah Jahan's ceremonial aigrette was valued at over a million rupees and his favourite rosary of perfect rubies and pearls was worth 800,000. It occurred to the emperor that such rare jewels should adorn the throne of the empire, thus 'beholders might share and benefit by their splendour and His Majesty might shine with increased brilliancy'. Shah Jahan worked closely with his jewellers to design a throne platform about three yards long and two and half wide, surmounted by a jewelled canopy five yards high. The outside of the canopy would be covered in enamel inlaid with jewelled arabesques of flowers and creepers while the inside, the part over the emperor's person, would be encrusted with gems, mainly rubies. Colour schemes were carefully thought out, and the supporting pillars, it was decided, would be studded with emeralds. Then came the final touch. Each pillar would be surmounted by that symbol of majesty and beauty in India, the peacock, created by gems inlaid to create rippling variations in colour.

The jewels in the imperial treasury seem to have been insufficient for such a huge task. Dealers in gemstones from the length and breadth of the country brought rubies, diamonds, pearls and emeralds weighing 230 kilos for the approval of the emperor. Jewels to the value of twenty million rupees were acquired with some additional exceptionally large stones worth over eight million. All made possible largely by income from taxation on agriculture and trade. Among the celebrated stones that Shah Jahan decided would embellish his throne, were the ninety-five-carat Akbar Shah diamond, the slightly smaller Shah and Jahangir diamonds, and the 283-carat Timur ruby, the second largest in the world; these, together with 1,150 kilos of pure gold. It took seven years to make the Peacock Throne, at a cost that was almost twice as much as Shah Jahan would spend on the Taj Mahal.

In the early eighteenth century, after the Mughal empire began to disintegrate, the Persian emperor Nadir Shah captured Delhi. Among the vast treasures he took back was the Peacock Throne. In the chaos that followed his death, the throne was dismembered by tribesmen, its fabulous jewels scattered all over the Middle-East. Although a few pieces were recovered in later years and used in the construction of a new Peacock Throne housed in Tehran's Gulistan palace, it does not compare with the original.

In addition to the huge treasure in the Agra Fort, estimated at over 300 million pounds sterling, Shah Jahan also had had repositories of riches at other secure locations. These were considered sacred trusts and it was said that those who misappropriated them came to grief. Akbar was believed to have placed a curse on one of his richest vaults, threatening anybody who mishandled the treasure with dire misfortune. Shah Jahan's second son, later Emperor Aurangzeb, harried by pressing financial straits and fear of a revolt among his unpaid troops, went to that particular vault and tried to avert the impact of the curse by avoiding the doors and breaking into the vault through a wall. But its effect dogged him. Aurangzeb's pay disbursements resulted in the distribution of so much gold that the bullion market crashed!

8

Teardrop on the Cheek of Time

> You knew, Emperor of India, Shah Jahan,
> That life, youth, wealth, renown
> All float away down the stream of time...
> Yet still one solitary tear
> Would hang on the cheek of time
> In the form
> Of this white and gleaming Taj Mahal
> —Rabindra Nath Tagore

Despite his considerable fortune, it behove Shah Jahan as emperor to undertake expeditions to extend his territories and further enhance his revenue. Like his father and grandfather before him he was anxious to conquer the Deccan for its legendary wealth, fabled diamond mines and fertile lands, all fiercely defended by powerful kingdoms. It was familiar territory for he had campaigned there on behalf of his father. Just under two years after he ascended the throne, Shah Jahan set off for the Deccan once again. Although she was three months pregnant with her fourteenth child, Mumtaz refused to be left behind. A large and well-cushioned litter was prepared for her comfort, luxuriously furnished and with enough space for attendants and a couple of her six surviving children to while away the hours of travel. Eight sturdy bearers, specially trained to carry the palanquin smoothly even over rough, undulating ground, ensured a comfortable journey. In palanquins alongside, musicians played for her diversion.

The journey was long and tedious but there were many stops for the emperor and his officials to attend to local matters, to hunt and to rest. Mumtaz, now growing heavier, stayed close to camp in her tent, cosseted by her ladies and spending time with her children. Jahanara, almost seventeen, was a woman already as was Raushanara, three years younger. They would never marry, following a custom initiated during the time of Akbar, when it was deemed that no one could be of sufficiently noble birth to marry a Mughal princess. Moreover, it was politically expedient to avoid adding claimants to the throne and further impetus to court intrigue. Mumtaz's sons were growing up fast. Dara and Aurangzeb were exceptionally talented. With his charm, erudition and strong interest in the spiritual, Dara, everyone's favourite, was three years older than the more intense Aurangzeb. Both spent hours at their books, Dara devouring everything he could find on Sufi and Hindu mysticism, while his brother concentrated on the Koran. The other princes, Shah Shuja and Murad, were less talented.

The royal entourage reached the strategic hilltop fort at Burhanpur, hub of the Mughal government of the Deccan, where Shah Jahan had decided to site the imperial headquarters. The accommodations were made even more comfortable by staff from Delhi who had travelled ahead.

On 16 June 1630 Mumtaz went into labour. Wazir Khan, the royal physician who had tended to her many times previously, was in attendance. Labour seemed normal enough, but when it became protracted, panic mounted. Although it was not unusual for women to have fourteen pregnancies, indeed many Indian Muslim women today have as many if not more, several of Mumtaz's had been during periods of incessant travel which had probably taken its toll. After thirty hours a girl child was born and her mother fell into an exhausted sleep. A few hours later, a messenger summoned the emperor—the empress was sinking. By the time Shah Jahan rushed to her side, her head had already been turned towards Mecca, and the solemn verses of the Koran were being chanted. Shah Jahan sat by her side, dazed, holding her hand till she passed on a few hours before dawn. During these precious hours, Mumtaz is said to have asked him to perpetuate her memory in a tomb such as the world has never seen, and to never marry again. She would probably have spoken of her great love for her husband and, as was customary, would have begged his forgiveness for any offence she may have inadvertently given him during their life together. Mumtaz Mahal would have left life as she lived it, with attitudes summed up by the inscription on a golden plaque found in a casket under her bed. A wedding gift from Nur Jahan, it proclaimed that loyalty and obedience to her husband were the finest treasures a woman could offer a man.

Mumtaz's ladies-in-waiting wrapped the body in the traditional five pieces of white cotton used for all women, be they paupers or empresses. Despite Islamic injunctions to the contrary, the weeping and keening would have continued, reaching a hysterical crescendo when a wall of the fort was broken open and the bier carried out. The large sorrowful cortege wound through Burhanpur to a garden. Mumtaz

Mahal was laid in a pavilion, her temporary tomb. A forty-day period of mourning was declared.

Shah Jahan's consuming grief is well documented. He locked himself in his chambers for seven days, refusing food and drink. Through the closed doors, a terrible moaning could be heard, like that of an animal in great pain. He rejected music, which he had loved, wore only white for a very long time and never again used the ittar that he had previously so enjoyed. His beard and moustache, which had only a few scattered grey hairs, became more than 'one third white,' says a court historian, and 'from constant weeping he was forced to wear spectacles.' Shah Jahan even thought of abdicating, but he considered his kingship a sacred duty above and beyond personal tragedy. 'Empire has no sweetness,' he insisted, however, 'life itself has no relish left for me now'.

Shah Jahan could not bear the sight of the new baby, Gohanara Begum. He held her responsible for her mother's death. She is said to have been brought up by her mother's friend and companion Sati-un-Nissa. Like her other sisters, Gohanara never married.

* * *

In early December, six months after Mumtaz Mahal's death, the body of the empress was taken to Dar-ul Khilafat Akbarabad as Agra was then called. Shah Shuja, her fifteen-year-old son, commanded its military escort. Sati-un-Nissa Khanam as well as the late empress's physician accompanied the bier. Along the way, silver coins and food were distributed to gathered crowds, who called out blessings on the soul of the empress. The cortege reached Agra in three months. Prominent citizens and members of the royal household would have joined the procession on its way to the riverside garden of Raja Jai Singh of Jaipur. Jai Singh was connected to the imperial family through his grand-aunt who had married Akbar, and his niece wed Jahangir. The Rajput raja offered the land as a gift but in accordance with Muslim law, he was given other properties in lieu of the garden.

Within a short period of his bereavement, Shah Jahan must have sublimated his grief to look for the perfect location for his empress's tomb. A riverbank site was considered crucial, both for the beauty and symbolism of running water as well as for the aesthetic consideration of the reflection of the planned mausoleum. A precedent had already been set in the riverside tomb of Shah Jahan's great-grandfather Humayun in Delhi, and more recently in that of Mumtaz Mahal's grandfather Itmad-ud-daulah in Agra.

I walk through the lovely Mughal garden that is a perfect foil for the great mausoleum, searching for the structure that sheltered the Empress's coffin while her tomb was under construction. I have to ask several times to find it, and many of those I speak to, all staff tending the gardens, are so programmed to focus on the Taj Mahal that they do not even know of the existence of Mumtaz Mahal's earlier place of burial. It is a small rectangular structure, now open to the sky. Just four walls remain, with arches slightly indented. There must have been a dome, but it has long since collapsed. The small tomb would have resounded each day to recitations of the Koran and prayers for the soul of the empress. By Islamic belief, if the empress had ever transgressed, there was still time to ask for divine forgiveness since celestial reckoning would commence only after the body was laid in the earth for the final time. The sacred cadences mingled with the sounds of frenzied activity, because the site began to swarm with workers, as hundreds of men prepared the foundations for the mausoleum already on the drawing board.

I discuss the process with Puneet Dan, who takes his career as a tour guide very seriously and has researched every aspect of the Taj so thoroughly that he is an expert on the subject. He has been coming here since he was in his teens and each time, he says, he sees something new. That is what has hooked him. Yet, to catalogue the individual marvels of the tomb does not do it justice. It is their coalescence that is so superb. He is a tough, chunky young man, with an irreverent sense of humour and a grin that lights up his entire face. He grew up in Agra, and like Neville Smith, knows many people in the city, though of a different generation. I tell him about my meeting with Yogesh at the Mankameshwar temple. 'Yogesh, a semi-mahant!' he laughs. 'I can't believe it, we used to chase girls together.'

His laughing persona becomes serious when we speak of the Taj. 'One of the many wonderful things about this building,' he declares, 'is the immense beauty that is revealed from different angles. After thousands of visits I still find aspects that I had not seen earlier. It could be the view from a side pathway, a trick of the light.' Puneet particularly enjoys taking visitors along one of the many side routes. 'It is another world,' he says, his face alight with enthusiasm, 'away from the crowds. You enjoy the garden, watch the birds, listen to them twittering in the trees and then you see the Taj. The sudden impact is stunning. Another thing that is special about the monument is that it looks wonderful both from a distance and on close inspection.' We sit together in the lovely gardens of the mausoleum, watching the changing patterns of light and shade, attempting to understand how such perfection was achieved.

Shah Jahan is said to have dispatched architects to the far corners of the empire to study existing tombs and to seek inspiration. Among the many places they visited, Isa Effandi, said to be the chief architect of the mausoleum (although Ustad Ahmad Lahori is also named), certainly spent time at Mandu, in central India, studying the tomb of Hoshang Shah, Sultan of Malwa in the early fifteenth century. It is one of the earliest structures of white marble and has a large dome, both aspects that would have interested the architect. I too had spent many weeks at Mandu developing a conservation plan, and recollect seeing the signature of Isa Effandi on the door jamb of Hoshang Shah's tomb. Orthodox Islam, of course, frowns upon mausoleums, and enjoins simple earth-covered graves. But temporal power circumvented this stricture and grand constructions crown the tombs of generations of sultans and Mughal royalty.

An imperial firman to do with the requisition of carts to transport marble from the Makrana mines in the Rajput kingdom of Amer, is dated as early as 21 January 1632, while the body of Mumtaz Mahal was on its final journey to Agra. The firman refers to previous correspondence and instructs Jai Singh to arrange for the transportation of marble 'in the earliest time'. Such urgency suggests that Shah Jahan had decided to build his empress's tomb of white marble within a few months of Mumtaz Mahal's death.

The emperor probably detailed precise parameters to govern the design of the mausoleum. It was to be of pure white marble, austere but decorated with flowers and plants. While it was grand and imposing, as befitted a memorial to the Empress of Hindustan, it was yet to appear ephemeral, floating. Perhaps the architect Isa suggested the edges be chamfered to diminish volume. Other ideas came quickly.

'Several experts,' Puneet reminds me, 'submitted concepts to Shah Jahan. Elements from these were combined and new designs created over and over again till they met with the emperor's approval, after which a wooden model was made.

Even this was repeatedly refined upon till the perfect proportions that the Emperor sought were achieved.' The Taj Mahal, then, is a synthesis of several great ideas. Even though Ustad Isa and Ustad Ahmad Lahori are believed to have been the main architects, Shah Jahan would have incorporated concepts that developed in brain-storming sessions that lasted through many nights. These ideas were not revolutionary, but evolved from the finest elements of Mughal as well as Hindu architecture.

* * *

A friend of a friend, makes an astonishing comment. 'The Taj Mahal,' he announces, 'was in fact a Hindu temple built by Raja Man Singh. Shah Jahan simply converted it into a tomb for his wife by adding a few Islamic elements such as calligraphy.' I have heard of this completely untenable theory but never dreamt I would meet an adherent. In the year 2000, the Supreme Court of India dismissed a petition that sought to declare that the Taj Mahal was a Hindu temple and issued a reprimand.

The friend of my friend is short, impeccably groomed and speaks in a distinctive, mellifluous tone. He goes on to inform me that the Taj Mahal is actually Tej-o-Mahalaya, a temple consecrated to Shiva in his manifestation as Agreshwar Mahadev, Lord of Agra. 'This,' he says, 'has not been much publicized because the government did not want to hurt the feelings of the Muslims. But there are 109 points that prove this was so. First of all, the name Taj Mahal is not found in any Mughal document.'

I attempt to explain that the mausoleum was originally referred to as 'Rauzah-i-Mumtaz Mahal', a name which certainly occurs in Mughal records of the time. The appellation Taj Mahal came into common use under the British when Taz or Taje Mahal, based on abbreviations of the empress's name common among Europeans, was corrupted into the present form.

'No, no,' he insists, 'Taje Mahal is a short form of Tej-o-Mahalaya.' I give up and sit back to listen. 'Most Mughal tombs, including those of Humayun, Akbar, Itmad-ud-Daula and Safdarjang,' Chandra says, 'are in fact captured Hindu mansions and temples.'

He offers further 'proof', in a very reasonable, almost measured tone. 'There are many Hindu symbols all over the area. The lotuses. The pots with flowering plants, for example, which you will find in Rajput palaces.' I interject to suggest that these were also widely used in Islamic architecture across the world. His voice rises a notch. 'Then there are those borders of sculpted Ganeshas on the main gateway.' These actually depict a series of interlocked acanthus leaves borrowed from classical western architecture. Only the wildest stretch of chauvinistic imagination could conceive of them as Ganeshas. 'And the flowers that are carved on the outer walls of the main structure,' he continues relentlessly. 'Notice these are in the shape of the sacred syllable *Aum*. What do you think of that?' I suppose you can contrive to see what you want to see. 'And that is not all,' he adds. 'There are gilded images of the sun in the main dome, and the sun, as everybody knows, is sacred to Rajputs.' The sun is also found in many Islamic structures, its representation said to be linked to early Zoroastrian associations. 'Also,' he insists, 'the four minarets at the corners of the plinth are actually lamp towers, *deepsthambh*, used in Hindu temples.' I realize that it is futile to point out that the muezzin called to the faithful from minarets which are obviously an important feature of Islamic architecture. He presents the clinching evidence. 'A piece of wood from a door to the underground chambers of the Taj was dated, using radio-carbon processes, to be from between 1270 and 1448. And work on the Taj is said to have started only in 1632.' I express the commonly held belief that there is considerable doubt on the authenticity of the sample, which he brushes away. 'So you see,' he concludes triumphantly, 'Shah Jahan did not build the Taj Mahal. He desecrated the Tej-o-Mahalaya temple, removed the idols and replaced them with cenotaphs and only added the inscriptions from the Koran, which took twenty-two years to inscribe.'

I bring up the obvious objection to his theory. If such a magnificent structure existed at such an early date, there would have been mention of it in some chonicle, Hindu, Mughal or even in the accounts of earlier European travellers. 'It is a conspiracy,' he exclaims, 'a conspiracy, I say, to hide the truth'. Although there may well have been pavilions in Raja Jai Singh's garden, these would have followed the Mughal pattern in being small structures to rest in during a day of leisure. While they could have been demolished in preparation for the tomb, there is no doubt whatsoever that work on the mausoleum began from the excavations of its foundation. A court historian summed it up, '… plans were laid out for a magnificent building, and a dome of lofty foundation which … will, until the Day of Resurrection, remain a memorial to the sky-high aspiration of His Majesty …. and which for strength will display the firmness of the intentions of its builder ….'

* * *

The precinct of the Taj Mahal was planned to frame and complement the tomb. There would of course be a mosque, but what of the other side? A replica called the *jawab*, the reply, was the solution, in the form of a kind of guesthouse, *mehmankhana*, for visitors. And while the mosque and its flanking structures would be magnificent, they would be built of rose sandstone so that they merged gently into the shadows.

The architect and his numerous assistants worked far into the night, preparing drawings, working out structural details, formulating the load, designing the foundations to distribute that weight, as well as to counter the thrust of the river. There were thousands of details: materials to source, workers to be employed, draught animals to be arranged and much more, and all in great haste, as the emperor would brook no delay. The vast recourses of the Mughal empire were brought to bear upon the construction. Hundreds, if not thousands of men, were employed to dig deep to the water level. And while they excavated the earth, bullock-carts laden with the stone and lime for the foundations creaked into the site day and night. Huge logs of sal are believed to have been laid at the water level in the Mughal manner, to create a raft-type structure of enormous strength on which the structure would rest. Within an incredibly short period, a firm foundation of lime and stone was laid. A series of great piers was built on this base, and from them gigantic arches rose to disperse the weight of the colossal mausoleum. This was the base for the main plinth of the tomb, the huge red sandstone platform called the *kursi*, the chair, on which the entire edifice rests. The bricks used in the foundations were soaked in hot fat to make them impervious.

Barely five months of work had passed when the first *urs*, commemorating the death anniversary of Mumtaz Mahal became imminent. The emperor would attend it as would the luminaries of the empire. Although debris would have been removed on a daily basis as part of the construction protocol, a final clean-up was probably necessary. More labour and innumerable bullock-carts were probably employed to remove any remaining rubble or left-over mud from the excavation of the foundations. This was dumped a short distance from the mausoleum, creating mounds now covered with grass, one of which is called Taj Khema, now a popular vantage point to view the monument.

Since records of expenses associated with the empress's mausoleum include an expenditure of Rs 2,252 on a sandalwood coffin during the first urs, it appears that the body, or perhaps the old coffin, was transferred to a new one. In the vicinity of the temporary tomb, 'heaven-like' tents and canopies of gold brocade and velvet, prepared in imperial workshops at the emperor's specific command, were set up, the ground laid with the finest carpets from Persia. Hundreds gathered. According to the court historian, they included 'great nobles, high ranking mansabdars, grandees and great men …. saintly persons and ordinary citizens'. The rituals were elaborate, involving recitations of the entire Koran 'for the merit of the lady', and prayers for the repose of the soul of the empress. A great banquet with every conceivable delicacy of the age would have been set out on brocaded cloths laid out on carpets, and all were invited to partake of it. 'Heaven was surpassed by the magnificence of the rituals'. Fifty thousand rupees were dispersed in alms to the poor, donations to religious scholars and to those who had recited the Koran and prayed for the empress. Jahanara, Raushanara and the ladies of the royal zenana would have followed similar rituals in the evening, after the men had dispersed, and spent the night before the temporary tomb, praying.

But to me, it is the second urs, on 26 May 1633, that was really significant. Peter Mundy, an agent of the British East

India Company, one among the more credible sources on the Taj Mahal, and who was present in Agra during this period, noted that an exquisitely decorated enamelled gold railing was installed around the empress's grave on this occasion. Court historians endorse his observation and record that the superintendent of the royal goldsmith's workshop, offered a gold screen worth 600,000 rupees on this date. Made of 40,000 tolas of gold, it was decorated with enamelled inscriptions and floral designs. Enamelled hanging lamps, specially crafted for the chamber in which the tomb lay, were also displayed. The railing was then installed around the grave of the empress, and the lamps suspended around it.

It is commonly believed, however, that the actual grave of Mumtaz Mahal is in the crypt below the cenotaph chamber. Since it was of course, impossible that the mausoleum was built in less than one-and-a-half years, the account of the second urs and the installation of the railing has led to a lot of confusion. The issue is actually quite easily resolved. On the second urs, Mumtaz Mahal was interred for the third and final time below the plinth in a second crypt in the underground chambers. This means that only the lowermost level of the mausoleum, with a grave chamber and perhaps surrounding apartments, would have been completed at this stage. An altogether believable exercise within even such a short time. According to ASI reports, the passages and chambers at the lowest level are decorated with paintings and gilt work with some stucco. Burial in the lowermost levels is also in keeping with Islam's injunction that the body must rest in the sacred earth.

Listings of expenses associated with the Taj Mahal refer to the costs of three sets of tombstones. Two sets are accounted for, one at the crypt, the other in the main cenotaph chamber. The last and real set of graves of both the empress and her husband were in the lowermost level of the mausoleum.

The use of cenotaphs to replicate the actual grave was a common practice among the Mughals. In Agra itself, there were precedents in the tombs of Akbar, Itmad-ud-daulah, Afzal Khan Shirazi (Chini Ka Rauza), even Kabutar Baba. In each case, the real graves were in basement crypts. False tombs are believed to have been developed to prevent anyone defiling underground graves by walking over them. They also enabled artistic expression and were the locale for prayers at a later date, after the real grave chambers were bricked up. Till the 1960s, prayers were regularly offered in the crypt till the area was closed to visitors.

The sombre ceremonial would have been attended by Shah Jahan, his sons and daughters, Sati-u-Nissa, the rest of Mumtaz's family, and senior nobles. The ladies would have probably participated in the ceremonial behind a screen. The enamelled gold railing was installed around the grave and the chamber was brightly lit by hanging lamps. The holy Koran was chanted as the assembly once again mourned their loss. The subterranean grave chamber was lovingly tended in the years that followed. Regular prayers and recitations of the holy Koran resonated, incense wafted from censers and the rich carpets would have been changed regularly. In later years, a similar regime was followed in the crypt.

The French physician and traveller François Bernier recorded in his memoirs that non-Muslims were not permitted to enter the basement, which he had heard contained a dazzling light. This was possibly from the lamps installed above the grave of the empress. In later years, Shah Jahan too was buried at this lower level and the crypt bricked up, as was customary, forever.

The gold railing is said to have been removed by Shah Jahan

on 6 February 1643 and replaced by a white marble screen. Another version of history says Aurangzeb replaced the railing with a marble screen after Shah Jahan's burial next to his wife. Although the gold railing could well have been removed from the subterranean grave chamber to accommodate Shah Jahan's grave, Aurangzeb's marble screen, if it exists, would be buried far below in the real grave chamber. Visitors are often told that the markings on the floor of the centotaph chamber indicate the location of a gold screen that once surrounded Mumtaz Mahal's cenotaph. This seems incorrect since it is unlikely that the gold screen would have been moved from the grave, where prayers were still said, to a mere cenotaph chamber. There is, however, yet another possibility. The record of removal could well have been a ruse to put off grave robbers who would have otherwise undoubtedly plundered the lowermost crypt. There is the intriguing possibility, then, that the gold screen and lamps are still there, sealed up at the lowermost level of the Taj Mahal.

* * *

By February 1633, when Peter Mundy visited Agra for the last time, the tomb under construction already drew many visitors. He recorded that the building 'goes on with excessive labour and cost, prosecuted with extraordinary diligence, gold and silver esteemed common metal and marble but ordinary stones'. Shah Jahan could well afford the expense as his land revenue alone was estimated at over fifty-six million rupees.

The enormous brick and mortar structure, that would be later clad with white marble, rose rapidly. A steady procession of elephants and sturdy carts, pulled by teams of twenty to thirty buffaloes, transported marble to the site. An army of stone-workers cut the huge blocks to the required sizes, numbering each according to an overall plan. Chips flew and the precinct resounded to the ring of hammer and chisel. As the slabs were completed, each seems to have been dragged along a ramp estimated to be fifteen kilometres long, and hoisted into place by a post beam and pulley system operated by labourers and teams of mules. Architects and draughtsmen finalized finer details, including the placement of inlay and carving. Scores of inlay specialists worked with assembly-line precision to hasten the process. Designs were traced on the marble by one group, after which others chiselled the grooves into which twenty-eight types of gemstones would be set, while still others shaped petals of carnelian, jasper, crystal, lapis lazuli, sapphire and many others. As many as forty-eight slivers of gemstones were used, in some cases, to create the subtle shading of a single flower.

* * *

Agra is well known even today for its marble inlay and I am curious to see how it is done. I visit the Subhash Emporium, lured by the promise of watching craftsmen at work. An ingenious and most effective ploy used by big shopkeepers all over Agra to draw in shoppers, and one to which I happily succumb. A group of artisans are working just inside the Emporium on different pieces of marble to demonstrate the varied aspects of their craft. Himanshu, a pleasant and personable young man, whose heritage this Emporium is, gives me a quick introduction. The work is called *pacche kari*. 'Pacche' means small chips of semi-precious stones and 'kari' is, of course, work. The creation of inlay is a long and laborious process, executed by small teams, each directed by a master craftsman whose art rests in in his ability to select gemstones appropriate for the shading that distinguishes the very best work.

Mohammad, a craftsman, works with a tiny blunt-ended chisel, in a gentle, rubbing movement that shapes the grooves into which the stones will be set. He has been performing this task since he was fourteen, and holds up his index finger with a big, boastful smile, pointing to a deep cleft on its tip. 'This I got from carving the grooves for the stones to be inlaid,' he says. In another group Arif shapes tiny slivers of amethyst on an emery wheel, an instrument as old as the art, turning each piece carefully to give it the merest hint of a curve, his forehead deeply scored by concentration. The stone is so small that I wonder how he is able to protect his fingers from injury. 'Experience,' says Himanshu, 'and many, many years of training'.

Himanshu points to another craftsman who is stirring the adhesive, a viscous paste of lime plaster, wax and honey, over glowing coals. 'The exact composition is not told outside the family,' Himanshu tells me. 'But it becomes rock solid when it cools.' The thick paste is inserted into the grooves and the stones placed piece by tiny, fragile piece. I count five different shades of white in a single minute flower. The work is excellent. More importantly, it has retained dynamism due to a growing market which demands new designs instead of static repetitions of old forms.

Arif, Mohammad and the others are descendants of craftsmen from Persia, where the art originated, who came to Agra to work on the Taj Mahal. Since the work on the great mausoleum took many years to complete, several families stayed on to settle here. Building activity burgeoned, inlay became fashionable and there was no dearth of work. But then the capital moved to Delhi. Times changed and the craft began to die. When Himanshu's grandfather started this work forty years ago there were only a few hundred craftsmen and most of them were looking for other trades for their sons. They were exploited by the shopkeepers and there was no aid from the government. Himanshu's grandfather, however, urged craftsmen to improve on what their fathers and uncles had done, and paid them more than they asked, as an added incentive. This restored pride in their work. Excellence became a goal once again.

Today, over 4,000 craftsmen are engaged in the marble inlay industry, many of them working from home. With an average of five dependants per family, around 20,000 people are supported by the industry. This includes the *pietra dura* work which is quite different from traditional pacchi kari, in that it uses power tools, bigger stones and bold designs. Many different kinds of hard stones are used in this work, with infinite variations of colour which enable the creation of stunning effects. And tourism accounts for almost 90 per cent of sales.

We walk through the emporium. Mind and eye are dazzled by the colour, the skill, the beauty displayed in an amazing variety of table-tops, lazy susans, bowls, vases, boxes of different shapes and sizes. Each piece with inlaid gemstones, and each with a different design. Prices range from ninety rupees to 25,00,000, though some pieces are priceless. Himanshu gestures to an attendant who cranks up the screens along one wall, a theatrical gesture that reveals glass-fronted cabinets that protect exquisite inlay, each piece of museum quality and of incalculable value. The collection was designed by Himanshu's uncle who has since passed away. My eye keeps returning to a simple rectangular, white marble table top with a border of superb artistry. Delicate, almost imperceptible hints of mother-of-pearl, used for the veins of the leaves, provide subtle accents which highlight the colours.

'The design,' Himanshu tells me, 'is adapted from that on the side of Shah Jahan's cenotaph'.

Much of the collection has been at least partly inspired by the Taj. 'The past gains meaning if it has a place in the present,' Himanshu says sagely. 'But mindless imitation is of no use. We may take the same motifs, but we use them in a different way.' Another table-top consists of a mesh of intricate arabesques interwoven with flowers. I look closely and see more detail: a parrot I had missed earlier, and then several more, tiny lifelike birds with emerald bodies and bright red beaks. I need to look at it repeatedly to see all the minute elements that contribute to the whole. 'Not surprising,' says Himanshu with his engaging grin, 'since it took seven years to make'.

A Taj Mahal made of mother-of-pearl has an arresting three-dimensional effect. I remark on the fine lines with which it is 'drawn'. Himanshu chuckles. 'It is black marble from Belgium, cut to the thickness of a single hair.' In one piece I find illusions of sunlight and shadow, in another, delicate tendrils and gently curving petals, in one case with the effect of a petal stirred by a breath of wind.

* * *

Work continued at a frenetic pace at the empress's mausoleum. Ustad Isa Afandi, the head draughtsman from Shiraz in Iran, worked far into the night, eyes straining in the lamplight. He, as well as his associate Muhammad Sharif, received 1,000 rupees a month, roughly equivalent to 500,000 rupees today. An amount, however, that was structured to include payments to the scores of assistants who participated in the preparation of various ground plans, cross-sections and elevations to guide the builders.

Dome-builders worked feverishly under Ismail Khan Rumi, so highly specialized that he and his team were paid the same amount as Isa Afandi. He had built several domes in his native Turkey. His father, and probably his father's father and many generations previous to them, had been builders of domes and he had grown up with the art, living and breathing the complex calculations associated with big domes from early childhood. By the time he reached his early teens, he was probably apprenticed to his father or some other relative for long years during which he honed his skills. He had come to Agra hearing of the great wealth of the Mughals and of their patronage of fine architecture. For such a major undertaking, Ismail Khan would have required several assistants trained like him in hereditary skills.

Kayam Khan from Lahore specialized in the construction of the small pavilions, the *chattris* that surrounded the main dome. These graceful and delicate structures, borrowed from Hindu architecture, were placed around the base of the dome to detract from its immense volume.

Thousands of workers came from across the country and from distant Iran and Turkey to support the endeavours of these masters. Qadir Zaman Khan, an expert in construction, turned his many skills and his huge crew of workmen to a variety of tasks ranging from the excavation of the foundations to masonry, from the lifting of the heavy blocks of marble by ropes and pulleys to the laying of stones, to maintaining plumb lines and an infinitude of other functions.

Master masons worked under the direction of Muhammad Hanif of Agra. Other than Muhammad Sajjad from Multan, whose name is remembered, these were anonymous men upon whose unsung skills the edifice rested. But they left behind little marks discreetly cut into the red stone slabs, on the pathways, stairs, plinths and pavements of the precinct with which individuals identified themselves. Thirty-six different motifs have been found, ranging from variations on Hindu symbols such as the swastik, lotuses, stylized fish and birds, to a variety of geometrical designs, including the star associated with Islam. Tenuous proclamations of self from illiterate but skilled men whose identity reaches out poignantly across the centuries. There is, of course, no truth to the story that Shah Jahan had the hands of the Taj's craftsmen cut off, or that the calligraphers were blinded to prevent them from creating a building to surpass the Taj.

Shakir Muhammad from Bukhara was an expert in the carving of stone flowers. Chiranjilal Pachchikar came from Lahore with his reputation as an inlayer. Ran Mal was the garden designer from Kashmir. Pira, a master carpenter of Delhi. There were hundreds more but these are among the twenty-five names that are listed in an old manuscript. We know how much they were paid; we also know that they were among the most proficient in their particular skill, that they were hard-working men who laboured to create great beauty. But we know nothing else.

* * *

One of the very few to actually put his name to his work, was a master calligrapher from Shiraz. Inscribed verses from the Koran in the main centotaph chamber conclude with the proud proclamation: 'Written by the insignificant being, Amanat Khan Shirazi.' He designed all the calligraphy of the mausoleum, including the famous black marble inscription inlaid around the high entrance gate where the calligrapy at the top is actually one-and-a-quarter times bigger than that of the sides, to make it all appear the same size. Other verses from the Koran are inscribed at different places of the mausoleum, deliberately structured to inspire visitors of the period with religious awe and reverence.

Calligraphy under Islam was an important decorative feature and a pleasing replacement for figurative art, which was forbidden. Based on complex rules, it developed forms of great beauty, with curved and vertical lines entwined to ripple in graceful arabesques. But there is more to calligraphy than just its beauty. According to Islamic tradition, the words of the Koran are sacred both in content as well as form. The inscription on Mumtaz Mahal's cenotaph reminds the faithful, 'Every soul shall taste of death, and ye shall have your reward on the Day of Resurrection; and he who....shall be admitted into Paradise, shall be happy; but the present life is only a deceitful provision.'

By 1636-7 the calligraphy in the main cenotaph chamber was complete and by early the next year, another outside the great western arched entrance to the mausoleum was also executed. This means that the mausoleum was more or less fully built by 1638/9, within about eight years of the death of the empress. The rest of the precinct and the gardens are what took twenty-two years to construct, not the Taj Mahal itself.

Though the art of calligraphy is still alive, it is slowly dying from lack of patronage. Shahzad Khan, among the few craftsmen left in Agra, squats on a ledge that projects over a drain outside his tiny shop at Sadar Bhatti, bent over a gravestone which he is carefully inscribing in English. He refers from time to time to a tracing that he has designed of the required words. A visitor, evidently a Hindu from his long loose dhoti drawn comfortably up to his skinny thighs, offers the odd comment.

The demand for calligraphy in Arabic is negligible. An altered demography caused by the migration of many affluent

Muslims to Pakistan has vastly reduced its use. 'But,' says Shahzad, 'mine is *shahi kam*, royal work. The very best.' He shows an inscription in the beautiful undulating Arabic script that he has just completed. It translates to, 'Every thing is the gift of God.' Some people put this up in front of their homes. There is almost no Persian work now, a little Arabic and Urdu, but mostly Hindi and English.

Shahzad is sufficiently literate to design calligraphy in five languages, Arabic, Persian, Urdu, Hindi and English, though he speaks only Hindi. But there is just not enough work. Or why would he be sitting over a drain under a thatch? There are plenty of excellent craftsmen, capable of excellent work, but people are just not prepared to pay them well. 'Why, Panditji,' Shahzad says to his friend, 'if we had the money we too could build a Taj today'. Panditiji pulls up his dhoti further and nods in agreement. 'Definitely, definitely. The skills are all there, it's a question of money and resources.' Shahzad continues, 'Now everything is so much easier. This tracing, for example, can be scanned on the computer and rendered to the appropriate size and then copied onto the stone.'

He needs to expand his business and is forward-thinking. 'Gravestones, I have heard, are in great demand in the West. Why can't we make them? There is no work like ours. We can carve or inlay, anything is possible in Agra. But where to find clients?' We talk about the possibility of trawling the Net to find funeral homes or cemeteries that could help him find commissions. I find the contrast moving: using the computer and the Internet to source business for handcrafted work learnt over the centuries.

* * *

Another marble memorial is being built at Dayalbagh about five kilometres north of Agra. It enshrines the ashes of the founder of the Radha Soami sect, but will also be a gathering place, a temple for his followers. I had gone there to meet Anurag Betai, whose name I had found on the Net while looking for mystic associations within Agra. Anurag and his family work with pyramids and pendulums for healing. They are also followers of the sect and live in the compound adjoining the great temple. His grandfather is president of the committee that governs the Radha Soamis of Soami Bagh.

We meet at the monolithic temple which, like the Taj, is being constructed entirely of marble, but of many different hues, ranging from white and grey to pinks and greens. It is an intriguing structure with an eclectic and sometimes startling combination of architectural styles ranging from the Islamic dome to Gothic arches and Doric columns. Work commenced in 1904 and current estimates indicate that it will probably be complete by around 2030. 'Yes, I know it is a long time. But consider this,' says Anuraj very earnestly, 'the number of man hours that will have taken to build this is less than the man hours for the Taj Mahal. We use 200 workers for eight hours a day, five days a week, for say even 100 years. That comes to 41,600,000 hours. As opposed to 116,800,000 in the twenty years it took to complete the Taj.' I consider pointing out that it took just eight years to complete the actual mausoleum, but I decide to let it pass.

Construction is slow for many reasons. First of all, the structure calls for blocks of marble of a particular size which are often difficult to procure. Moreover, until relatively recently, there wasn't even a crane. Huge blocks of stone were lifted by pulleys in the old way. And then of course there is the sheer volume and complexity of the work.

Anurag has a quiet, considered demeanour; he is serious

but with flashes of humour. 'Soami Bagh', he tells me, means the 'Garden of the Lord'. This is the place where the first guru of the Radha Soami faith lived. 'Just as the sun's rays are the greatest at the equator,' he tells me, 'the energy emanating from the Supreme Being is focussed at Agra. That is one of the reasons our guru established the Radha Soami movement here.' After each guru passed on, succession was often disputed and different gurus established break-away groups. As a result, there are many different sects associated with the Radha Soamis. One among these is the sect to which Mr Agam Prasad Mathur is guru. Another is that of their neighbours, the Dayal Baghis. Anurag smiles ruefully. 'We have been in litigation with them for decades over the rights to the temple. The case was first heard before Independence in the Privy Council in London.

The Soami Bagh sect has had no guru since 1949 when the last guru passed on. They believe a guru will reveal himself when the time is right. Anurag pauses to think through his next words. 'We also believe that the guru is always present. He becomes manifest in deep meditation.' He grins, struck by another idea. 'Even a hundred years is no big deal in cosmic time.' Meditation, contemplation, singing *bhajans* in praise of the Lord, chanting the first guru's name and reading from the scriptures—these are the practices enjoined upon the Soami Baghis. One of the fundamental teachings of their scriptures is detachment from the material world. 'Only then can you connect with the Lord,' Anurag explains. I consider the irony implicit in this grand temporal structure to perpetuate the memory of a guru who advocated such detachment.

The din of dozens of hammers and chisels draws me to craftsmen sculpting delicate flowers from huge blocks of marble. One is working on an enormous rose, with large, fragile petals probably less than a millimeter in thickness, a marvellous continuity of skill. His father and his grandfather worked at this site and he is training his teenage son to take over. He stands up and stretches to ease the kinks in his back. 'Then it will be four generations,' he says wearily. 'This rose has taken me almost eight years to carve.'

Anurag walks me around the soaring cathedral-like space that will be the main prayer chamber of the temple. The dome is not yet in place, but towering Doric columns on all sides are topped by enormous stone flowers, fruit and vegetables, all exquisitely worked and very lifelike. A wide canal, rather like a reflecting pool, is planned around the building. I am unable to fully understand how it will all come together, so Anurag takes me to see the model that has guided construction. An enormous dome is its centrepiece, covered in a gold mesh and topped by an ornamented finial also of gold. Tapering minarets flank the temple, in much the same way as at the Taj Mahal. Except that in the foreground, a towering structure in two tiers, rising almost to half the height of the dome, resembles a church spire. Pointed arches with strong Gothic overtones alternate with conventional arched arcades and a domed gateway. Anurag tells me the model was created in 1928.

* * *

The Dayal Bagh ashram across the road from Soami Bagh is a cool leafy place with big, old trees and a sense of serenity balanced by dynamic resolve. Streams of people returning from their morning worship walk purposefully past, all in similar kurtas of white with a thin orange stripe, 'all woven at the ashram,' says Mishraji at whose insistent invitation I have come here, 'and sold at cost'. There are people at work everywhere. One large group is weeding an open space as large as a football field, others are at work on smaller patches. Two old ladies, at least in their eighties, are sitting on low stools pulling out weeds. Mishraji smiles. 'We believe in manual labour, at least two hours of it, every morning, after prayers.' This is in keeping with the belief that work is worship. At this time of the year there is not much to do in the extensive fields owned by the ashram, which is why devotees are working on the grounds, but usually every one would be in the fields at this time.

Mishraji is actually Mr S.P. Mishra, who is a friend of Harsh Bhaskar's shoe manufacturer father. He runs both a profitable business enterprise in Agra as well as the weaving centre at the ashram. A golf cap covers a shock of white hair, glasses front his twinkling eyes, and a white moustache frames a generous, smiling mouth. Dayal Bagh, he explains at length, is almost entirely self-sufficient in food, clothing and many other necessities of everyday life. It also has its own watch-and-ward arrangements, waterworks, electric supply system, internal telephone exchange, newspaper, post office, cooperative bank and hospital. Schools, colleges and vocational institutions, established and run by the ashram, provide value-based education to mould the next generation. Several small industries, established to provide 'honest earnings' and prevent idleness, produce articles of everyday use ranging from textiles to footwear, Ayurvedic medicines and toiletries. They even have a kind of marriage bureau which helps residents find suitable spouses. Weddings are arranged by yet another body, which keeps the costs well under control. Mishraji adds, 'My daughter's wedding cost me just 15,000 rupees, as opposed to the around 10,00,000 that I would have had to spend elsewhere.' Dayalbagh is a world away from the world but complete in every sense, sustained by its own efforts. Mishraji sums up in the words of a previous guru, 'Wealth does not flow here but neither is there hunger or deprivation; there are no opulent homes nor are there dilapidated huts; no one is great, nor is anyone insignificant.'

We walk through the large compound, past orderly rows of small houses built by the ashram at the expense of each householder on the strict understanding that there is no ownership, only assured lifetime occupancy. The houses are tiny, two small rooms and a kitchenette, yet many are tenanted by the rich and famous accustomed to much more. We stop frequently as Mishraji gives and receives greetings, short endorsements of affection and respect. An elderly man, probably in his early seventies, is sweeping the roads with a long-handled broom. He works with an impressive thoroughness, sweeping with long strokes slowly, almost meditatively. He speaks impeccable English and neatly sidesteps my queries. 'Why don't you get her a book,' he suggests, 'that will tell her something about us'. Mishraji explains the man's reluctance. 'Not all of us are learned enough to explain everything. Also, we have found that reasoning and argument are tedious processes that may be used endlessly with no result. For us it is enough to feel blessed with an inner experience that has changed us in a way that can only be described as fundamental.' He thinks for a moment. 'It is as though a spiritual light has illuminated and purified our hearts, elevating and expanding our souls, making it possible for us to realize the Fatherhood of God and the brotherhood of man.' The teaching at Dayalbagh is directed towards achieving a higher level of consciousness which, they believe, changes one's life.

We walk on through the campus still buzzing with devout workers. A large sign, quoting His Holiness Huzur Mehtaji Maharaj, the previous guru, reads, 'If you want to eat, you must sweat first. If you want self-government, you must learn to govern yourself first. If you want to deserve anything, you must learn to serve others.' A cyclist pedals by furiously, calling out urgently in a low voice. Mishraji asks me to move closer to the far edge of the pavement. Several people rush out. 'There,' Mishraji says in hushed reverence, 'there is our guru Mahrajji. You are most fortunate.' A man in white kurta pyjama cycles slowly by, his head down, deep in thought, and at a suitable distance behind him, thirty yards or so, an escort cycles at the same pace. All those gathered along the way offer obeisances as their guru cycles on. Mishraji has a beatific expression. 'My guru, he is everything. I am non-existent in his presence.'

We drive some distance away from the ashram campus to a new settlement, past the educational institutions, vocational training centres and vast tracts of land, 1,500 acres in fact, that belong to the ashram. The fields are immaculate, completely free of weeds. The people here only cultivate as much as they need and sell to their people at cost. The profit motive is completely absent.

I meet a gentleman, debonair and fit in shorts and a black shirt, who brushes aside, but with great charm, my queries as to why he made the move from Delhi. His wife, a comfortable-looking, smiling lady in a well-filled salwar kameez, a big maroon bindi on her forehead, tells me about her day. 'I wake up at 2.30 a.m.,' she says, smiling her warm smile, 'and reach the central prayer hall a few kilometres away by 3.30. We have half an hour of personal meditation, followed by prayers with our guruji from 4 to 5.30 a.m. after which we do two hours of physical labour, working in the fields or on the compound. Home for a quick breakfast, shower and change and by 9.30, I am at work till 4.30. Then tea, household chores, an early dinner and bed.' We talk about the pettinesses of everyday life. 'There simply isn't the time,' she laughs.

* * *

It is earlyish in the morning and the day is only just beginning in Agra as the car I have hired bumps and jolts along narrow streets. Life beats around every corner. Mouth-watering fragrances waft from steaming cauldrons crowded around by men having a quick breakfast on their way to work. A little further, milk is being sold by the yard, measured at arm's length into foaming containers. A group of girls in navy pinafores and white blouses are on their way to school. Their headscarves proclaim them to be Muslims. Two men play chess in a patch of sun. Vegetable-vendors wheel their carts down narrow streets, pausing while women make their choice. The colours are fresh and vivid; green peas, red Indian carrots, purple brinjals, fresh spinach—a perfect subject for a still-life. Small shops on the way sell miniature Taj Mahals and other bric-a-brac, including kangaroos and *Jurassic Park*-inspired dinosaurs.

Workshops along the road are already open, each surrounded in a cloud of white dust. A man bends over blocks of white stone in a small, dark room. The dust of the stone covers the floor, the shelves; it sifts through every crack, coats every object. The man's limbs are covered in the fine white powder, even his hair is white. He has been living with the stone, breathing its dust since he was a child, for close to forty years now and there are many, many more like him.

'What are you making?' I ask. He looks up. 'The Taj Mahal,' he says, 'what else?'

Abdul Hamid uses soapstone, which is cheaper and far easier to work on than marble. He makes three little replicas a day and sells them for Rs 185—a fairly good business. I mention the belief that the Taj is a tomb and hence an inauspicious object for domestic use. 'That is a tomb,' he says, 'this is a work of art'.

He saws the soft stone into segments, the thickness of slices of bread. 'These will be the sides,' he says. I shall work in the arches and decorative details later. Then they will be fitted into the base and later the dome. The completed 'replicas' are about six inches high. But the work is shoddy, catering to the lower end of the market. Similar pieces are being made in little rooms all along the road. One workshop is on top of a roof. Men saw away at the stone while the household unfolds around them. Chickens peck in the stone dust, washing is hung out, as miniature Taj Mahals, the sources of sustenance, come into being.

9

Only for a Pitcher

Shah Jahan's eldest daughter and favourite child, the princess Jahanara, was just seventeen when her mother died. Yet, she put aside her own sorrow and tended to her devastated family. Her sweet temper and gentle, loving nature gradually brought to their lives and to that of the court, a semblance of normality. Jahanara assumed her mother's place as the senior lady of the realm. One of her first tasks was to make arrangements for the wedding of her beloved brother, Dara Shikoh, in the spring of 1633. It was the first family celebration since her mother passed away and Jahanara ensured it was both joyous and magnificent. The Fort came alive with festivity, and music reverberated from its palaces, while Shah Jahan put aside his mourning and dressed in the rich robes of a bridegroom's father. The entire riverfront was cleverly lit and boats were decorated to resemble birds and animals. There were firework displays, banquets and rich gifts for all. Jahanara paid half the costs of the extravaganza, which ran to a million rupees, equivalent to the cost of building the Red Fort at Delhi with all its palaces.

As the years went by Jahanara became the fulcrum of her

father's life. She managed the affairs of the harem and of the imperial household with maturity and dignity. Although she loved her brother Dara best, she often intervened on behalf of the younger Aurangzeb whom their father sidelined in favour of Dara. The charming rooms allocated to Jahanara in the Fort are located close to the emperor's bedchamber, the Khas Mahal, with the river on one side and the splendid Anguri Bagh garden on the other. Another similar apartment is said to have been used by her younger sister Raushanara. Both, covered by attractive curved roofs typical to those in Bengal, were built by Akbar, who enjoyed experimenting with indigenous forms of architecture. Shah Jahan recognized the beauty of these chambers, which were among the few structures that he did not demolish. Jahanara's apartment is of the red sandstone that Akbar favoured but was then embellished by shining *araish* plaster.

Jahanara would have spent a lot of her time in and around the white marble Khas Mahal. It is a large, airy, pillared chamber with murals of gold and blue and the graceful cusped arches that identify Shah Jahan's building. Fountains played in the pool just outside the Khas Mahal, and the subtle fragrances of the perfumed water drifted inside the royal bedchamber.

Anguri Bagh, in front of the Khas Mahal, was a popular garden retreat, where Jahanara strolled among parterres of fragrant flowers. She would have paused at the central pond, trailing her fingers in its cool waters and strolled along the water channels enjoying the soft gurgling. Other ladies from the zenana apartments that enclosed the garden on three sides, would have joined her, their soft laughter rippling through the evening air. The name Anguri Bagh, meaning 'garden of grapes', is associated with Shah Jahan, who created a pattern of vines, inlaid with precious stones, in the corner close to the Jasmine tower. But the garden was initially laid by Akbar and is one of the few at the Fort to survive the years.

One evening in 1644, just after her 31st birthday, Jahanara was returning to her apartments after her father retired. I imagine her hurrying across the marble terrace of the Khas Mahal, brightly lit by flaring torches and candles. Suddenly, the night was shattered by anguished screams. Her flowing muslin robes had brushed against a lamp on the floor and caught fire. Jahanara was enveloped in flames. Four of her attendants flung themselves on her to put out the flames, but they too sustained serious burns and two of them died within a few weeks. With third-degree burns on her arms, back and sides, Jahanara lingered between life and death for over four months.

Shah Jahan summoned every physician of the realm who claimed to have a salve to heal the burns. The emperor stayed at Jahanara's bedside most of the day, limiting the daily durbar to only urgent matters. Great sums were given out to charity to atone for any sins that may have brought this terrible retribution. One thousand and one silver rupees were placed under her bed each night and distributed in the morning to holy men and mendicants, in the hope that their blessings would cure Jahanara. The emperor prayed by his daughter's bed far into the night. Eventually, a slave named Arif is said to have prepared the salve that healed Jahanana's tortured skin. According to another version, she was cured by Dr Gabriel Broughton, from the East India Company's factory in Agra. In reward, it is said, he asked and received permission for the company to trade in Bengal.

* * *

Dusk begins to seep into the sky behind the impressive domes of the Jama Masjid, that Jahanara built. Flights of pigeons swoop towards their evening roost and the call of the muezzin hangs in the still air. *Allah ho Akbar,* God is great. It is a particularly fine voice, full, rich and reverberant. In a previous time it would have summoned the faithful without the aid of the microphone that diminishes it somewhat, but is now necessary to overcome the ambient sound of the modern day: the cacophony of horns, the roar of vehicles, the stutter of generators.

The big domes above the sanctuary are very beautifully proportioned. Stairs up the high plinth lead to a spacious courtyard surrounded by arched arcades. There is a large water body with a fountain in the centre where the faithful fulfil injunctions to cleanse themselves before they pray. A group of men have gathered around the water. A man in a lungi and kurta, with the beard typical to the Indian Muslim, in this case coloured with henna, scrubs his legs and feet, his arms and hands. The ritual of cleansing the body also helps centre the mind, gradually stripping away everyday cares and enabling a focus on the divine.

A chant has already begun. Several men, all with their heads covered, stand in a line on a long narrow carpet, facing the decorated *mihrab* wall towards the west, the direction of Mecca. The mullah leads the prayer, his voice rising and falling in a cadence typical of a chant in any religion. I am the only woman present. In the old days, ladies in purdah would have participated in the prayers through the fine stone lattices at the end of the arcade. The congregation, today a mere twenty, would have been much larger in Shah Jahan's day. Since the mosque was close to the Fort and its large population, there would have been soldiers in uniform, nobles in rich robes, together with common people, all standing together in brotherhood before God. The zenana section would have been similarly crowded, filled with the rustle of rich silks; fragrant with different ittars.

'Only Sunnis can worship at Jama Masjid,' says a voice behind me. 'This is because the Shias have a different namaz and the timing of their prayer is also different. While we regard Hazrat Mohammed, peace be on him, as the wellspring of our faith, Shias see Hazrat Ali, his son-in-law, who was martyred at the battle of Karbala, as the one who brought Islam to the world. Also, they are governed in all things by a council of twelve scholars headed by an imam. Where we Sunnis have scholars and jurists who offer opinions, not diktats.' The speaker is Siraj Qureshi, a big, middle-aged man with a high forehead and eyes lined with antimony. 'The Mughals were of course Sunnis,' he tells me, 'as is the entire Arab world, except for the Iraqis, who are mostly Shias'. Qureshi sahib was chairman of the Sunni Waqf Board at Fatehpur Sikri.

The Waqf Board has claimed ownership of the Taj Mahal, and I seize the opportunity to hear more about the controversy. 'Wherever there is a grave or a masjid, it is considered to be the property of the Waqf Board,' Qureshi sahib elaborates. 'The Taj is world famous; huge sums of money are associated with it. The thought came to the Board: "Why should we not take it over?" Why do they want the Taj?' he declaims, pausing dramatically. 'Only for the income and the publicity.'

'How can you say this as a Muslim and as a Sunni?' I enquire. His reply is prompt. 'I am an Indian first. The Taj Mahal is Hindustan's pride. It cannot be taken care of by the Waqf Board, only by the Archaeological Survey. The Board has around 4,000 properties in Agra, and most of them are neglected.' The controversy caused him to resign. 'Money, it dominates everything,' he says furiously. 'Take this Jama

Masjid, for example. Two separate committees are contesting their rights to the mosque in court. It is the rentals from the shops around the monument that interest them.' He throws his arms up. 'Will you believe it, in spite of the heavy income, the financial affairs of Jama Masjid are in a terrible mess. Electricity bills are in arrears to the tune of over 300,000 rupees.'

Mr Qureshi is also the general secretary of the Hindustan Baradari, established in 1927 to promote brotherhood among Hindus and Muslims. In 1996 he received the Kabir award for his work towards communal harmony and national integration. Qureshi sahib was motivated by the Koran, which, he explains, tells Muslims: 'Belong to where you are, for only then are you true to Islam. If you live in India and praise Pakistan, even though it is a Muslim country, you are not true to your faith.' He continues with short staccato sentences. 'God is everyone's. We should do our own religious duties without criticizing the faith of others. Help everyone, irrespective of their caste or creed.'

According to Mr Qureshi, different peoples co-existed in Agra for centuries. But Partition altered old equations. Many homes of Muslims, vacated when they left for Pakistan, were taken over by migrant Hindu Punjabis who came here with the baggage of hurt and resentment against Muslims. This introduced a feeling of unease that lingered till about 1950. Gradually, things settled down, helped by India's defeat by China in 1962, which caused a general insecurity and brought both communities closer together. New tensions erupted after the war to liberate Bangladesh in 1971. Thousands of Pakistani prisoners of war were released following the Shimla agreement between the two countries. Muslims were happy at the release of co-religionists, while Hindus were angry that India did not get any tangible benefits in exchange. Politicians nurtured the hostility to develop their vote banks, and antagonism grew.

Then came the 1990s and the demolition of Babur's mosque at Ayodhya by Hindu fundamentalists, which caused great resentment among Muslims and celebrations among some Hindus. Twelve Muslims were shot during police firing to disperse rioting crowds. Some Muslim homes were burnt and the fear psychosis thus engendered encouraged many to live in ghettos, for protection. Communalism grew in Agra. The differences were papered over but there is still a miasma of suspicion and mistrust.

During the post-Babri Masjid riots, Qureshi sahib says he rescued eight Hindus who were caught short by the curfew. 'Local Muslims wanting to avenge the death of their friends tried to attack them, but using the goodwill I have in the community, I managed to get them away. There was a lot of media coverage of this,' he says with satisfaction. In another incident, forty children between six and twelve years old were stranded at a madarsa in a predominantly non-Muslim area. Mr Qureshi went to their rescue with the district magistrate and a contingent of police. The madarsa was torched that very night.

Life has not always been easy for Mr Qureshi. When he was a boy he had to help out in the family's leather business because his father was ailing. He would wash leather for hours, even in winter. And then, to earn more money, he distributed newspapers and delivered blocks of ice which he carried on his head to small cold drink outlets. He made enough money to pay for the weddings of four sisters and three brothers and then finally his own. 'No work is too big or too small,' he says, happy with his achievements.

Qureshi sahib is currently working towards encouraging Hindus and Muslims to participate in each other's festivals.

'In our Muslim area we all celebrate Holi,' he says proudly. 'The clouds of red *gulal* powder are so thick, it looks like a Hindu settlement.' During Ramazan, Hindu families are encouraged to host *iftar* parties during which Muslims break their fast. Mr Qureshi has even persuaded the district magistrate to give an iftar party in the last week of Ramazan. 'I am the organizer,' he says modestly. 'I chose the district magistrate to host this annual event because this is one office that must be widely perceived as secular. When an invitation comes for a party at his home, everyone is happy to attend.' He sighs deeply. 'There are, of course, fundamentalists on both sides. But if Babri Masjid had not happened terrorists would not have gained strength. The feeling developed that the state would not protect Muslims, that Muslims must take care of their own, that if one Muslim is killed we must kill twelve Hindus.'

* * *

Jahanara is said to have had her own haveli on the outskirts of the city. A garden palace, where she could stroll unfettered by the boundaries of the harem. There, away from her many duties at court, she could write poetry or study the mystic Sufi writings that that so moved her. Jahanara was said to have met with secret lovers in her garden. There are many stories about the men she is said to have secretly entertained. Niccola Manucchi, a gunner with claims to medical skills, and an inveterate gossip, who claimed to be 'deep in the confidence of the principal ladies and eunuchs in her service', insists that she drank with them, so much so indeed, that 'sometimes she….had to be carried to bed.' There was even a bazaar rumour about her incestuous relationship with her father. Almost all European chroniclers also refer to it.

Tavernier, writing many years later, says that some nobles endorsed the liaison, claiming, 'it would have been unjust to deny the king the privilege of gathering fruit from the tree he had himself planted'. Whatever the truth, Jahanara's dignity was unimpaired and she remains in the pages of history as a beautiful, cultured and most remarkable woman.

Shah Jahan, however, was more tainted. He is said to have emerged from mourning with a voracious sexuality. Even the permissive Mughal court was scandalized by his dalliances with the common Kashmiri dancing girls who performed in the squares of the city. Opinion was especially outraged when he took one of them as a concubine. Shah Jahan is said to have justified his enjoyment saying, 'Sweetmeats are good, whichever shop they come from.' He visited the annual eight-day Meena Bazar, to search for women who titillated his fancy among the wives and daughters of the nobility. The emperor would be seated on a throne carried by several Tartar women surrounded by matrons and eunuchs. According to Manucchi, 'when a lady caught his eye, he would go up to her stall and make some purchases, and if she met his expectations, he would make a sign to the matrons, who would then ensure she was later brought to the king ....'. If the emperor desired a noble's wife, the husband was expected to immediately divorce her and send her to his liege. Such ladies were legion. Some stayed a few days and returned home laden with rich gifts, others remained in the harem as imperial concubines. The women had no choice in the matter, their feelings were of no consequence.

Shah Jahan is said to have dallied with these ladies in the lovely Sheesh Mahal, where the ceilings and walls were inlaid with tiny pieces of convex mirrors from Aleppo. Candles, reflected hundreds of times in the tiny mirrors, illuminated the rooms with shimmering light while Shah Jahan and his ladies splashed in the shallow marble pools. Shah Jahan's *amours* were no secret. And when his favourite Farzana Begum's palanquin appeared, beggars in the city would call out, 'Oh, breakfast of Shah Jahan, remember us.' Apparently, Jahanara was not only aware of her father's liaisons, but actively helped him meet the women he desired. Among these was the wife of her mother's younger brother whom she invited to a feast after which Shah Jahan spirited her away.

* * *

'Sexuality,' Manju tells me, 'simmered under cover in the Mughal harem, and many princesses and concubines had secret lovers. Take Raushanara, for example, favourite sibling of the puritanical Aurangzeb. On one occasion she had nine young men concealed in her apartment for miry enjoyment'. She laughs at my surprise at her phraseology. 'That's a direct quote from a book on Mughal women,' she informs me. 'The incident came to light when Aurangzeb's daughter wanted to borrow one of the young men. Furious when her aunt refused, she tattled to her father.' Manju is a delightful young woman with a risqué sense of humour despite her conservative Bania background. Her gamine persona goes well with the trousers she prefers over saris reserved for formal family occasions. She embarks on another story, this time about Zeb-un-Nissa, Aurangzeb's daughter, who fell in love with Aquil Khan, the empire's governor in Lahore. On one occasion, when she was inspecting a pavilion under construction in her garden, her lover appeared dressed as a mason, carrying a trowel to complete his disguise. On another occasion, and after a long separation, Aquil Khan visited the princess in Delhi, circumventing all the guards. 'I have to read it to you,' Manju giggles. 'It was a wonderful meeting, tempered with high emotion and love, as if heaven was virtually coming down to the two maddened lovers.' Unfortunately, spies informed Aurangzeb, who arrived on the scene. Aquil hid in a large cauldron. 'What is in the *deg*?' the emperor asked. 'Only water to be heated,' Zeb-un-Nissa replied. 'Then light the fire under it,' her father instructed. As the water heated, the princess whispered to her lover to remain silent to protect her reputation, a request the brave man is said to have honoured even as he boiled to death.

Despite all her modernity, Manju lives, like many others of her community, in a joint family in a huge sprawling home. Four brothers live with their parents, along with their wives and children, but in separate apartments, complete with kitchenettes. Other than breakfast, however, the entire family has most meals together, cooked in the main kitchen in the parents' part of the house. That helps hold the family together, the sharing of meals.

Like the Khandelwals of the riverside haveli, her husband's family is not as well off as it once was, though by outward appearances they seem very wealthy. Manju wears large solitaire diamonds in her ears. 'Each costs more than a Maruti' she grins cheerfully. But most of the wealth is asset-based. There is not much liquid cash. The family business is also jointly owned and managed. That worked well in the old days but today it sometimes causes problems. One brother does not pull his weight, or another's wife feels her husband works harder than his brothers and deserves more from the family kitty. 'It's especially hard on the women,' Manju complains. 'The husbands have at least bonds of blood, but the wives come from different families and often, it's difficult for all the sisters-in-law to get along. Also, we have very little to do. There is household help, we don't have to worry about cooking, and we are discouraged from going out to work, so

there tends to be time to bicker and brood.' Manju's in-laws
are wonderful people—they don't play favourites among their
sons' wives, which helps—but there is still friction. A lot of it
centres around the children, and the competitiveness among
the ladies on their achievements. Then there is the money.
Not that she lacks for anything, Manju adds hastily, 'but if
any one of us wants to buy something, we have to ask our
mother-in-law for the cash. It is awkward, although she never
refuses; it's rather like being a child again and asking for
spending money.'

* * *

Shah Jahan regarded kingship as a sacred duty and worked
hard to do justice to his high office. The emperor was
awakened at four each dawn in the splendour of the Khas
Mahal, to music softly played in the raga of the morning,
Bhairava. After performing the ablutions that must precede
worship, he faced Mecca and recited the morning prayers.
Later, he dressed and went to his personal mosque, probably
the white marble Nagina Masjid, one of his most beautiful
creations, completed around 1635. The tiny mosque, attached
to the zenana, holds a feeling of great sanctity, canonized by
the devotions of worshippers. It is entirely of white marble
but on a scale that is relatively small, almost intimate. Slender
pillars support the cusped arches and far above them, the
domes rise in searing perfection. In these exalted surroundings,
the emperor spent two hours on his knees in prayer.

Further into the morning, Shah Jahan greeted his subjects,
as his father and grandfather had before him, at the
Muthamman Burj, an octagonal pavilion on a bastion that
projects over a large clearing below. A murmur rustled through
the gathered crowd, growing to a roar as they greeted their

sovereign. '*Padshah salamat*,' they shouted in one voice, 'we salute our emperor'.

Later, he reviewed the cavalry, a ritual that all the Mughal emperors, seasoned horsemen themselves, particularly enjoyed. On occasion, the elephants were also paraded and Shah Jahan inspected each one. He would have known several by name. This diversion was followed by the daily durbar. Before the emperor stepped out on the high platform of the great hall of public audience, the magnificent new Diwan I Am, the royal herald would announce his imminent arrival: 'Behold the Protector of the Realm, the Shadow of God on Earth, the Scion of the House of Timur, the second Lord of the Twin Conjunction, the Emperor Shah Jahan.' Crowds of courtiers awaited their king. The more senior ones stood respectfully within a silver railing, leaning on silver walking sticks, hands folded, heads bowed, while others thronged the hall, each individual positioned according to the strictest protocol. The huge pillars, edged with gold, were hung with rich drapes of silk and brocade. Musk and ambergris, burning in sensors, mingled with the fragrances used by the Mughal grandees.

A roll of drums heralded the emperor's arrival. As he stepped onto the throne platform, the assemblage placed their right palms to their foreheads and bowed low before their ruler. The emperor settled down on the Peacock Throne flanked by guards and attendants bearing the Mughal insignia on long gold staffs, while others wielded yak-tail fly whisks brought from distant Tibet. Dara, to whom his father had granted the supreme privilege of being seated during durbars, stood beside his gold chair just below the Peacock Throne. Shah Jahan was not close to the other princes. He ignored Aurangzeb and seldom gave him the accolades he worked so hard to receive. Of Murad and Shuja, the emperor said,

'Murad Baksh has set his heart on drinking; Muhammad Shuja has no good trait except contentment'. But Shah Jahan could not bear to be parted from Dara. And when he deputed his three other sons as viceroys in various parts of the empire, he kept his eldest son by his side.

A handsome man, polite and gracious, urbane and engaging, Dara was popular with the people but had little patience with the sycophants at court. Dara's special concern was to establish connections between Hinduism and Islam. To this end, he studied the Hindu holy texts and had them translated into Persian. He was especially impressed with the Upanishads, which he considered to be not just 'in conformity with the Holy Koran' but interpretations of it—a view that outraged orthodox Muslims. The ulema branded Dara a heretic, a crime punishable by death.

Asaf Khan, chief noble of the realm and father of the empress, positioned on a lower marble dais, introduced issues for the emperor's attention and read out petitions. Shah Jahan listened gravely and gave instructions. He spoke softly, never raising his voice even when angered, his self-control always absolute. The emperor reviewed the progress of his armies as they ranged across the empire under the command of his sons. He attended to matters in the provinces and dispatched orders. Punishments were meted out upon guilty officials, while those that performed well were rewarded. Accounts were examined and expenditures allocated. Shah Jahan's revenue had increased over three times since Akbar, to around Rs 220 million, but expenditures were four times as much.

Later in the day, the emperor held court in the Diwan-I-Khas, the hall of private audience, where he received visiting kings and envoys or met his nobles to discuss secret affairs of state. An inscription compares this magnificent chamber embellished with exceptional carving and inlay, to the highest heaven, while the emperor is equated with the sun, a simile endorsed by rays of gold that once decorated its silver ceiling.

After the midday prayer, Shah Jahan withdrew to the harem for a light meal, prepared under the supervision of Jahanara. He rested for a short while, before another durbar at the Diwan-I-Am, followed by further sessions at the Diwan-I-Khas, finally retiring only late in the evening. Shah Jahan and his predecessors all worked hard to govern their people well and with justice. But there remained the reality of poverty, of exploitation, of venal officers, of all the disparities and contradictions that continue to beset modern India.

* * *

Now that the palaces in the Fort were complete, and the building of the mausoleum for Mumtaz Mahal was well underway, Shah Jahan's obsession with architecture found another focus in plans for a new Mughal capital at Delhi. Work commenced in April 1639, the year the Taj itself was nearing completion. The court finally moved from Agra to the new capital, named Shahjahanabad after the emperor in 1648. Although Agra's political importance diminished, the city continued to be an important centre of trade and commerce. It also retained a considerable military and administrative presence as the headquarters of an important province. Agra's Fort, too, continued to be vital as the repository of one of the largest treasuries of the empire. But things were never the same again.

* * *

Delhi did not always suit Shah Jahan, who was ageing and

often unwell. On his physicians' advice he returned to Agra for a change of air with Jahanara and Dara. Agra flowered with the emperor's presence, but the bazaars were rife with rumours. It was whispered that his illness was brought about by his continued use of aphrodisiacs, and his desire to remain virile despite his advancing years. He was already sixty-five, older than any of his predecessors. News began to filter into Agra of the princes stationed in the far-flung corners of the empire who had grown alarmed at the consequences of Shah Jahan's ill health and age. They were concerned over Dara's influence, and were fearful that in the event of their father's death, they would lose not only the throne, but also their lives. Shah Jahan had, after all, ascended the throne after having all potential claimants murdered. All too soon, messengers galloped into the Fort with word that Shuja, Murad, as well as Aurangzeb, were each marching on Agra.

Armies were dispatched to stop the princes. But the emperor cautioned his commanders to be lenient towards his sons. Lack of decisive action allowed Shuja to escape and caused the army sent to check Aurangzeb to be defeated. The latter advanced on Agra with his brother Murad. Dara prepared for war. He took ceremonial leave of his father in the great Diwan I Am, while Jahanara watched from behind the purdah. Shah Jahan embraced his beloved son and beseeched Allah for Dara's safety. The rattle of battle drums echoed through the magnificent hall as the prince mounted his chariot at the head of an army of over 50,000. The people of Agra turned out in their thousands to wish him Godspeed.

Dara's army met Aurangzeb's and Murad's forces in the scorching heat of summer at Samogarh, thirteen kilometres from Agra, close enough for artillery barrages to reverberate through the Fort. Victory at first veered towards Dara. But everything changed in a matter of minutes. Dara dismounted briefly from his war elephant. His soldiers, seeing his howdah empty, thought he had been killed. Aurangzeb's forces seized the moment and his drums signalled victory. The imperial army lost heart and fled. News of the defeat reached the city far ahead of the dispirited Dara. Among the people of Agra there was grief and the wailing of widows, for many among their men had died in battle. Over 10,000 had fallen. Dara reached his riverside palace at nine at night and fled with his family to Delhi.

Aurangzeb demanded his father surrender the Fort and fired a fusillade at the great citadal. Shah Jahan's guns boomed in reply, while the people of Agra left the city in droves or huddled in their homes in terror. After a few sallies, Aurangzeb realized that Akbar's Fort was still impregnable. It could withstand bombardment as well as siege. Then, an idea struck him. He cut off access to the river. The fountains of the Fort fell silent and its gurgling waterways went dry. Thousands of pampered occupants were now suddenly tormented with thirst, their agony worsened by the heat. Shah Jahan wrote to Aurangzeb in poignant Persian verse:

Yesterday I had an army of nine hundred thousand,
Today I am in need of a pitcher of water!

Aurangzeb's son, Muhammad Sultan, assumed charge of the Fort. He paid his respects to his grandfather, who finally broke down and sobbed. Muhammad took possession of the coveted treasury and confined Shah Jahan to his palace, following his father's orders to completely isolate the deposed emperor. Murad and Shuja were imprisoned. Dara was captured almost a year later, brought to Delhi, humiliated and eventually stabbed to death and beheaded. Life at Agra resumed, though the palaces at the Fort were shorn of their pomp and no longer echoed with merriment. Shah Jahan was restricted to his personal apartments. Jahanara insisted on sharing his captivity and continued her tender ministrations. There were also the other ladies of the harem as well as the attendants, the singers and dancers. And on occasion, the sound of ankle bells and the thrum of music echoed from the marble palaces.

But the gaiety was forced and soon abandoned. Shah Jahan turned to religion, and solemn recitations of the Koran replaced the sound of revelry. Petty humiliations were heaped upon him by the new governor, a eunuch who took pleasure in humbling the erstwhile emperor. Shah Jahan's slippers even wore out and repeated requests for a new pair were ignored, forcing the emperor of Hindustan, once the wealthiest man in the world, to shuffle through his palaces in tattered footwear. Aurangzeb, who now possessed the legendary jewels of the Mughals, pressed his father to give him his personal jewellery, especially a diamond thumb ring and a rosary of perfect pearls. Shah Jahan gave up the ring but threatened to grind the rosary to dust rather than surrender it.

Eight years passed. In January 1666, when Shah Jahan was seventy-four, the ailments that had brought his kingship to an end, recurred. Years of dissipation took their final toll. His fever rose and the pain in his abdomen became unbearable. Lying in the lovely octagonal room that he had created for his wife, he realized his time had come. Readings of the Koran had already commenced in his room, and Shah Jahan, ruler of the universe, prisoner of his son, quietly departed this world. Aurangzeb sent word to the chief eunuch of Agra to delay the burial till his emissary arrived. The imperial representative passed a heated iron over Shah Jahan's feet, to make sure that he was really dead, because he had once escaped a difficult situation at Bijapur in a coffin. The grand funeral that Jahanara had planned was not permitted. At dawn on 2 Febuary 1666, a sandalwood coffin bearing the remains of Shah Jahan was carried out of his palace and placed on a boat that carried it down the Yamuna to rest in the earth at the lowermost level of the magnificent mausoleum he had built. His grave, to one side of Mumtaz Mahal's, and off centre, seems to me to be deliberately planned by Shah Jahan to relegate himself to a secondary place for all eternity. This contradicts the suggestion that Shah Jahan built the Taj Mahal as a vainglorious memorial to himself.

It is still said in Agra that Shah Jahan's personal elephant, Khaliqdad, sensed the passing of his master and died even while his last rites were being performed. An era that had left its mark on Agra, forever, had ended.

10

Rule Britannia

After Aurangzeb's death in 1707, the Mughal empire slid into steady decline. North India, and with it, Agra, was plunged into a continued insecurity as ambitious marauders, lured by the imperial treasuries held at the Fort, strove to establish control. Finally, Suraj Mal, legendary leader of the martial Jats from nearby Bharatpur attacked Agra. Finding Akbar's Fort impossible to breach, Suraj Mal bribed its commander to open the gates to his men, who carried away incalculable riches. Jat soldiers camped at the Taj Mahal, lit fires inside the mausoleum to keep themselves warm and made off with its silver gates and finest gems.

Agra, under the later Mughals, was dominated by a legion of transient rulers who sought quick gains and loot. Then in 1803, British forces defeated the Maratha governor of Agra and quickly established a military presence in the city, fulfilling long-held ambitions to expand their sphere of influence. The Presidency of Agra was created by a decree of the British Parliament and the city went on to become the headquarters of the North-Western Provinces. In later years, Agra lost this position to Allahabad, but the city remained the headquarters of a commissioner's division. The British Raj at Agra was represented by the commissioner, the collector, the public works engineer, the district forest officer and the superintendent of police. They differed vastly from the trader adventurers that had come before. Most of these officials were from the British upper classes and brought with them a sense of noblesse oblige, reinforced by feelings of racial superiority, which impelled them to work towards uplifting the native population.

The new administrators lived far from the crowded bazaars of the old city, in the Civil Lines, carefully laid out with avenues. The military moved troops from the Fort, in the heart of the city, to cantonments on the outskirts, with separate barracks and facilities for European and native soldiers. A comprehensive effort to distance the rulers from the ruled. Sprawling colonial bungalows wrapped in deep verandahs, crouched in quiet compounds encased in shrubbery and girded by herbaceous borders. Here they fashioned a way of living that incorporated the little social rituals of Britain in a lifestyle that was light years away from India. Generations dressed for five-course dinners and dined by candlelight, hand-pulled punkhahs stirring the air, an army of well-trained native servants anticipating every need. Loose Indian garments, previously worn, were rejected in favour of the many layers of tight-fitting European clothing that proved such a torture in hot Indian summers. British officialdom and their wives gathered at clubs where no natives other than servants were permitted, and at churches where a smattering of Anglo-Indians served to reinforce their exclusivity. There were balls and picnics, horse-riding, fox hunts, pig-sticking and shikars. The British played tennis, croquet and rugby, and organized gymkhanas to promote sport.

But above all, they built, adapting the neo-classical styles to local conditions in monolithic structures that were emphatic statements of power and dominance. One of my favourites is the Baptist School, a beautifully proportioned Palladian building with soaring Doric columns that are imposing and yet graceful. Today, its peeling facades and dusty grounds are testimony to venal caretakers who skimmed donations from overseas, leading to disillusionment among patrons and eventually a cessation of contributions. Later incumbents even allowed large chunks of land to be encroached upon, so much so that the church lost huge and valuable real estate for paltry considerations. Congregations which ignored the ongoing neglect were also to blame for their silence that implied tacit endorsement. The school, too, which was once self-supporting, fell on bad times and accepted a government grant which meant that teachers became government employees. All incentive vanished and, with it, any interest in teaching. The students suffered. Values that were to be inculcated in school disappeared from the curriculum. And even though education was free, students left for better schools.

A less commanding but charming relic of the period is the Lauries hotel built in 1854. It is single-storeyed and sprawling, fronted by colonnaded, shady verandahs that acted as a buffer against the heat and filtered the harsh summer light. Rajesh Lal, who owns it with his brothers, explains that a recent study described it as a perfect example of an adaptation of the colonial bungalow and an elegant application of the English Palladian style. Lauries Hotel is one of the oldest in India. 'Hotels were rare curiosities in the mid-nineteenth century,' Rajesh explains, running his hands through thick greying hair that frames a youthful face. 'Although Agra was a military and civil station of considerable importance at that time, the main reason for opening a hotel seems to have been the demand created by visitors eager to view the Mughal monuments.' The hotel was host over the years to thousands of visitors, including distinguished guests such as Alfred Hitchcock who even sketched a self-portrait in the visitors' book in the bar. 'Our bartender was particularly famous,' Rajesh says with nostalgia. 'He was said to make the best cocktails east of the Suez, and was written about in many travel books and magazines. Sadly, he passed on, and many stories died with him.'

The Lal family bought Lauries Hotel in 1975, when there was only one other nice place to stay at in Agra. Business was good, but then terrorism reared its ugly head. Bomb blasts, the demolition of the Babri Masjid, all these created an instability that affected the tourism market. Tourism is an unpredictable business. If a politician on either side of the border sneezes, cancellations roll in. The old days, when guests spent four to five days savouring the monuments of Agra, are long gone and now every one is rushing to cover as much as possible in a day or at the most two.

* * *

The Suez Canal opened in 1869, reducing the arduous voyage between England and India from four months to a mere six weeks. Missionaries who now flocked to India, fired with the zeal to civilize heathens 'sunk in vice and misery'. In their ignorance they maligned Islam and Hinduism and propagated a new kind of religious fundamentalism, in the name of the one, the only Christian God. But they also brought medical care and education, invaluable contributions to people who had not previously been beneficiaries. Englishwomen, who also began to come out to India, were engulfed by culture shock and came to regard all natives as somehow subhuman, dirty and 'nasty'. The amity during the heyday of the Mughals was forgotten and it was the differences that dominated. Change was rapid. Harsh judgement and moral superiority gained ground. Englishmen, secure in their notion of superiority, expressed a general contempt of the locals. Governor General Cornwallis emphatically stated, 'Every native of Hindustan, I verily believe, is corrupt.' To his successor, Wellesley, the natives were, 'vulgar, ignorant, rude, familiar and stupid ....' The contempt was not confined to the people, but also to their culture, including its expression in architecture. Large parts of historic Agra were demolished.

British forces overran the marble palaces of the Fort. The commandant was billeted at the Diwan-I-Khas and exquisite palaces were overrun by his officers. Extensive demolitions were conducted all over the Fort to make space for utilitarian barracks, ammunition dumps and other military infrastructure, till only thirty of the original 500 palaces now remain. The Diwan-I-Am was used as an arsenal and its soaring arches were bricked up. General John Colvin, who died of cholera during the uprising of 1857, was buried in a marble grave that continues to be an eyesore in front of Shah Jahan's magnificent Hall of Public Audience.

Indian wives and Anglo-Indian children became the target of the moral indignation of Englishwomen and came to be regarded with acute embarrassment. An order was issued debarring individuals with an Indian parent from employment in the civil, military or marine branches of the East India Company. Caught between two worlds, they belonged to neither.

Thomas Macaulay, president of a committee on public instruction, expressed the goals of colonial imperialism and urged the development through education of 'a class of persons, Indian in blood and colour but English in taste, in morals and in intellect'. And so the Agra Collegiate School was established in 1832. Even though plague devastated the city in 1839 and a year later, a famine left a thousand dead, reducing Agra's population to one-tenth, the construction of public buildings continued relentlessly. St Patrick's School and St Peter's College were set up in the 1840s and St John's College by 1850.

Dr Neville Smith, whose academic career brought him into contact with most Agra colleges, tells me that St John's quickly developed a reputation for excellence and has several distinguished alumini, including a President of India. A handsome red sandstone building with Indo-Saracen turrets, St John's is impossible to miss. At closer quarters, its vast expanse of foreground is almost completely treeless, and while it is evidently earmarked for sport, there are no court markings and no sign whatsoever of recent use. Dr Smith walks at a fast clip down a beautiful but dusty arcade, past even dustier classrooms all thronged with chattering coeds, their vitality in startling contrast to the general air of languishing decline.

But these students represent a small fraction of those actually enrolled at St John's. Attendance is extremely low. According to one school of thought this is because there is no compulsion from the university. Earlier, it was mandatory for students to attend at least seventy-five per cent of all classes and the university called for attendance records every three months. That is not done now. However, the problem, I have been told by older staff members who are retired, is primarily due to the general deterioration in college management. Previously, there was no religious discrimination and many of the faculty were non-Christians. This changed over the years and religion overtook merit. Gradually, the quality of teaching became poorer and, inevitably, students lost interest. Yet, in spite of attending few classes, students clear examinations. Scores of coaching classes and private tutors have sprung up, who guarantee a certain percentage. The promised results are achieved by unofficial links to people in the university, who leak examination papers. A racket that continues to undermine higher education throughout the country.

In tribute to the respect that Dr Smith still commands, we are quickly shown into the office of the principal. A large, airy room dominated by a picture of the Sacred Heart of Jesus. Dr Prasad received his doctorate in agriculture, a subject that is not part of the curriculum of this college. Dr Smith later explains that, being a Christian establishment, it is considered meet that the principal and as many of the staff as possible be of the faith. And with the migration overseas of the better-educated Anglo-Indians, qualified applicants are few and far between.

St John's has more than 4,000 students, the majority enrolled in Bachelor of Commerce courses as this is perceived as a good qualification for employment. There is even a special evening session for B.Com students who are unable to get admission in the standard course. Of course, the college also offers all the arts subjects as well as the sciences.

Dr Arjun Das, head of the department of commerce, joins us. 'I have been at St John's since I was a student in 1962. I topped the university in my M.Com and was immediately invited to join the faculty.' Many things have changed in the intervening years. Salaries were a mere 250 rupees in 1963. Today, a new member of the faculty starts at Rs 10,000 and within ten years, the figure rises to around Rs 20,000, plus a pension of half the last-drawn salary. Despite this hike, salaries of teachers both in colleges and schools are a poor reflection on the value placed on education. Until this changes, the quality of scholarship will continue to suffer.

The other big difference since the 1960s is in the number of girls who now attend college. 'I remember the days,' Dr Das says, 'when there were just one or two girls in the class. Now, they form over fifty per cent of the student body. And they are far more diligent than the boys.'

The principal and Dr Das are called away and I am passed on to Dr Madhurima Sharma, one of the few woman non-Christian teachers at St John's. She is very attractive, with a wide, persistent smile that shows her even white teeth. We walk to the assembly hall as we talk. Dr Sharma's father was in education and all her four sisters have also acquired Ph.Ds. 'Even in Mughal times,' she says, 'Agra was a centre of learning'. She heads the department of Hindi. Her particular interest is poetry in the dialect of Pali, from nearby Mathura; its subject, the Lord Krishna. 'It is so elevating,' she smiles. 'There is so much to learn from it. The philosophy of Krishna is the philosophy of love, *prem marg*. Without love there is nothing. ' She pauses to greet students who touch her feet in respect. Evidently, Hindi literature and, perhaps, the manner in which Dr Sharma teaches it, have earned their appreciation. Later, she explains the reasons for her popularity. 'I encourage my students to discuss their personal problems with me. Many of their families are conservative and children are too embarrassed to approach their parents with any problems they may have. I advise the students on their relationships, on careers, on the many issues that bother the young.'

Dr Sharma's real calling is social work and her passion, politics. 'People say intellectuals are not suited to politics,' she says indignantly. 'Are intellectuals, then, just to be heroes in drawing rooms, always talking, but not doing anything? In the current Indian situation, everyone must take responsibility. And yet, people are so passive, so uninvolved, they won't even go out and vote.' Of particular interest is the issue of reservation of seats for women in Parliament to protect their interests and to better equip them to win elections. 'But male Members of Parliament are blocking this move,' she says. 'They fear that if women are empowered, they will surge far ahead. More women must come out of their homes and become teachers, engineers, doctors and so forth.' Higher education among women in Uttar Pradesh is low, at just fifteen to twenty per cent, and among Muslims as well as the poorer sections, it is not even two per cent. Dr Sharma is passionate about her belief: 'Education is information and information is power.'

Several schools were established by the British and, together with the colleges, made Agra an important centre of education. Christian schools are still considered excellent and most old Agrawallahs that I have met were all educated in missionary institutions. It was the English medium of education that parents saw as an advantage they wanted for their children. Moreover, there was the dedication of the nuns and priests who taught as a vocation. They came from a position of giving, where the low salary normally paid to teachers was not of consequence. In the long term, Macaulay's strategy paid off. In terms of the spread of Western education, values and of course, language.

Such education was restricted to a small group, including myself and many of my contemporaries. Our intellectual inputs were entirely British. We had no exposure whatsoever at school to the Indian epics, classics or the exquisite poetry of the Vedas, no knowledge of Panini, Aryabhatta, Bhaskar or Bhaskaracharya. Indeed, we learnt well to dismiss our own culture as based on superstition or hyperbole. We were intellectual Eurasians.

* * *

As power grew, so did British arrogance, which impelled a policy of territorial expansion that gained momentum in the 1840s. A series of kingdoms was arbitrarily annexed, leading to public outrage. The final indignity came when native soldiers were expected to bite off the top of cartridges greased with pork lard, repugnant to Muslims, and beef fat, forbidden to Hindus. The army revolted in 1857 and Indian soldiers fell upon British officers and their families with dreadful savagery. However, the revolt did not seriously impact Agra. This was because, unlike other areas such as Jhansi and Lucknow, ruled by traditional dynasties which the British had overthrown, the Mughals had never been replaced by a long-term local power base. As such, there was no ruler in Agra who could rally the people. As a precautionary measure, however, the British residents sheltered at the Fort, where they lived in comparative comfort and security. Indeed, there are stories of parties and merriment that went on far into the night.

The revolt ultimately failed, but in retaliation, British armies swept across the land on missions of vengeance. All standards of honour and chivalry were abandoned in a campaign of retribution from which even civilians were not exempt. Neither side would ever really forgive the other.

Conversation in the courtyard of Jahanara's Jama Masjid is still charged with indignation. A fiery young man ironically sporting a bandana of the Union Jack—chosen only for its colourful and non-figurative design—takes centre stage. 'Can you believe it, British forces seized our Jama Masjid, claiming that the holy building had sheltered mutineers,' he protests, gesticulating widely. 'They blew up its porch and laid mines in the mosque itself, planning to destroy it completely because they said it was a threat to the Fort.'

'But,' says another, 'they realized the Muslims of Agra

would revolt. That is the only reason they did not carry out their plans.'

'Still,' says the first, 'for almost six years Muslims were forbidden to worship here on pain of death.'

Then there were the demolitions. To ensure a clear field of fire for guns mounted at the Fort, the main market of the city, which stood between the Jama Masjid and the Fort, was razed to the ground. In the 1870s, railway tracks were laid, placing a barrier between the two previously linked and interdependent structures, forever changing the context as well as the topography of the Mughal city. It also divided Agra into the ordered British-occupied cantonment and Civil Lines, and the 'native' city. Plans are currently underway to restore the connection between the Fort and the mosque. But it will be a long and difficult manoeuvre as there has been haphazard development, including the establishment of a fish market and several small eateries.

One of the consequences of the uprising of 1857 was the change in the pattern of British governance. Queen Victoria was declared Empress of India and a Viceroy appointed to govern the jewel in her crown. But the changes did not do much to improve the lot of the common people. The incidence of famine rose sharply in the nineteenth century, causing over twenty-one million deaths. Food shortages were accentuated by the reduction of buffer stocks caused by the export of grain. The situation was aggravated by the conversion of food-producing land to plantations of cash crops such as indigo for the British market. Unfair and discriminatory trade practices added to the devastation of the land and worsened the plight of the people.

In the late seventeenth century, cloth merchants in England affected by the rising demand for Indian cottons, pressured their government to ban the import of cottons from India.

British cottons soon flooded the Indian market and thousands of artisans, ginners, weavers, dyers and printers were forced into penury. Indian merchants were similarly affected, trade languished and the economy was devastated. British motivation naturally lay in the interests of their nation across the seas which was fundamentally different from the attitude of the Mughals, to whom India became home. While the Mughals had worked hard to develop and upgrade local craft skills, the British saw these as competition that needed to be contained if not destroyed. To make matters worse, income tax was introduced to fund the functionaries of empire. Resentment against the British mounted, manifest in the burgeoning movement for freedom.

* * *

Dr R.C. Sharma, erstwhile head of the department of history at St John's College, is closely associated with the Shaeed Samrak Samiti commemorating martyred revolutionary Bhagat Singh. The famous rebel lived for a time at two locations in Agra where he manufactured the bombs he later threw into the Legislative Assembly. Dr Sharma is a slight man with a small moustache, who looks to be in his forties, although he retired from St John's several years ago. He speaks very softly, but with great intensity. Several people of his generation, and also some contemporaries of the freedom fighter, believed it was important to perpetuate Bhagat Singh's memory. The committee they formed was allotted land near the old Central Jail where many freedom fighters were imprisoned. In association with the Agra Development Authority, the committee created a rather attractive three-winged contemporary sculpture. The Shaeed Samrak Samiti runs a library and reading room on the premises and holds seminars and lectures, but public interest is low. Funds are always a problem and staff salaries are largely funded by contributions, though there is also a small grant. The garden in which the memorial is set, however, is a popular place where local people take their morning walk.

There are meetings on the first Sunday of each month, attendance is thin quantitatively, but the few people that come are a committed lot, ready to spread the word. In 2006 the focus was on schools, with familiarization camps, talks and so on. 'Sadly,' says Dr Sharma, 'the Bollywood films on the life of Bhagat Singh have probably done more to generate awareness than years of such endeavour'.

The original idea was quite inspiring. It was an attempt to generate consciousness of Bhagat Singh's ideals. 'Politics in India after Independence,' Dr Sharma says, sighing deeply, 'have been such that it is difficult to retain any principle. Bhagat Singh's concept was that there should be in India a society free from exploitation, where everyone should be able to live reasonably well.' Dr Sharma speaks very softly and I have to strain to listen over the roar of traffic passing outside his home. 'The way our political system is being run leaves much to be desired. No political party, including the Left, is truly interested in establishing a society free from exploitation. They are all only interested in power.'

There were many others like Bhagat Singh who challenged British dominance, but not until 1947 could a new epoch be established. British reluctance to leave India was summed up by the famous words of Lord Curzon, Viceroy of British India, in 1894: 'India is the pivot of our Empire .... If the Empire loses any other part of its Dominion we can survive, but if we lose India the sun of our Empire will have set.'

Dr Sharma talks slowly and contemplatively about the high values, the deep commitments, the sacrifices that were current in the run-up towards Independence and the erosion that occurred afterwards. 'In the beginning it was rather like the Taj Mahal, with the culmination of centuries of culture,' he says, sitting on his hands, a mannerism perhaps adopted to avoid gesticulating. 'After that, things began to go downhill. The wonderful palaces of Delhi were a brief exhalation of the same spirit but then it petered out and the dynasty diminished, the creative momentum was exhausted and the aesthetics worn out. In the same way, the creative impetus of years of struggle, arrested by the horrors of Partition, never regained its momentum.'

* * *

I have been repeatedly told that Partition destroyed the ethos of Agra. Dr Smith's brother Mr Ronald Smith, fills me in. 'I was quite young at the time,' he muses, 'but many images are indelibly etched in my mind.' There was of course a lot of stress and unease; an unsettledness, as families who had lived in Agra for generations contemplated their future. It affected all communities. 'Even my mother,' Ronald says, scanning memory, 'wondered what would become of us in the new order. She used to say it will be the *kabristan*, the graveyard for us. Her Hindu as well as Muslim neighbours often reassured her and told her Christians would be welcome in both countries.' One of the first things Ronald remembers about the time is his school friend Feroz sketching a map of Pakistan on the wall under the tamarind tree near his house. 'We will go away to Pakistan,' Feroz had announced, 'but then we will return riding on horses to reclaim the Fort'.

The map was a bit of a shock at first; the reality of Pakistan had not struck home till then. Ghatia Azam Khan, the locality where the Smith family still lives, was a predominantly

Muslim area but with a mix of Hindus and Christians. Each followed their own ways of life but mingled with others, as neighbours should. Ronald's friends, for example, were both Hindus and Muslims. And so were the girls they ogled.

Suddenly, everything changed. There were reports of riots in the city. Communities resentful of the new circumstances, even fearful, erupted into violence. Curfew was imposed. Police jeeps with microphones rolled by, asking people to clear the streets. There was a rumour that the local grain shops had been looted, and some other shops too. Whenever curfew was lifted, the market was crowded with shoppers stocking up against emergencies. Ronald and his friends bought enough kites to keep them busy till the next day, when there would be a six-hour relaxation. Ronald smiles gently. 'I remember my mother, who was addicted to her paan, finding it very difficult to go without.'

Ronald and his friends looked out from the balconies of their homes during the curfew, while their grandmothers, mothers and sisters peered from behind them. Bibi Behan called out that they were all one and no harm would befall them. Khudijia Apa and may others joined the chorus of approval. 'Reality hit us,' Ronald says, with a faraway look in his eyes, 'when Babu Bhisti, the water-carrier, a gentle man who was a popular figure in the neighbourhood, was murdered by a group of turbaned and bearded men wielding swords.' He adds sadly. 'We didn't even know he was Muslim till then.' People in the mohalla were outraged and a whole group rushed out, all bent on vengeance, but the assailants could not be found. 'Why did they have to kill a harmless old man,' asked Panditji, who lived in the temple under the banyan tree. Someone saw Babu Bhisti's son, a big-built man armed with a lathi, looking for his father's killers. A few days later we heard that the youngest son of Nawab sahib, the most important man in our locality, had gone out on his motorcycle, found the murderers and had them arrested.

Calm returned by 14 August. 'Babu Paanwalla decorated his shop with garlands of currency notes and flowers,' Ronald tells me. 'So did many others. There were celebrations in every street. Hindus and Muslims embraced and the aroma of festive foods wafted from every kitchen.' He smiles broadly in recollection. 'Chaman doled out lassi at half rates, Kesho sold sweet, sticky gulab jamuns for a song. Nazro offered cold drinks, Matto Mal distributed Gandhi topis and Buddhi Masterji tailored new clothes for the occasion.' The bazaar was open all night. Around 11.30, a crowd gathered in front of the house of the nawab. He was the only one who had a radio. Just before midnight, Nehru delivered his famous speech. 'There was a hushed silence,' Ronald says. 'Not even the mohalla dogs barked. Even those who did not speak English seemed to absorb its meaning. Soon afterwards, our Muslim neighbours started leaving for Karachi. Feroze went and so did Sultana, the prettiest girl in our mohalla, and so many other friends. But the map of Pakistan remained on the wall for many years to come.'

11

The Moonlit Garden

The flat-bottomed boat drifts slowly down the river, propelled by the pole of the boatman. It smells of water, weed and wind. A few buffaloes wallow in the turgid flow while sandpipers and stilts forage at the water's edge. The Yamuna is strangely lifeless, in hibernation as it were, till better days roll around. The dams upstream, and the pollution, are only decades old, the river has existed for eons. Perhaps this period of degradation will be just a brief episode in her life. We drift slowly past the Taj, rosy in the late evening light. The mausoleum dominates the skyline, its reflection ripples in the water, immaculate, beatifying. The eye and the mind are riveted; there is nothing else.

I am privileged to take a boat from the pier at one side of the Taj to Mehtab Bagh, which means 'moonlit garden', in the company of Dr S.C. Yadav, director of the horticulture department of the ASI, who was responsible for its restoration. A tall thin man, he walks with a slight stoop, eyes focussed earthwards as though he were always examining his plants. He fills me in on the background. 'There were eleven gardens that we know of between the fort and Mehtab

Bagh, which is the last in the chain,' he says. 'This garden was probably in existence long before the Taj Mahal was even conceived of, probably even before Mumtaz Mahal was born.' It is said to have been originally developed by Shah Jahan's great-great-grandfather, Babur, as part of his attempt to make life at Agra more bearable. In later years it seems to have been the special refuge of a Rajput princess married to one of his descendants who, perhaps in nostalgic memory of the *chandini* or 'moonlit' gardens of her desert homeland, planted Babur's garden with night-blooming fragrant white flowers that gleamed in the moonlight. 'We believe,' says Dr Yadav, 'that Mehtab Bagh later came into the possession of Raja Man Singh Kacchawa of Amber, who also owned the land on which the Taj Mahal now stands.' The connection is reinforced by the name of the village in the vicinity of the garden, Kacchapura. Mehtab Bagh was in imperial ownership by the time the Taj was built and was probably acquired by Shah Jahan when he requisitioned the land on which the Taj is built.

Dr Yadav speaks of his early passion for horticulture and his decision to study landscape architecture. 'In those days,' he laughs deprecatingly, 'no one had heard of such a discipline. I was the first landscape designer to join the Government of India.' He studied many different kinds of historical gardens, Hindu, Buddhist and of course Islamic, and advised the ASI on period gardens.

The boat bumps gently against a wide stretch of sand which we trudge across up into Mehtab Bagh. Just a few years ago, Dr Sharma tells me, the garden was a huge mound of sand that blew in great clouds whenever there was a strong wind. This was believed to affect the Taj, acting like sandpaper on the white marble. Accordingly, the horticulture department of the ASI was instructed to move quickly to develop the area as a green belt, an important segment of the buffer zone surrounding the monument. Mehtab Bagh is also part of the heritage zone which will link the Taj and Agra Fort. The horticulture department had to design the plantings carefully. If they were too dense, the view of the Taj would be obscured. Since it was crucial to stabilize the site quickly, Dr Sharma planted a mix of fast-growing shrubs, with the traditional slower-growing fruit trees of a Mughal garden in addition to some local variety of grass. Lawns were a much later British innovation, but there was always some kind of meadow-type ground cover in Mughal gardens. Of course, the actual restoration of Mehtab Bagh as a Mughal garden will follow further studies. Water will always be a problem, so future plantings will have to be carefully considered. Water channels, too, must be adapted to function as a closed loop, which though not completely authentic, are necessary, given current environmental realities.

Tons of earth were excavated in the roughly seventeen-hectare plot to level the ground and, as the sand was removed, they found traces of the original garden. Dr Sharma and his team excavated some parts of the water system that irrigated Mehtab Bagh and also found remnants of two pavilions. But most important of all, they discovered a huge octagonal pool in which twenty-four fountains once played.

Suddenly, Mr Sharma stops at the head of a broad path and says with the air of a conjurer, 'Look.' There at the end of the path is the Taj, perfectly centred, as if it were at the end of the garden. The river is not visible, just the Taj, subtly framed by the red sandstone domes of the mosque and the Mehman Khana. It is a completely different aspect, a view unimpaired by the thousands of visitors that throng its precincts.

'This garden,' Dr Sharma explains, 'is perfectly aligned

with those of the Taj. Even its main water channel is positioned in continuation with that of the mausoleum.' He adds that Mehtab Bagh was integral to the design of the Taj Mahal complex. Mumtaz Mahal's great white marble tomb would then have been at the centre of the two gardens—as was usual in the layout of Mughal mausoleums—instead of standing at the head of the garden as it had seemed. But Shah Jahan added another element. This garden was developed to view the Taj by moonlight, while the other was its setting for the day. Mehtab Bagh was, therefore, different in composition and focus to the gardens in the foreground of the Taj. It was to be enjoyed at night, a garden of white flowers that would release their scents in the cool evening air. Instead of using red sandstone for paving, as in the gardens in front of the Taj, the walkways here would have been white, for moonlight strolling. But the most remarkable feature of this garden was the octagonal tank positioned to reflect the white mausoleum. Dr Yadav says with quiet pride, 'I was there when the tank was filled for the first time. It was the night of a full moon, and believe me, I shall never forget it, the pool held a perfect reflection of the Taj Mahal.'

Perhaps the building of this garden and its pavilions formed the basis for the legend of the black Taj. The French jeweller Jean Baptist Tavernier, who was prone to reporting rumours, recorded in his memoirs that Shah Jahan had begun to construct his own tomb on the other side of the river, opposite the mausoleum he built for his empress. This myth was embellished over the years till it was said that Shah Jahan planned to build a replica of the Taj Mahal for himself, but entirely in black marble. While it is a seductive story, extensive excavations in Mehtab Bagh were unable to uncover any evidence of even the foundations of such a structure. Tavernier's theory could well have been prompted by seeing workmen constructing water channels and garden pavilions.

Mehtab Bagh was at a lower level than the Taj and was often flooded by the river, especially during heavy monsoons. The flooding was probably a recurrent problem which, Dr Sharma tells me, led to the garden being abandoned, probably as early as the late seventeenth century.

Evening has drawn in. Shades of indigo seep into the land, obscuring its features, but across the river the Taj shimmers, opalescent in the night. I am reminded of Mrs Sleeman who, in the late 1800s, told her husband Major-General Sir William Sleeman (celebrated for his suppression of ritual murders by the Thugs), that she would be happy to die the very next day if such a monument be erected to her memory.

* * *

Not everyone in the new empire was that appreciative. Lord William Bentinck, the first governor-general of India, had planned to remove the marble facades of the Taj—for sale in London. Shah Jahan's imperial hamam in the Fort was the first to be stripped, and wrecking machinery was moved into the grounds of the Taj. But the governor-general was informed that the auction of the hamam panels had not been successful. The cost of demolishing the Taj could not be recovered.

During British rule, the Taj Mahal became a popular spot for outings to relieve the tedium of life in Agra. Garden parties and bazaars made use of the gardens, and concerts as well as open-air balls were held on the great marble terrace in front of the main entrance to the mausoleum. Chinese lanterns decorated the precinct, and powerful lanterns illuminated the dance floor, brass bands played and the ladies and gentlemen of the station danced the night away. It was during one such convivial evening on the 23rd of February 1833 that Barbara

Duncan, the thirty-one-year-old wife of James Duncan, civil surgeon of Agra, sat on the narrow parapet around the terrace, lost her hold, fell to the *chameli farsh*, the marble plinth on which the mausoleum rests, and died. On another occasion, a British Major found his wife in the arms of her lover on a moonlit night at the Taj, and shot her dead. The minarets also saw several tragic suicides.

When Governor-General Auckland and his entourage, including his spinster sister the Honourable Emily Eden, an accomplished water colourist and prolific letter writer, visited Agra towards the end of 1839, a reception was held at the Taj Mahal attended by about 100 people. They dined in what was probably the Mehman Khana. Emily Eden, who thought it was a mosque 'desecrated many years ago', recorded in a letter to her sister in England that she found 'rather shocking our eating ham and drinking wine in it'. She was happy, however, that they were in Agra in the cold season, for she had heard that during summer it 'is avowedly the hottest place in India'.

Sir Charles Mallet records that on his arrival in Agra he was directed to proceed to the 'Taje Mahl .... which was the place allotted .... for my accommodation'. Other officers were billetted on the premises, and at least one in a minaret. In later years, the Jawab or Mehman Khana was also rented out to honeymooners. Lord Curzon, the first viceroy of India, who was passionately interested in the Taj, noted that previously, 'it was not an uncommon thing for the revellers to arm themselves with hammer and chisel, with which they whiled away the afternoon by chipping out fragments of agate and carnelian from the cenotaphs of the Emperor and his lamented Queen ....'

Some of the stones pried out of the inlay were replaced under the direction of Lord Curzon, who brought time, energy and passion to the restoration of the Taj Mahal. Cracks in the minarets, caused by a massive earthquake in the early nineteenth century, were also repaired. The marble façade was cleaned and the garden was restored with the aid of old plans that had been discovered. Overgrown trees were pruned, water channels revived, flowerbeds laid out, and trees replanted. The entire precinct received attention till, as he records, 'the group of mosques and tombs ... are once more as nearly as possible what they were when completed by the masons of the Shah Jehan. Every building in the garden enclosure of the Taj has been scrupulously restored ...', at a cost of more than 12,000 pounds. In a speech made from the terrace of the Taj Mahal, Curzon said, 'If I had never done anything else in India, I have written my name here, and the letters are a living joy.'

* * *

Conservation has been an ongoing and dedicated process ever since. Year after year, damaged inlay and crumbling stone are repaired and replaced with the same techniques once used by Mughal craftsmen. More recently, concern over the discolouration of the marble led to an innovative solution, implemented under the supervision of Dr K.K. Muhammad of the ASI, Agra. The Taj received a face pack!

Studies of Mughal texts revealed that in Akbar's time, *multani mitti*, an absorbent lime-based clay, somewhat similar to fuller's earth, was used to clean marble. 'Our chemists worked to adapt an ancient recipe,' Dr Muhammad says. 'It consists of multani mitti, cereal, milk and lime, a mixture used for centuries by Indian women to cleanse their skins.' Of course, it was first necessary to sterilize all the ingredients to eradicate any bacteria that could harm the marble. 'Then we made a paste which was brushed on in layers till it was an inch thick and left it on for twenty-four hours before washing it off. It made a huge difference,' Dr Muhammad says with a brilliant smile. 'The surface was restored and so was its lustre. The tests we conducted showed that deposits of phosphates and carbonates caused by pollution, as well as grease from the sweat of visitors' hands, were all removed. It was a fantastic discovery.' Dr Muhammad adds, 'Scientists from Rome observed our work and are now working on similar methods to clean marble statues in Italy.'

A plan is being drawn up to take the conservation process forward and also to develop that much-needed boost to tourism: a visitor-friendly infrastructure. The Taj Mahal Conservation Collaborative has been initiated by the ASI in conjunction with the National Cultural Fund and the Indian Hotels Company (which owns the chain of Taj Mahal hotels). Urgent matters to do with restoration as well as visitor facilitation, ranging from signage to tourist access, restrooms and so forth will be addressed in the first phase. Other components include the upgrading of the existing museum as well as the development of Mehtab Bagh while future plans involve tackling the development potential of the area around the Taj. These will incorporate a tourism centre with interpretation facilities, waiting lounges and much else.

While the association of private institutions with conservation is both laudable and appropriate, it is important that the involvement remain restricted to such activities and the corporate profit motive be eliminated. Hidden benefits of goodwill, image-building and publicity inherent in this partnership are of incalculable value. 'However,' says Amita Baig, project co-ordinator, 'the Indian Hotels, and indeed all their consultants have decided that since the issues the collabarative seeks to address are so much bigger than themselves, it is not appropriate thatany participant be named.'

All efforts to address long-range development around the Taj must note that the people of Agra are central to such development, and have the right to a substantive number of the jobs that will arise. It is also crucial that methods to alleviate poverty receive urgent attention, otherwise begging, hustling and other undesirable side effects of tourism will grow. Improved facilities may attract tourists, but they may also attract people who prey on them.

Boosting tourism does fill hotel rooms and bring in revenues but there is the fallout to consider. The exhalations and sheer number of footfalls of visitors could pose, in the long term, a danger to the marble at the Taj. The site is already crowded and visits are not always pleasant, involving jostling one's way through great crowds. Some serious thought will have to go into developing measures to control the swelling numbers at any given time, while ensuring that the less privileged of those who come to gaze in wonder at the Taj Mahal not be kept away, for the monument is after all their heritage.

Methods will have to be devised to ensure that crowds of visitors do not converge on the Taj at the same time. Timed ticketing, with built-in incentives, is among the viable options. In addition, alternate approaches to the mausoleum through the less frequently-used parts of the gardens on either side of the monument would alleviate overcrowding and make a visit to Taj more enjoyable. Viewing the Taj from Mehtab Bagh, or from a boat on the river, should be assiduously promoted.

* * *

The commissioner of Agra is a remarkable man. He has fractured a vertebra but conducts his office from his bed with formidable dedication to duty. A meeting with his staff is concluding when I arrive. Mrs Kumar keeps me company while I wait in her husband's large, wood-panelled office. She is delightfully informal—refreshingly different from the stiff wives of important officials who wear their husband's positions with ponderous pretension. Unlike such ladies, she has her own career path, and we are soon in deep discussion over her efforts to convert farmers to organic agriculture. She is a hands-on person and has spent a lot of time working in the field, literally. Marketing of produce is now her concern.

Dr Kumar's PA tells us that the commissioner is now free and his lady ushers me across the house, through a lovely high-ceilinged drawing room to the spacious master bedroom. It is the first time I have ever conducted an interview in these circumstances, but Mrs Kumar puts me at ease with her bright chatter. Her husband, in a comfortable kurta pyjama, is lying in bed wrapped up in a sheet. He is fair, with a high forehead accentuated by a receding hairline, and seems to be tall. He is also very articulate.

The people of Agra, I recall from previous conversations with others, have high hopes of him. He is, they said, an Agra boy. Dr Kumar laughs when I tell him that. 'I also completed my post-graduation in Agra,' he clarifies, 'at St John's actually, and then taught physics at Agra college for a year'. He identifies strongly with the city and its problems. Foremost on his crowded agenda are the supply of drinking water, cleaning up the city, repairing roads, improving drainage and dealing with sewage.

The shortage of potable water has been a huge problem for years. 'The Yamuna at Agra contains hardly any water, just the waste of Delhi and Haryana,' Dr Kumar says ruefully.

'No treatment can make it drinkable, and chemical additions are injurious to health. So, the Yamuna is not a long-term solution. My constant view has been that the solution to Agra's water woes is water from the Tehri Dam.' The installation of a 132-kilometre conduit to bring water from the Ganga to Sikandara, on the outskirts of Agra, will deliver approximately 150 cubic centimetres of water per second, the current requirement of the city, and will be supplemented by water from the upstream Gokul Barrage at Mathura. 'After all,' says Dr Kumar, 'the population will grow and water needs will expand in the future. Both measures together should ensure that Agra will have sufficient clean drinking water for the next fifty to sixty years.'

The people of Agra often complain that huge sums of money are spent on the Taj, while the city itself, its ongoing decay and the many other issues that plague its citizens are largely ignored. At last there seems to be an official who cares about Agra and addresses himself with sincerity and commitment to alleviating its woes. Garbage collection is next on the commissioner's schedule, as well as a special focus on improving cleanliness in the old city. Segregation, threshold collection and composting are all on the anvil. Instead of hiring more staff, Dr Kumar plans to enlist the help of local non-governmental organizations as also the poorer segments of society. This will enable collection charges to be a low ten to fifteen rupees a month. It will also reduce overall costs from the projected ninety-five crore rupees to just twenty-six. Awareness camps are planned, since public participation is crucial. After all, the family has to segregate its garbage.

Plans are well under way to sewer sections of the old city and to develop sewage treatment plants to reduce pollution of the Yamuna. Potholed and dug-up roads will also be problems of the past if Dr Kumar has his way. 'Bad roads,' he explains, 'are the result of constant interference with the surface after the road is laid. Despite administrative strictures, various agencies dig up the roads. One day it is to lay pipes, the next for broadband cables and so on. The big problem is lack of co-ordination and the absence of responsibility,' he says, shifting uncomfortably in his bed. 'The tele-communciations industry is also a big offender. Various service providers seek permission to lay their cables, but although the repair of the road damaged in the process is incorporated in the provisional permissicns, they often get away without implementing it.' Dr Kumar recently insisted on the arrest of one such offender to establish an example and show that he means business.

Much of the money needed to fund these and other projects in Agra will be funded by various national and international agencies, supplemented by the toll tax that is added on to the entrance fee to monuments by the Agra Development Authority. We talk about the controversial dual pricing of tickets. I strongly feel that it is justified. The Taj is the heritage of every Indian, including the most poor, the vast majority of whom could not possibly afford to pay anything higher than the twenty rupees currently charged. Yet, there is no reason why entry charges should not be on par with those levied elsewhere in the world, particularly since money has to be raised to preserve the monument. Dr Kumar, however, is working towards adding value to the enhanced fee for non-Indians. Free mineral water and shoe covers are already provided, but he would like to see improved toilet facilities, especially outside the premises, and the provision of other amenities, including roads, parking space and so on. Another pet project is to shorten queues for higher value entrance tickets by making them available at some hotels, the airport, perhaps even on the Net. In addition, the separate queues for higher-value tickets that exist only theoretically, simply must be implemented.

Dr Kumar burnt a lot of midnight oil to secure permission for night viewing of the Taj. Now he is working on getting permission for night tourists to be able to walk midway to the monument. 'Visitors are permitted night entrance only in eight batches of fifty,' he says, 'and there are hundreds of security people to ensure there can be no threat to the mausoleum.' Plans are also afoot for a night market to give tourists something to do in the evenings. The quality and variety of products on sale will be carefully monitored. And finally, Agra's commissioner plans to develop the city's Mughal gardens, a project that is close to my heart. 'There were so many gardens in Agra,' says Dr Kumar, 'that many place names still retain the suffix "bagh", for "garden"'. The Shah Jahan gardens between the Taj and the Fort, both world heritage sites, are to be gradually restored under the supervision of experts. Regular monitoring as well as accountability will be integral to the project. Dr Kumar has the vision and the will to make all these dreams come true. While he is in place, there is hope for the city.

* * *

By the time the Portuguese friar Sebastian Manrique visited Agra in the winter of 1640-41, the mausoleum was more or less complete and work on the garden seems to have been progressing, for he records that 1,000 men, mostly overseers, officials and workmen, were largely busy 'laying out ingenious gardens, planting shady groves and ornamental avenues'. The flanking structures and the completion of the gardens would take several more years.

Khadims, the attendants of the tomb, would have already assumed their duties, their prayers believed to ensure peace to the departed and mercy on the day of judgment, when the body rose again. As such, Shah Jahan had made arrangements for the khadims and other religious personnel at the empress's tomb to receive regular and generous earnings from the *waqf* or trust set up for the upkeep of the mausoleum. The waqf received an annual income of 300,000 rupees from the revenues of thirty villages as well as taxes generated by trade at the bazaars and caravanserais just outside the complex. Towards the end of the nineteenth century and well into the twentieth, descendants of khadim families were employed as caretakers by the ASI, but have now been replaced by more professional management.

On the tenth anniversary of the death of the empress, a great urs was held to pray for her soul. The emperor joined the congregation in the prayers and presented a pearl canopy for her grave. In the years that followed, Shah Jahan was not always present at Mumtaz's urs, initially because he was busy building Delhi, and later, because he was imprisoned in the Fort by his son Aurangzeb. But even in his absence the imperial coffers amply provided for the recitations of the Koran, for alms-giving and other associated expenses.

* * *

In 1653, Prince Aurangzeb noticed that the big dome of the mausoleum had developed cracks, which had led to leakages. There were also cracks above the arches in the vaults around the grave chamber. Aurangzeb informed his father, who ordered necessary repairs be carried out. Other recorded renovations were executed in 1810, although only in the superstructure, since the lower sections were now bricked up.

A series of military and public works department engineers supervised further repairs over the years, but the cracks developed yet again. Finally, an advisory committee was established for the restoration and conservation of the Taj Mahal.

An alarming segment in Agra expert R.N. Nath's book deals with stress and damage and indicates that there is a strong possibility that the Taj is sinking. The chameli farsh has a slight incline, according to Dr Nath, towards the river. Although it is widely held that the slope, which is of just 3.5 centimetres, was probably deliberately contrived for drainage, Dr Nath believes that the angle of inclination is increasing, though very gradually. He is concerned that this could indicate a gradual destabilizing of the entire structure and lead to cracks at the apex of the underground arches and vaults of the foundation. Cracks, he insists, have already appeared near the base of the huge piers that support the plinth. Most experts, however, say there is no substance to Dr Nath's report of cracks in the foundation piers. The 'marginal' increase in the incline of the chameli farsh is explained as an inevitable consequence of the settling of such a large building.

R.N. Nath's book also dwells on how the minarets are all slightly out of plumb. The differences between the base and the top range from 20.32 centimetres on the south-west minaret, to 3.8 and 7.6 on others.

While the minarets were designed to lean out, partly to ensure that they fell away from the mausoleum in the event of an earthquake, Maurice Rogers supplies further clarifications by e-mail: 'The inclination of the minarets has to do with an optical illusion first discovered by the Greeks, when building temples such as the Parthenon. They found that perfectly straight columns seemed slightly concave to the human eye. To rectify this they made columns that were slightly convex. The term for this is "entasis" and it ensued, I understand, from the way that the back of the human eye is not flat (in contrast to a camera) but curved. As a result, straight lines are interpreted as slightly curved, while lines with a slight convexity are seen to be straight.' According to Dr Nath, the incline seems to have increased by 1.27 centimetres in the south-east minaret and .25 in the three others, over a twenty-five-year period. However, detailed periodic surveys conducted by the ASI did not find any structural damage.

The distinguished doctor of history is a small thin man, with thick white hair centrally parted and more white hair coming out of his ears. He has dedicated his life to the Taj, researching and studying it for many years. Dr Nath is irascible on the subject of the great mausoleum as he believes that the monument is not being handled with the care it merits. 'Read my books,' he snaps, when I bring up his theories. After I assure him that I have, he is more amenable to discussion. 'In 1940,' Dr Nath explains, 'an advisory committee on the maintenance of the Taj was established. It set up 104 benchmarks and stipulated that each year, the relevant parts of the monument be measured on these parameters. By 1965, twenty-five years after the committee was set up, the incline of the minarets had increased.' He pauses to drink a glass of water. 'These complex measurements were conducted by the Survey of India till 1968 or 1969. After this, sincerity vanished and the Survey functions as a government department.'

He thinks for a moment. 'The Yamuna and the Taj are inseparable,' he says emphatically. 'The Taj was designed with a free-flowing river in mind. In fact, the stability of the monument derives much from the river. It is essential that water be released from upstream dams to maintain a certain quantum of flow. If the river dies, the Taj will not stand.'

The UNESCO draft report of 2003 also stressed the importance of the hydraulic pressure and flow of the river in the structural design of the Taj Mahal.

'De-silting of the riverbed is crucial. Around 3.6 metres of sand need to be removed,' Dr Nath insists. 'This can easily be financed by the large amounts earned from entrances to the Taj. Rs 550 of the 750-rupee ticket costs goes to the Agra Development Authority. The Authority receives an annual amount of at least fifteen crore. And the amount could be much bigger, but a large portion ends up in the pockets of those along the way. People go in groups of, say, thirty, and bribe the staff into issuing only fifteen tickets to cover them all. This kind of thing happens all the time. We should rename the Taj, the 'Gold Mine', because that is what it has become.'

Dr Nath is outraged at the commercialization of heritage. 'People holding concerts with the Taj as a backdrop!' he exclaims. 'Yes, even if they *are* far away, it is a violation of the monument. It is a form of cultural vandalism, a cheap publicity stunt. Is the music not good enough on its own? Does it need props?' He turns his ire on Agra. 'Who are the managers of the city?' he demands to know. 'Some 80,000 generators are operating in Agra and it is the generator lobby that prevents us from getting proper electricity. The little power we receive is consumed by thousands of illegal connections. To add insult to injury, officers and politicians get free power.'

* * *

Around 1872, an English artist, William Hodges, painted the first known picture of the Taj Mahal, a view from across the river, similar to that from Mehtab Bagh. He described the mausoleum as the, 'most perfect pearl on an azure ground', and said he had never experienced such impact from any work of art. Hodges records that the fountains played and the gardens were in fairly good repair during his visit. Paintings by Thomas Daniell and his nephew William, executed in 1887, show that this continued to be so, except that some overgrown trees impeded views of the monument. The Daniells had come to India at the invitation of the East India Company, and though overwhelmed by the Taj, they were forced to work swiftly and move on as the region was in turmoil. Their camp had even been attacked on two occasions. Despite the pressure of time, they made hundreds of drawings later published as aquatints, that became vastly popular and introduced the Taj Mahal to the West.

Photography, introduced in France in 1839, increased visual access, and interest in the mausoleum burgeoned. Priyalal and Sons, the first photographic studio in Agra, and one of the earliest in India, opened in 1878. I walk through the same doors over a hundred years later to meet Ravi Khandelwal, the grandson of the original owner. Ravi is not very familiar with family history, and telephones his father, who is at home surfacing from an afternoon nap, and asks him to join us. While we wait, he shows me around the state-of-the-art facility. Upstairs in the studio, three ladies are attending to another who is to be photographed, adjusting the folds of her sari for the perfect drape. Mr Priyalal Khandelwal joins us. Though stooped with age and slightly out of breath, he comes alive when we talk about photography. The first camera, he tells me in a quavering voice, came to India in the 1840s. It was at the height of British power, when all the latest innovations of Western civilization were coming into the country: the rifle, the railways and, yes, the camera. At that time his father was at Bharatpur. It seems that the Raja acquired a camera and allowed Mr Priyalal senior to use it. He quickly became an adept. Then when Kodak came to India, the company suggested he start an agency. In those days, after soaking the negative in developing fluid, it was exposed to sunlight till the print evolved. Sometimes it was over-exposed, sometimes under. Mr Priyalal junior gets a faraway look in his eyes. 'Father took a packet of a hundred papers and said, "I have to get it right." From that day on, he worked towards mastering printing.'

Then he started the studio. There was of course no electricity, so he put in a huge skylight and big glass panels on the walls with sliding shutters that could be adjusted. 'I watched him and I learned,' Mr Khandelwal says. 'My training began in the dark room. I learned my ABC there and my one-two-three also.' Finally, in 1948, he took his first photograph. It was of the Baptist school. Many photographs followed. When someone came into the studio for a portrait, he would take five or six shots, just to practise. Then he made a series, 'Pictorial Agra'. Not many of those have survived but he forages among old files and produces two views of the Taj. 'They were old field camera shots,' he explains, 'using the plate camera, with glass negatives'. One photograph, taken from the opposite bank, shows the Yamuna as still a full-bodied river, with water-lilies in the foreground. Another shot from a height, perhaps from the top of the entrance gate, he doesn't remember, shows huge spreading trees, their branches partially obscuring the monument.

'I was never very good at this kind of photography,' he apologizes. He specialized in people. His favourite subject? He sucks his gums contemplatively. 'Young girls,' he smiles sheepishly. 'I like to capture youth, to immortalize youth.' On many occasions he has taken wedding portraits of three generations of brides from the same family. People come from far away for such portraits.

* * *

Puneet and I circumambulate the monument as members of the imperial family and countless visitors have, paying our respects to the empress and wishing her the peace and repose in death that she seldom had in life. The slope by the riverside is littered with plastic mineral water bottles by tourists who clearly did not perceive this as a site of any sanctity. Across the river and far to the left is the Fort and, in the foreground, the river. In a previous time the imperial barge would have been visible as it made its slow and stately journey from the Fort, while Shah Jahan sat on the deck under a jewelled awning contemplating his creation and thinking of the woman it immortalized. More humble river boats would have been hastily paddled aside to make way for the emperor and show reverence for the royal personage. The royal barge would have docked at the landing below the mausoleum and Shah Jahan probably swept down the stairs to the subterranean grave of his beloved wife, to pray for her soul.

I look up towards the mausoleum, and on the edge of my vision, securitymen in the minarets of the Jawab Mosque are silhouetted against the evening sky, their rifles in sharp profile. Puneet tells me that many more in plainclothes mingle with the crowds, watching for the first sign of trouble. These are new and troubled times and the Taj Mahal is a prime target for terrorists. I look more carefully at groups of men scattered in the precinct. Are those young men who seem to be tourists out for fun, really policemen? And that middle-aged man sitting on his haunches squinting into the sun? Security cameras have now been installed to monitor any suspicious activity. Discreetly located, they do not intrude on the monument and yet have a wide and comprehensive sweep.

Strangely, one of the main threats to the Taj, especially to its interiors, comes from the breath and body moisture from the thousands of visitors each day. That is why the crypt on the third level, which was earlier open to visitors, has now been closed. In addition, acid residue, from the hands of visitors who cannot resist touching the monument, damages the marble surfaces. 'But,' Puneet says with laughing eyes, 'the greatest peril the Taj Mahal has ever faced was in the early 1940s, when an American air force cargo plane took off from Agra airport and almost crashed into the big dome'. It's a piece of Taj trivia that he came across in an old issue of *Reader's Digest*. The pilot had landed at the Agra military airfield to refuel his aircraft. When he took off, he found that the plane was very slow to rise and suddenly, to his horror, right in front of him was the Taj Mahal. With tremendous effort, he was able to turn the aircraft and missed the big dome by a mere hundred feet. The aircraft was so close that the pilot said he could see the shocked faces of workers on the scaffolding of the dome which was under repair. Apparently, the plane had been loaded with excess fuel, a mistake that occurred because the Indian Air Force calculates in kilograms while the American pilot had put in his request in pounds. The aircraft was carrying almost double the required fuel!

In another minaret there is a continuous air-monitoring station set up by the Central Pollution Board. Puneet tells me it has replaced the old manual system and, in addition to monitoring the level of pollution in the vicinity of the Taj, will also study the wind to identify the direction it is coming from. Pollution at the Taj has risen sharply in the last fifty years and has caused considerable damage to the marble. In

1999 it was found that pollutants from the refinery at Mathura, fifty-eight kilometres away, as well as soot from the coal-fired iron forges and wood-burning crematoria in the immediate vicinity of the monument, were five times higher than the permitted level. Small-scale industries had risen from a mere eighty-four in 1997/1998 to well over 6,000 in 2001, the year that Agra's vehicles also reached a record. Public interest litigations by heritage organizations focussed attention on the problem. Stringent emission control measures were put in place at the refinery, river bank crematoria were moved and nearly 300 coal-based industries were told to change to natural gas or to relocate outside the protected zone by 1997. Generous compensations for workers were to be included in the package.

There was an uproar in Agra. Businessmen and workers were pitted against environmentalists and conservationists, the need to conserve heritage in strong opposition to the need to provide jobs. The former US President Bill Clinton once commented, 'Pollution has managed to do what 350 years of wars, invasions and natural disasters have failed to do. It has begun to mar the magnificent walls of the Taj Mahal.'

Rajeev Lal provides insights into the environmental issues associated with the metal forges. He doesn't claim to be a historian or an authority on Agra, but he applies sound commonsense and insight into many issues. We explore the reasons that made the city such a major focus for the industry. 'I think it is the soil,' he says. 'It has a high clay content and mixes well with the molasses which is used to make moulds. The Agra clay is also very heat-resistant, which is important, since molten iron is poured into the moulds.' He believes that the industry had its beginnings under the Mughals with the need to cast cannon for the army. A plausible theory, that couples the present with the past, forging links across the centuries.

I think of Akbar's Armenian forger, Shah Nazar Khan, buried in the Roman Catholic cemetery, who was well known for his genius in casting heavy cannon. He designed and fabricated the famous 45-metre-long Zamzammah, immortalized in Kipling's *Kim*: 'Who hold Zamzammah, that fire-breathing dragon, hold the Punjab, for the great green-bronze piece is always first of the conqueror's loot.' It is still displayed on the Mall in Lahore. Only expert forgers could cast cannon, but hundreds of lesser ones, perhaps the forefathers of those who now work the forges, would have fabricated the cannon balls so crucial to Mughal battle strategy.

A new gas line has been laid to fire furnaces for the foundries in Nunhai, Agra's industrial area. A demonstration of governmental will, which, however, is difficult to implement as many technical problems are associated with the gas furnaces. The bangle and glass industry in Ferozabad, around forty kilometres from Agra, and within the polluting zone of the Taj, made the change to gas easily. But ferrous forges are more complex and the technology has not been fully adapted. Some forges have been able to access the requisite technology and switched to electric furnaces, but the electricity requirement is huge and in a power-deficient state such as Uttar Pradesh, the cost of production soars. Many other forges have moved to places beyond the forty-kilometre limit, severely impacting the economy of Agra.

* * *

I often wonder how the Taj, for which accolades have resounded through history, is perceived by the people of the city. I find my answer unexpectedly at a *mushaira*, where the city's poets gather to share their newest compositions on the second and fourth Sundays of every month.

During Mughal times, poetry was part of life, a form of expression that was a sign of distinction and education. The poetic sensibility was highly developed and the ability to think and speak in similes and metaphors, to string entire garlands of words, was fundamental to polite society. Language, in turn, gained tremendous flexibility, able to encompass subtle nuances of feeling. Most noblemen and women supported accomplished poets who were often part of aristocratic households. They initiated children of the family into the intricacies of composing poems, but had enough leisure to further their own creativity. These and other more famous poets presented their newest compositions at mushairas.

The mushaira, an important aspect of the social and cultural life of the city, was held in palaces and havelis throughout Agra. Great chandeliers and innumerable candles converted night into day. White sheets spread over soft mattresses were scattered with brocaded bolsters and cushions. A candle was placed by attendants in front of a participant, usually at the behest of the host, indicating it was his turn to recite. The recitation was often interrupted by enthusiastic exclamations of appreciation and if a poem was particularly well received, there were requests for an encore, so that every nuance could be fully appreciated. Outstanding presentations were well rewarded and trays of silver and gold coins were showered upon the poet. Women participated, but from behind a screen, sending out notes to request specific poems from a reputed poet in attendance.

Even after the Mughal empire disintegrated, the mushaira continued to hold its own though the language used was less often Persian and more usually the increasingly popular Urdu, which combined the local Hindi with the more formal idioms of Persian. Mirza Ghalib, often called the Shakespeare of Urdu poetry, was born in Agra although he moved to Delhi at the age of thirteen. The city was also said to be the birthplace of the renowned Mir Taqi Mir as well as that of Nazeer Akbarabadi. The latter was apparently so fixated on the Taj Mahal that he was unable to leave Agra even for more lucrative employment elsewhere. The rich poetic tradition, however, was seriously impacted by Partition and the migration of many of Agra's literary Muslim families.

I find the hotel where the mushaira is to be held with some difficulty and am directed to a small door leading to the basement, a long dimly-lit, cavernous room that echoes to the sound of recitation. A group of men and women is seated on green plastic chairs in a pool of light at the far end of the room. A youngish man, perhaps in his thirties, is reciting a poem. He is wearing a pale blue shirt with large brown checks, anonymous black trousers and sturdy black chappals. The audience interrupts with exclamations of pleasure which he acknowledges with a beaming smile and *taslim*, the traditional gesture of the hand to the forehead. But I am still too disoriented to tune in to the nuances of his poem.

The master of ceremonies directs the action to an older man, who launches into an ironic poem about assuming responsibility for one's own life. It's a very interesting composition, with a superficial flippancy hiding a deeper intensity. 'Don't blame the koels for work done by the cows,' he repeats, to make sure the point has been understood. He recites in comparative silence as the audience unravels the varied levels of meaning before erupting into rapturous acclamation.

The four women sit on one side of the group bunched together, the ten men on the other. Everyone is serious and focussed, intellectually stimulated.

Kamala Saini, her hair in a French roll, recites a poem on shared joy. She has a big diary filled with poems. Her discerning audience often anticipates the next words or phrase of her poem, and aesthetic appreciation peaks. There is a short tea break. Conversation dwells on poetry. 'It is our life breath,' says Ahmad. 'To earn a living getting poetry published these days is very difficult, but it is something we just have to do.' Others join in. 'In the past, poets had patrons who covered all their expenses, and all they had to do was write superb verse. That enabled them to reach heights of excellence that we will never be able to aspire towards. Except for a few, especially among the women, who do not have the burden of bread-winning, there simply isn't the luxury of time.' Many among the gathering have jobs in media, in television or the press. Others are school or university teachers. I eavesdrop on a conversation between two of the men. One asks another whether he has seen a popular film. '*Yaar*,' is the reply, 'I find it increasingly difficult to watch movies. The visual is too facile, it does not engage the mind, only diverts it.'

Finally, it is time for the subject of the day. The lady next to me, in an attractive cream cotton salwar kameez with a baby pink sleeveless cardigan, explains that after each session, they decide on a subject for the next meeting. 'This forces the lazier among us to compose new poems, to stretch our minds.' And the subject of today's mushaira is the Taj!

The recitations begin with Shail Bala Agrawal, tiny diamond earrings twinkling in her earlobes as she moves her head to make a point. Hindi poetry is difficult to translate, and I can only approximate the meaning. 'Agra has been abandoned on the pages of history,' she declares. 'The sparkling Yamuna is polluted ... the sweetness has gone out of life ... gentleness and consideration have vanished ... so has trust ... industries are being compelled to move [to protect the Taj] and for us the Taj has lost its allure ....' Shailbala's husband Kanaiya Lal is next. 'Ah, my beloved,' he laments, 'the Taj is not what it was, when we used to meet there ... now there are ticket-collectors, metal detectors and body searches ... now the Taj is packaged, marketed and sold. It is for the pleasure of tourists now ... my beloved, don't invite your friends to the Taj.'

The next recitation is by Sashi Taneja, who warns visitors they have made a mistake in coming to the city of the Taj, where roads are broken and potholed, where there is often no electricity or water. There seems to be a plot, she insists, to allow Agra to decay.

As poem follows poem in different styles and meters, my astonishment increases. There is not one on the beauty of the Taj. Every poet without exception presents compositions that are variations on the theme of the difficulties the Taj has brought to the people of Agra. 'Surely the people of Agra have received some benefits from tourism,' I ask. A flurry of conversation erupts. The trickle-down effect does not work, because a large number of employees in starred hotels, and transporters, are not from Agra but outsiders from large national corporations. Tourism too is not growing as it should. Although Agra has almost 4,000 upmarket beds the occupancy is only around sixty per cent, since thousands of visitors come to Agra just for the day, and also because it is too hot for almost six months of the year. Things are better now but tourism is sensitive to disturbances ranging from political upheavals to outbreaks of chicken flu in Maharashtra, more than 2,000 miles away.

And because of concerns regarding environmental deterioration that could affect the Taj, measures have been taken to remove activities that could impinge upon air quality. 'The refinery went to Mathura,' complains one. 'It is a loss of thousands of jobs,' adds another. 'And now the iron foundries have moved, because they used coal-fired furnaces that smoked and were thought to endanger the Taj.'

The room is charged with excited indignation.

Thanks to Rajeev Lal I am familiar with the subject and feel empowered to interject, 'Surely not so many jobs have been lost. The foundry workers were contract labour, moving from one site to the next. So the numbers affected are not so high.'

The reply comes quickly. 'Yes, but they haven't considered the truckers, their families....the numbers affected are about four times those calculated by the government.'

Shailbala adds, 'A couple of thousand are affected directly, but indirectly, many, many more. Thousands more in related jobs and affected families.'

'And tourism is no substitute.'

'Anyway, all tourism creates are cadres of elite providers and a culture of touts.'

'Yes, the Taj is not good for Agra.'

'But,' I protest weakly, 'all the measures of closing the foundries and banning furnaces are measures that control pollution, to improve the air you breathe, the air your children breathe.'

'What difference does clean air make if your children go to bed hungry because you cannot get work?'

The general consensus is that Agra needs more industries. 'The population is almost two million,' says Ahmad, 'and yet there is hardly any industry worth more than a crore'.

'Shoes and carpets,' I remind them, but am informed that many of these businesses have been destroyed in family disputes. What often happened was that one great visionary in the family set up the facility, which came to be later run by his sons. Differences grew, till by the time the grandchildren came to inherit the business, it was fraught with dissension and usually sold for the value of the real estate.

There is still one more poem to be presented. A woman clears her throat and begins to recite. Her voice echoes in the cavernous room and the emphasis is chilling.

> *How does the past affect the present in Agra?*
> *How does the past affect the present in Agra?*
> *It is the city's strength but also its weakness*
> *The Taj is Agra's strength and its weakness*
> *It is our pride, it is India's pride*
> *But because we consider the Taj to be everything*
> *Anything else is scorned*
> *Even the plight of the common man*
> *Whenever there is any thought of advancement in Agra*
> *It is the Taj, always the Taj, only the Taj*
> *The Taj is like a coffin in which the people of Agra are*
>   *buried alive.*

* * *

Later that same evening, still shaken by the verdict of the poets, I take a cycle rickshaw to the Taj with Puneet. This is one of the categories of non-polluting transportation from the car park to the Taj, mandated by the Supreme Court in 1994. There were previously many cycle rickshaws in Agra, popular for their low cost, but they all but disappeared because they were deemed to clog traffic.

It is a pleasant way to travel, slow, with plenty of time to take in my surroundings and to make the transition from the hurly-burly of Agra to the Taj. My rickshawwallah, though, is loquacious. 'The Supreme Court's ban on motorized vehicles near the Taj Mahal has been a boon to us,' he says. 'Of course, there are also the electric buses and horse-drawn tongas, but we rickshawwallahs have a new life. This is a new improved rickshaw,' Ram Chander, my charioteer explains. 'It is lighter than the old ones and see, it has gears, so I no longer have to struggle to pedal up the hills to the Taj. I can do several trips each day without getting tired.' The rickshaws are now also more stable and safer that those of yore. The ride is smooth now, as well as less perilous.

'These rickshaws are all made in Agra,' Ram Chander informs me, turning back to check that I have registered the information, with complete disregard to oncoming traffic. 'And since around 40,000 new rickshaws are produced every year, that is a fair amount of jobs.' Not bad money, either. Ram Chander makes around 100 to 150 rupees each day. And vehicles such as his eliminate the sulphur dioxide emissions from motorized traffic, which settles on the marble facades, forming a fungus called marble cancer.

* * *

Finally, I am back at the Taj with Puneet Dan. The great mausoleum flushes gently in the evening light and the clamour of the poets' acrimony begins to recede. Since I have no words, those of Mathew Arnold come to mind: 'Human affection never struggled more ardently, passionately, and triumphantly against the oblivion of death ....' I am deeply conscious of the woman, the daughter, the sister, the mother, the wife, the empress the mausoleum commemorates. Still, after much searching, I find Mumtaz Mahal elusive. Since she died in childbirth, she is, according to Islam, a martyr, and her memorial is a sacred site. Shah Jahan is said to have emphasized this aspect in a poem:

> Prayers are here answered
> The roses of pardon bloom throughout the gardens
> Even sinners are here cleansed of their sins.

This belief, Puneet tells me, is reinforced by symbolic parallels to Paradise throughout the Taj Mahal. 'The great entrance,' he explains, 'represents the gate to Paradise. This is endorsed by the calligraphic message which invites the faithful to 'gather in the garden of Paradise which is below the throne of God'. It also marks the transition from the outer to the inner world, which devotees are expected to experience in the holy memorial. 'Even the form of the Taj Mahal,' he informs me, 'was structured to recall the pavilions of Paradise, its edges chamfered, not just to diminish bulk but also to create a roughly octagonal shape inspired perhaps by the octagonal pavilions of the Islamic heaven described in the holy Koran. The throne of God is supported by the four elements, which are here, represented by the minarets.' I am astonished at his erudition. He grins sheepishly. 'I got it from a book.'

He continues in a more serious tone. 'The Taj itself is likened to the throne of God and the garden is an attempt to translate the perfection of heaven into terrestrial terms.' The lotus pool at its apex, perfectly positioned to reflect the Taj Mahal, according to Puneet, symbolizes the Lake of Abundance, the source of the four streams of milk, honey, wine and water that sustain life and ripple through Paradise. 'Thus is God presented through the garden, as the source of all good things.' he concludes triumphantly. 'The image of these precincts as Heaven, is endorsed in the inscription on

Shah Jahan's cenotaph which describes him as Rizwan, the Guardian of Paradise.' The sanctity of the site was reinforced by prayer, its sacred cadences rising and falling from the grave chamber in the early years, and after it was bricked up, from the crypt on the third level. 'The entire structure was designed for resonance,' adds Puneet. 'The passages and the rooms around the chambers act as conduits for sound, conducting it into every corner of the mausoleum where visitors participating in the urs would be seated.' The sound would be drawn out, ululating, gently fading away into a resonant silence.

Slowly, I turn my attention to the hundreds of visitors that throng the monument, taking in the wonder on their faces. They number, in one year alone, almost three times the population of Agra. Life in the shadow of the Taj Mahal may not be easy, but such beauty is surely its own compensation and belongs not just to Agra but to the world. The Taj is a memorial not just to a king's love for his queen but also to the thousands of men who conceived, designed and laboured to create this, the world's best-known monument. Most importantly, in its inspired blending of Hindu and Muslim forms, the Taj Mahal is an expression of the broadness of vision we seek in ourselves.